Spatial Learning Strategies
Techniques, Applications, and Related Issues

EDUCATIONAL PSYCHOLOGY

Allen J. Edwards, Series Editor
Department of Psychology
Southwest Missouri State University
Springfield, Missouri

Published

Charles D. Holley and Donald F. Dansereau (eds.). Spatial Learning Strategies: Techniques, Applications, and Related Issues

John R. Kirby (ed.). Cognitive Strategies and Educational Performance

Penelope L. Peterson, Louise C. Wilkinson, and Maureen Hallinan (eds.). The Social Context of Instruction: Group Organization and Group Processes

Michael J. A. Howe (ed.). Learning from Television: Psychological and Educational Research

Ursula Kirk (ed.). Neuropsychology of Language, Reading, and Spelling

Judith Worell (ed.). Psychological Development in the Elementary Years

Wayne Otto and Sandra White (eds.). Reading Expository Material

John B. Biggs and Kevin F. Collis. Evaluating the Quality of Learning: The Solo Taxonomy (Structure of the Observed Learning Outcome)

Gilbert R. Austin and Herbert Garber (eds.). The Rise and Fall of National Test Scores

Lynne Feagans and Dale C. Farran (eds.). The Language of Children Reared in Poverty: Implications for Evaluation and Intervention

Patricia A. Schmuck, W. W. Charters, Jr., and Richard O. Carlson (eds.). Educational Policy and Management: Sex Differentials

Phillip S. Strain and Mary Margaret Kerr. Mainstreaming of Children in Schools: Research and Programmatic Issues

Maureen L-Pope and Terence R. Keen. Personal Construct Psychology and Education

The list of titles in this series continues on the last page of this volume.

Spatial Learning Strategies

Techniques, Applications, and Related Issues

Edited by

CHARLES D. HOLLEY
Department of Medical Education
Office of Evaluation Services
Texas College of Osteopathic Medicine
Camp Bowie at Montgomery
Fort Worth, Texas

DONALD F. DANSEREAU
Department of Psychology
Texas Christian University
Fort Worth, Texas

with Foreword by
HAROLD F. O'NEIL, JR.

1984

ACADEMIC PRESS, INC.

(Harcourt Brace Jovanovich Publishers)

Orlando San Diego San Francisco New York London
Toronto Montreal Sydney Tokyo São Paulo

ACADEMIC PRESS, INC.
Orlando, Florida 32887

United Kingdom Edition published by
ACADEMIC PRESS, INC. (LONDON) LTD.
24/28 Oval Road, London NW1 7DX

Library of Congress Cataloging in Publication Data

Main entry under title:

Spatial learning strategies.

   (Educational psychology)
   Bibliography: p.
   Includes index.
   I. Learning, Psychology of. I. Holley, Charles D.
II. Dansereau, Donald F.
BF318.S63 1984   153.1'5   83-15715
ISBN 0-12-352620-5

PRINTED IN THE UNITED STATES OF AMERICA

84 85 86 87   9 8 7 6 5 4 3 2 1

Contents

Part I Overview and Theoretical Perspectives

Chapter 1 The Development of Spatial Learning Strategies

CHARLES D. HOLLEY
AND DONALD F. DANSEREAU

Chapter 2 A Theoretical Framework for Spatial Learning Strategies

JOOST A. BREUKER

Chapter 3 The Role of Spatial Strategies
in Processing and Remembering Text:
A Cognitive–Information-Processing Analysis

ERNEST T. GOETZ

Part II Spatial Strategies: Techniques and Evidence

Chapter 4 Networking: The Technique and the Empirical Evidence

CHARLES D. HOLLEY
AND DONALD F. DANSEREAU

Chapter 5 Networking: Application with Hearing-Impaired Students

GARY LONG AND STEPHEN ALDERSLEY

Chapter 6 Concept Structuring: The Technique and Empirical Evidence

JOSEPH L. VAUGHAN

Chapter 11 The Representation of Knowledge: Curricular and Instructional Implications for Science Teaching

JAMES H. STEWART

Chapter 12 Evolving a Description of Text through Mapping

DIANE L. SCHALLERT, SARAH L. ULERICK, AND ROBERT J. TIERNEY

Chapter 13 Graphic Postorganizers: A Spatial Learning Strategy

RICHARD F. BARRON AND ROBERT M. SCHWARTZ

Part IV   Spatial Strategies: A Critique

Contributors

Numbers in parentheses indicate the pages on which the authors' contributions begin.

STEPHEN ALDERSLEY (109), *National Technical Institute for the Deaf, Rochester Institute of Technology, Rochester, New York 14623*

THOMAS H. ANDERSON (189), *Center for the Study of Reading, Champaign, Illinois 61820*

BONNIE B. ARMBRUSTER (189), *Center for the Study of Reading, Champaign, Illinois 61820*

RICHARD F. BARRON (275), *School of Human and Educational Services, Oakland University, Rochester, Michigan 48063*

JOOST A. BREUKER (21), *COWO, University of Amsterdam, 1012 GC Amsterdam, The Netherlands*

JAN VAN BRUGGEN (163), *COWO, University of Amsterdam, Amsterdam, The Netherlands*

BERT CAMSTRA (163), *COWO, University of Amsterdam, Amsterdam, The Netherlands*

DONALD F. DANSEREAU (3, 81), *Department of Psychology, Texas Christian University, Forth Worth, Texas 76129*

ERNEST T. GOETZ (47), *Department of Educational Psychology, Texas A&M University, College Station, Texas 77843*

CHARLES D. HOLLEY (3, 81), *Department of Medical Education, Texas College of Osteopathic Medicine, Fort Worth, Texas 76107*

GARY LONG (109), *National Technical Institute for the Deaf, Rochester Institute of Technology, Rochester, New York 14623*

W. J. MCKEACHIE (301), *The University of Michigan, The Center for Research on Learning and Teaching, and Department of Psychology, Ann Arbor, Michigan 48109*

MARCEL J. A. MIRANDE (149), *The Centre for Research into Higher Education, University of Amsterdam, 1012 GC Amsterdam, The Netherlands*

DIANE L. SCHALLERT (255), *Department of Educational Psychology, The University of Texas, Austin, Texas 78712*

ROBERT M. SCHWARTZ (275), *School of Human and Educational Services, Oakland University, Rochester, Michigan 48063*

JAMES H. STEWART (235), *Department of Curriculum and Instruction, School of Education, University of Wisconsin–Madison, Madison, Wisconsin 53706*

JOHN R. SURBER (213), *Department of Educational Psychology, School of Education, University of Wisconsin–Milwaukee, Milwaukee, Wisconsin 53201*

ROBERT J. TIERNEY[1] (255), *Graduate School of Education, Harvard University, Cambridge, Massachusetts 02138*

SARAH L. ULERICK[2] (255), *Department of Educational Psychology, The University of Texas at Austin, Austin, Texas 78722*

JAN VAN BRUGGEN (163), *COWO, University of Amsterdam, Amsterdam, The Netherlands*

JOSEPH L. VAUGHAN (127), *College of Education, East Texas State University, Commerce, Texas 75428*

CLAIRE E. WEINSTEIN (293), *Department of Educational Psychology, The University of Texas at Austin, Austin, Texas 78712*

[1]Present address: Center for the Study of Reading, University of Illinois, Champaign, Illinois 61820.

[2]Present address: Department of Geology, University of Oregon, Eugene, Oregon 97403.

Foreword

Whether one takes as an indicator a report of prestigious study groups, or the anecdotal studies from industry, the military, or academia, educational problems in America are being recognized and reviewed. Approximate measures of national educational quality, such as the Scholastic Aptitude Test scores, show a consistently downward but fluctuant trend; and high school effectiveness, as measured by the class of tasks appearing on required statewide proficiency tests, is questionable at best. Because the technological sophistication of our society has continued to accelerate, it seems likely that these problems in education and training will be encountered with increasing frequency.

Although the surface features of American education show little cause for optimism, there are other reasons for hope. Since the mid-1970s, research in the areas of learning, instruction, and training has been proceeding at a rapid rate, and the findings of these efforts are beginning to merit application in public schools and other training environments. Of particular note has been progress in the broad area of cognitive psychology, including the work of those psychologists, educators, and computer scientists who have been attempting to understand how and under what conditions learning takes place. In attempting to synthesize the critical importance of cognitive psychology for instruction, one is led in one of two important directions.

First, the area of artificial intelligence has included the investigation of expert and learner knowledge and inferencing strategies, in an attempt to formulate appropriate computer program models for learning strategies. Powerful programming environments and personal computational facilities have been developed. Thus, applications of intelligent computers in instructional settings have become a reality. The second area of importance is that of learning strategies, the topic of this book. Learning strategies are used by learners to facilitate the acquisition, storage, and/or use of information. The focus of this field is on making the student an active learner, not a passive one driven either by a teacher's instructional strategies or by a computer's. The learning strategies approach is more than a simple point-of-view shift, as from third to first person in literature. The stress on the learner represents a convergence of approach from behavioral and cognitive psychology, one that emphasizes the active processing requirements of performance rather than the process of teaching. By reducing the salience of the teacher's role, learning strategies immediately benefit students: Student learning strategies minimize the fuzzy translation of teacher strategies and the subsequent loss of effectiveness before teacher strategies reach learners. Therefore, the instructional context is broadened to include a wider range of options than are usually considered in teacher-mediated instruction. This volume suggests ways in which learning strategies (e.g., spatial and semantic-network representations) may be more powerfully instantiated in text design and technology applications. Some of the most promising work in the field of learning strategies is documented. The chapters collectively represent the best statement of the state of the art in this field.

HAROLD F. O'NEIL, JR.

Preface

The contents of this book are largely based on four premises:

1. The cognitive activities that students engage in when encountering academic or technical learning tasks are of crucial importance.
2. These activities can be modified through instruction, training, and testing to make them more effective.
3. Teaching strategies or materials should be oriented toward the facilitation of these cognitive activities.
4. Networking and other spatial mapping techniques can be used as vehicles for developing desired cognitive activities.

In our previous writings we have been critical of the historical emphasis of educational research on teaching methods. This criticism is particularly oriented toward teaching methods that may lead to inadvertent reinforcement of inappropriate and nontransferable learning strategies. For example, many teaching and testing methods implicitly encourage rote memorization by specifying exactly what must be learned, rewarding verbatim answers on tests, and putting little emphasis on the relationships between incoming and stored information.

Rote memorization usually involves multiple readings of the material, with little or no effort devoted to assimilating the information. Consequently, the material that is "learned" is not meaningfully related to other stored information, thereby limiting the facility with which such information can be retrieved at a later date. Such a strategy, although perhaps useful in many educational environments, is maladaptive in many job situations, where understanding is more important than mere storage. Although the limitation of rote memorization has been emphasized, the same arguments probably apply to a large number of other strategies developed by students to cope with a teaching-oriented education.

By not stressing learning strategies (or not orienting teaching strategies toward the desired cognitive activities), educators, in essence, discourage students from developing and exploring new strategies and, in so doing, limit students' awareness of their cognitive capabilities. This lack of awareness not only retards the individual's performance on cognitively oriented tasks but can also extract a large emotional toll. Most of us are familiar with students who spend inordinate amounts of time rote memorizing college or high school materials and who are still barely getting by. Such an individual's personal, intellectual, and social development must certainly suffer from the pressures created by this use of a relatively inefficient learning strategy.

This historical emphasis on teaching methods stems directly, we believe, from the behaviorist (stimulus–response) influences that pervaded psychology until the mid-1950s. Advocates of behaviorism have traditionally ignored the organism and have concentrated on establishing relationships between stimuli presented (inputs) and subsequent responses observed (outputs). To most behaviorists, the organism represented an inscrutable black box, which was not amenable to scientific investigation. In the 1950s there was an increasing interest in more complex behaviors, such as problem solving and language processing, and it was the failure of behaviorism to deal adequately with these higher-order activities that stimulated the growth of a new school of thought: cognitive psychology.

The cognitive psychologists, unlike the behaviorists, stressed the role of the organism's covert manipulations of the incoming stimuli in predicting responses. The cognitive approach has replaced behaviorism as the dominant school of thought in experimental psychology, but, as is usually the case, application has lagged behind basic research. Only since the early 1970s have cognitive findings had a substantial impact on education—and this impact has been relatively small compared to the possibilities for such an influence. Much of the untapped potential lies in the area of learning-strategy improvements, both by focusing directly on the teaching of effective learning strategies and by reorienting teaching strategies and materials to produce desired cognitive activities.

Each of the contributions in this volume is oriented toward use of spatial mapping techniques to explore this untapped potential. It should be noted that, to date, the research with mapping techniques has been somewhat sparse. By presenting a book containing a sampling of the available information on these techniques, we are hoping to stimulate other research to further explore this domain. Chapters 1 (Holley & Dansereau), 2 (Breuker), and 3 (Goetz) provide some of the theoretical underpinnings for using spatial strategies in this role. Chapters 4 (Holley & Dansereau), 5 (Long & Aldersley), 6 (Vaughan), 7 (Mirande), 8 (Camstra & van Bruggen), and 9 (Armbruster & Anderson) report on specific spatial techniques that have been developed for use by the learner. Chapters 10 (Surber), 11 (Stewart), 12 (Schallert, Ulerick, & Tierney), and 13 (Barron & Schwartz) are geared toward using specific spatial techniques to reorient teaching strategies and/or materials to produce desired cognitive activities. Finally, Chapters 14 (Weinstein) and 15 (McKeachie) provide a critique of the foregoing chapters and explore some implications for education and applied research.

We would like to express our gratitude to a number of people who have assisted in the preparation of this volume. Allen J. Edwards originally conceived the idea for the book; we are grateful for both his inspiration and his confidence in the product. Harry F. O'Neill, Jr., has been a key figure in many learning strategies research programs, including our own, and was kind enough to write the foreword for this volume. We extend our appreciation to each of the chapter authors for their contributions, and for their patience and assistance with our editorial efforts. We would also like to thank M. J. O'Desky, Dolores Murray, Shirley Barnes, Maxine Shoffner, and Leah Flowers for their various contributions to this effort. Additionally, we would like to express our gratitude to the editorial staff at Academic Press for their pleasant attitudes and professional production work. Finally, we would like to acknowledge the following funding agencies for financial support of the research program that permitted the development of this book: (1) Defense Advanced Research Projects Agency (MDA-903-76-0218), (2) National Institute of Education (NIE-G-79-0157), and (3) Army Research Institute for the Social and Behavioral Sciences—Basic Research Division (MDA-903-82-C-0169).

Spatial Learning Strategies
Techniques, Applications, and Related Issues

PART I

Overview and Theoretical Perspectives

CHAPTER 1

The Development
of Spatial Learning Strategies

CHARLES D. HOLLEY   DONALD F. DANSEREAU

INTRODUCTION

Although psychologists' concerns with the organization and representation of knowledge in human memory have a rather lengthy history (e.g., Wertheimer, 1970), major advances in this area are relatively modern. These advances are the result of several interrelated phenomena, such as the decline of behaviorism in psychology, the merging of psycholinguistics and psychology, and the rapid development of computer technology. In 1972, Tulving presented a major distinction that has helped to clarify and guide much of this research and its applications. Specifically, Tulving (1972) developed the concepts of *semantic* and *episodic* memory and argued that

> episodic memory receives and stores information about temporally dated episodes or events, and temporal–spatial relations among these events. Semantic memory is the memory necessary for the use of language. It is a mental thesaurus, organized knowledge a person possesses about words and other verbal symbols, their meaning and referents, about relations among them, and about rules, formulas, and algorithms for the manipulation of these symbols, concepts, and relations [pp. 385–386].

3

SPATIAL LEARNING STRATEGIES
Techniques, Applications, and Related Issues

Tulving conceived of these as two interdependent information-processing systems that (1) selectively receive input information, (2) retain various aspects of that information, and (3) retrieve and transmit that information when it is needed. The two systems appear to differ in the types of information that is stored, the conditions and consequences of retrieval, and possibly their vulnerability to interference (Bourne, Dominowski, & Loftus, 1979). Because of their potential importance for text-processing issues, the primary focus of the next two sections of the present chapter is on semantic memory structures and processes. Although the validity of the structure–process distinction has been questioned, it still provides a good organizational scheme for describing semantic memory. These two sections provide the conceptual framework for a discussion of learning strategies that capitalize on our existing knowledge about the operating characteristics of the human memory system. The basic premise is that learning and processing strategies will be more effective and efficient, if they encourage students to perform activities and create structures that are congruent with memory system operations.

SEMANTIC MEMORY STRUCTURES

One of the first functional models of semantic memory was proposed by Bartlett (1932). The basic assumption of this model and its many variants (e.g., Ausubel's [1963] subsumption theory) is that humans process information in accord with hierarchically inclusive schemata and subschemata. A *schema* can be described as the abstract prototype of a class of objects, events, or situations. Schemata are usually viewed as being recursively embedded; that is, one schema can be a component of another schema. As an example, a face schema would contain placeholders for eyes, ears, nose, mouth, and so on (Palmer, 1975). When the appropriate placeholder for each of these objects is activated during either retrieval or encoding, the placeholder is said to be *instantiated*. (See Rumelhart & Ortony, 1977, for a detailed description of schema theory.)

Schema theory has proven to be useful in providing a framework for studies of prose processing where activation of appropriate existing schemata facilitates comprehension and recall (e.g., Bransford & McCarrell, 1974). However, the theory does not have the precision necessary for providing a basis for detailed predictions in educational settings or for development of explicit learner strategies for acquiring schemata. Part of the problem is that schema theorists have typically not described *in what form* prototypes and subschemata are stored. Theorists working from a somewhat different per-

FIGURE 1. Diagram of node–link relationships.

spective have attempted to develop detailed representational schemes for semantic memory. The most prevalent among these is the node–link structuring principle. (Node–link representational schemes can be viewed as more precise extensions of schema theory; see Frijda, 1972.)

Quillian (1968, 1969), one of the early node–link formulators, suggested that human memory may be organized as a network composed of ideas or concepts (*nodes*) and the named relationships (*links*) between those concepts. For example, the relationships (links) between the concepts (nodes) *dog, Doberman,* and *loyal* can be expressed as "A Doberman is a *type of* dog," and "A Doberman can be *described* as loyal." These node–link relationships can be represented spatially, as illustrated in Figure 1.

Based on this notion, Quillian developed a computer simulation program that "comprehended" textual input by relating the text information to a structured semantic memory network. While the psychological validity of some of the characteristics of the model underlying this program have been questioned by researchers (e.g., Conrad, 1972; Frijda, 1972; Landauer & Freedman, 1968; Landauer & Meyer, 1972; Schaeffer & Wallace, 1969; Wilkins, 1971), the model has proved to be a powerful starting point for subsequent theorizing. In particular, it has led to more refined network schemes such as those of Winograd (1972) and Rumelhart, Lindsay and Norman (1972; Norman, Rumelhart, & Lindsay, Norman, Rumelhart Research Group (LNR) 1975).

Closely associated with these network models are models based on propositional structure (e.g., Anderson & Bower, 1973; Kintsch & van Dijk, 1978). In general, these models represent the relationships between information units as grammatical propositions. Propositional models, which contain linear strings of propositions, are typically transformable into two-dimensional networks, and vice versa (Anderson & Bower, 1973).

Network and propositional models have been shown to be predictive of a variety of human memory functions and problem-solving activities (see Baddeley, 1976; Bourne *et al.*, 1979; Ellis, 1978; Newell & Simon, 1972). Some of the possible processes involved in the formation and use of these types of representation are discussed in the next section.

SEMANTIC MEMORY PROCESSES

In this section the three most prominent classes of models of processing associated with semantic memory are briefly described. These three classes are (1) depth of processing, (2) top-down/bottom-up processing, and (3) reorganization.

DEPTH OF PROCESSING

Craik and Lockhart (1972) proposed a depth of processing (DOP) view of memory. In this model, surface processing is concerned with physical characteristics of the stimulus (e.g., brightness, lines, angles), while deeper levels of processing are concerned with semantic aspects of the stimulus. This model also proposed an association between depth of processing and duration of the memory trace. Specifically, trace durability was assumed to be completely dependent on level of processing, with rote rehearsal maintaining a trace but not strengthening it.

The original formulation of the model was relatively simple and straightforward. It involved a single, central control mechanism (primary memory) and viewed learning entirely in terms of moving through ever-deeper levels of processing (Baddeley, 1976). Although a number of experimental studies provided support for hypotheses generated by the model (e.g., Craik & Tulving, 1975; Craik & Watkins, 1973; Woodward, Bjork, & Jongeward, 1973), it soon became evident that the original model was an oversimplification. For example, certain neuropsychological findings were inconsistent with the DOP model (see Milner, 1968; Shallice & Warrington, 1970; Warrington & Shallice, 1969; Yin, 1969). Equally critical to the model was experimental evidence indicating that some types of meaningful processing were associated with poor retention (e.g., Mandler & Worden, 1973).

Consequently, the original model was expanded to include the notions of breadth of processing or degree of elaboration (Craik & Jacoby, 1975; Craik & Tulving, 1975), discriminability of stimuli (Lockhart, Craik, & Jacoby, 1976), and contextual effects (Jacoby & Craik, 1979). The reformulated model emphasizes the following: (1) *depth* refers to qualitative differences in encoding processes—semantic processes are more abstract, less tied to specific inputs, and more interrelated; (2) greater depth and greater degrees of elaboration result in a more distinctive or discriminable trace; and (3) encoding and retrieval processes share many similar properties—greater degrees of elaboration at input result in a more distinctive trace. Because distinctiveness is relative to a particular context, this dimension must be reinstated at retrieval (Jacoby & Craik, 1979).

The reformulated DOP model, which appears to correct some of the flaws inherent in the simpler model, contains several implications for the development of effective learning strategies. First, the learning strategy should require encoding activities that compel the learner to process the material in greater semantic depth. Second, the strategy should provide a vehicle for achieving greater degrees of elaboration during encoding. Third, the strategy should also represent a retrieval mechanism for reconstructive retrieval of the memory trace.

Top-Down/Bottom-Up Processing

Some information-processing approaches to the comprehension of text have posited the presence of conceptually driven (top-down) and data driven (bottom-up) processes (e.g., Lindsay & Norman, 1977; Rigney & Munro, 1977; Rumelhart, 1977). *Top-down processing* is a strategy whereby the individual proposes possible inputs (i.e., develops expectations presumably derived from previously stored schemata) and then determines whether or not these occur in the input data. *Bottom-up processing* is a strategy whereby the particular pattern of processing is determined primarily by the stimulus properties of the input data (Rumelhart, 1977). Comprehension involves an interaction of the two strategies, whereby conceptually driven expectations are revised via the data, and bottom-up processing is revised via the expectations.

The notion of top-down and bottom-up processes originated in work on artificial intelligence and has been used with such models as the HEARSAY system (Reddy, 1975) and the Augmented Transition Network (ATN) (Bobrow & Fraser, 1969; Thorne, Bratley, & Dewar, 1968; Woods, 1970). The latter model, in particular, was originally developed as a device for computer processing of natural language but was subsequently applied as a model for human language comprehension by Kaplan (1972, 1974), Stevens and Rumelhart (1975), and Wanner and Maratsos (1974). Kaplan (1973) developed a "general syntactic processor" for the ATN model, which allowed both top-down and bottom-up sources for its hypotheses.

Applying the foregoing concepts from artificial intelligence research to text processing by human subjects, Munro and Rigney (1977; Rigney & Munro, 1977) argued that the nature of the external stimuli would influence the type of processing. Specifically, these researchers argued that due to the limited capacity of the (assumed) central processor, the nature of the prose stimulus material would dictate which strategy would predominate. Familiar narrative prose is usually processed top-down and unfamiliar nonnarrative prose (including expository text) is usually processed bottom-up. The implication for a text-learning strategy would appear to be the development of a technique to facilitate the bottom-up extraction of top-level schemata.

REORGANIZATION PROCESSING

The importance of stimulus organization in processing verbal material has been well demonstrated both for word lists (e.g., Bousfield, 1953; Bower, Clark, Lesgold, & Winzenz, 1969; Cofer, 1965; Mandler, 1967; Melton & Martin, 1972; Thomson & Tulving, 1970; Tulving & Madigan, 1970; Voss, 1972; Wood, 1969) and for prose (e.g., Balser, 1972; Bower, 1974; DiVesta, Schultz, & Dangel, 1973; Frase, 1969a, 1969b; Friedman & Greitzer, 1972; Musgrave & Cohen, 1966, 1971; Myers, 1974; Perlmutter & Royer, 1973; Schultz & DiVesta, 1972). Based on the rather robust evidence that an organized stimulus presentation produces better recall than an unorganized one and that subjects attempt to create organization in the absence of an organized presentation (Bower, 1972), a number of investigators have explored the effect of reorganization on performance with prose (Shimmerlick, 1978).

The encoding variability or differential encoding hypothesis of Melton (1967) and Martin (1968) provide the theoretical basis for postulating that encoding information through two different organizations would improve prose performance. This hypothesis predicates that variability of encoding increases the number of potential retrieval cues, thereby increasing the likelihood of correct recall. (This line of reasoning also is supported by Tulving's [1968, 1978] work on encoding specificity.) With respect to prose, empirical studies have provided evidence both for (e.g., DiVesta et al., 1973) and against (e.g., Perlmutter & Royer, 1973) the encoding variability hypothesis. According to Shimmerlick (1978), the weight of the evidence appears to favor the value of reorganization with more complex material. Given this assumption, it seems clear that learning strategies should encourage learner-based organization of the text information. It should also be noted that reorganization or encoding variability can be viewed as an aspect of DOP because this is one technique by which depth and breadth of elaboration can be achieved (cf. Craik & Tulving, 1975).

The foregoing brief and selected reviews of semantic memory structures and processes provide a theoretical framework for approaching the notion of developing and training learning strategies. Although such strategies can and do take many forms (see O'Neil, 1978; O'Neil & Spielberger, 1979), the development of spatial strategies seems to be of particular import because they tend to capitalize on many of the implications suggested by the formal models. Some of these implications include (1) compatibility with n-dimensional representations of long-term memory, (2) requiring encoding activities that compel the learner to process the material in greater semantic depth, (3) providing for the achievement of greater degrees of elaboration during encoding via reorganization or dual encoding, (4) providing a reconstructive retrieval mechanism for the memory trace, and (5) providing for the bottom-up extraction of top-level schemata. In the next section the types of nonlinear representations that have been explored with learners are described.

TYPES OF NONLINEAR REPRESENTATIONS EXPLORED WITH LEARNERS

Nonlinear representations that have been explored with learners may be generally categorized as either concrete or abstract. Concrete representations such as drawing–imagery (e.g., Dansereau, Long, McDonald, Actkinson, Collins, Evans, Ellis, & Williams, 1975; Kulhavy & Swenson, 1975; Levin & Divine-Hawkins, 1974; Rasco, Tennyson, & Boutwell, 1975) and photographs (e.g., Dwyer, 1973a, 1973b; see Dwyer [1978] for a comprehensive review) may be further categorized as *isomorphic* (a true representation of the entity) or *metamorphic* (a caricature of reality).

While concrete spatial representations have a fairly robust experimental history that indicates their effectiveness with short, imageable prose, they have several potential shortcomings with respect to improvement of processing with typical educational textbooks. Specifically, such schemes can depict only a limited number of relationships and they tend to be episodically rather than semantically oriented (in terms of Tulving's [1972] distinction). Additionally, concrete representations with text input tend to be associated with local processing, as opposed to abstraction of a text macrostructure. Holley (& Dansereau, McDonald, Garland, & Collins, 1979) and Dansereau (& Holley, 1982) argued that with ecologically oriented text, abstraction of a text macrostructure was an important feature of effective learning strategies. The effectiveness of concrete representational strategies may be attenuated by the length and type of prose stimulus.

Abstract representational schemes tend to be generally categorizable based on whether they are relatively content dependent (e.g., graphs, flowcharts) or content independent (e.g., matrixing, networking). The most generalizable spatial strategy would seem to be one that is abstract and content independent, but has the flexibility to incorporate other categories of processing strategies as appropriate. In other words, for a given task, content-dependent or concrete representational strategies can be superior to content-independent strategies; thus, the generic strategies need to be able to capitalize on the beneficial aspects of the specific strategies. Three generic strategies are briefly described in the next section.

THREE UNCONSTRAINED
REPRESENTATIONAL SYSTEMS

In this section three abstract, content-independent representational strategies, which have been independently developed as part of long-term research projects are reviewed. Because each of these methods is detailed in subsequent chapters, the review is brief.

NETWORKING

Over the past several years the authors and their colleagues have developed, evaluated, and modified components of an interactive learning strategy system (see Dansereau 1978, 1980; Dansereau & Holley, 1982; Dansereau *et al.*, 1977; Dansereau, Collins *et al.*, 1979). This system is composed of *primary* strategies, which are used to operate directly on the text material (e.g., comprehension and memory strategies), and *support* strategies, which are used to maintain a suitable cognitive climate (e.g., concentration strategies). Assessments of the overall strategy system and system components indicate that strategy training significantly improves performance on selected text-processing tasks (e.g., Collins, Dansereau, Holley, Garland, & McDonald, 1981; Dansereau, 1978; Dansereau, Collins *et al.*, 1979; Dansereau, McDonald *et al.*, 1979; Holley *et al.*, 1978, 1979).

Networking forms the basis for the primary strategies in the learning strategy system. During acquisition, the student identifies important concepts or ideas in the material and represents their interrelationships and structure in the form of a network map. To assist the student in this endeavor she or he is taught a set of named links that can be used to code the relationships between ideas. The networking process emphasizes the identification and representation of (1) hierarchies (type–part), (2) chains (lines of reasoning–temporal orderings–causal sequences), and (3) clusters (characteristics–definitions–analogies). A schematic representation of these three types of structures and their associated links, and an example of a summary map of a nursing textbook, are given by the present authors in Chapter 4. Application of this technique results in the production of structured two-dimensional maps that provide the student with a spatial organization of the information contained in the original text materials. While constructing the map, the student is encouraged to paraphrase and/or draw pictorial representations of the important ideas and concepts for inclusion in the network.

When faced with a test or a task in which the learned information is to be used, the student is trained to use the named links as retrieval cues and the networking process as a method for organizing the material prior to responding. Assessments of networking (Dansereau, McDonald *et al.*, 1979; Holley *et al.*, 1978, 1979) have shown that students using this strategy perform significantly better on text processing tasks than do students using their own methods.

Concomitant with the development of networking, two other laboratories had also embarked on longitudinal research projects to develop similar spatial strategies. These laboratories are at the University of Illinois (Urbana-Champaign), which developed a technique called mapping, and the University of Amsterdam, which developed a technique called schematizing. Like networking, each of these techniques requires the student to convert prose material into two-dimensional, concept–relationship diagrams. These techniques, along with networking, are particularly noteworthy in that they provide a formal, easily learned, flexible system for representing text material. Unlike more content-dependent techniques (e.g., matrixing, flowcharting, constructing pictures), these systems can be used with a wide variety of text. Further, they can potentially be used to enhance not only learner activities, but teaching and testing activities as well.

Mapping

Mapping was developed at the Center for the Study of Reading, University of Illinois (Urbana-Champaign) by T. H. Anderson and his colleagues (e.g., Anderson, 1979; Anderson & Armbruster, 1981; Armbruster, 1979; Armbruster & Anderson, 1980; Armbruster & Schallert, 1980). Anderson (1979) credits Hauf (1971) and Merritt (Merritt, Prior, Grugeon, & Grugeon, 1977) with developing precursors to mapping. In particular, Hauf (1971) used an elementary approach to mapping, which involved placing the central idea of a passage near the middle of a note page and attaching the subsidiary ideas in a concentric fashion, thus producing a product resembling a road map. Anderson (1979) argued that any mapping scheme "should have the flexibility and simplicity of the one discussed by Hauf (1971), but also should be capable of succinctly representing a variety of relationships" (pp. 93–94).

In *mapping*, the student learns a set of relational conventions or symbols. These experimenter-provided symbols depict seven fundamental relationships between two ideas, for example, *A* and *B*. These relationships are (1) *B* is an instance of *A*, (2) *B* is a property or characteristic of *A*, (3) *A* is similar to *B*, (4) *A* is greater than or less than *B*, (5) *A* occurs before *B*, (6) *A* causes *B*, and (7) *A* is the negation of *B*. Additionally, two special relationships identify *A* as an important idea or a definition; the connectives *and* and *or* are also used. Application of mapping results in the production of structured two-dimensional diagrams; Armbruster and Anderson provide an example of this in Chapter 9.

The experimental support for mapping is sparse, but the few studies that have been conducted indicate that the technique facilitates delayed recall of short narrative prose (e.g., Armbruster, 1979; Armbruster & Anderson, 1980).

The principal differences between mapping and networking appear to be that the former strategy (1) emphasizes local organization rather than abstraction of an overall framework or schema, and (2) employs spatial representation of relationships rather than labeled relationships. With respect to the first difference, Anderson (1979) argued that application of mapping to entire text chapters was too time consuming and recommended that the strategy be employed for each important task outcome (e.g., potential test-item on a chapter test). However, Holley *et al.* (1979) argued that the abstraction of an overall framework (macrostructure) for ecologically oriented passages (e.g., textbook chapters) was an important feature of a mapping strategy (i.e., networking). With respect to the second difference, whether the relationships are depicted graphically or labeled may be irrelevant—as long as they are depicted. The superiority (if any) of one method over the other will probably be determined by which method is eventually demonstrated to be simpler for students to comprehend and apply.

SCHEMATIZING

Schematizing was developed at the Center for Research into Higher Education (COWO), University of Amsterdam (e.g., Breuker, 1979, 1980; Camstra, 1979; Mirande, 1979, 1981; van Bruggen, 1980). According to Breuker (1979), the theoretical underpinnings for schematizing are an eclectic blend of node–arc representations (e.g., Frijda, 1972), schema notions (e.g., R. Anderson, Spiro, & Montague, 1977; Winograd, 1975), macrostructure (e.g., van Dijk, 1977), episodic–semantic memory distinctions (e.g., Tulving, 1972), and artificial intelligence (e.g., Winston, 1977).

Schematizing involves the labeling (and, where appropriate, the clustering) of concepts and the depiction of relationships between concepts by lines that are annotated to reflect seven types of relationships (Mirande, 1979). These relationships and annotations are presented in Table 1. Application of the technique results in the production of serially organized (left to right), two-dimensional diagrams of a passage. An example of a schematization is presented by Mirande in Chapter 7.

Schematizing is similar to networking, and different from mapping, in that it uses annotated lines to depict relationships between concepts and

TABLE 1

Relationship Symbols Employed with the Schematization
Technique[a]

Relationship	Symbol
Similarity	
Interaction	
Denial of similarity	
Denial of a static relation	
Denial of a dynamic relation	
Negative influence	
Positive influence	

[a]Lines represent static relationships (e.g., classifications, properties, time–space, comparisons); arrows represent dynamic relationships, (e.g., conditional, cause-and-effect).

emphasizes the extraction of an overall framework or macrostructure. It is
different from networking in the types of relations depicted, the method of
annotation that is used (as previously argued, such differences may be irrelevant), and the organizational structure of the resulting diagrams (serial vis-à-
vis hierarchical). The importance (if any) of this latter difference has not been
demonstrated.

As with mapping, little experimental evidence is available to support (or
refute) the effectiveness of schematizing. The majority of studies that have
been conducted are of a "field study" nature and are more along the lines of
formative rather than summative evaluations. Nonetheless, the technique has
been shown to be an effective processing aid in the context of a general study-
skills course (Camstra, Metten, & Mirande, 1979). (The empirical evidence
supporting schematizing is detailed by Camstra & van Bruggen in Chapter 8.)

SUMMARY AND OVERVIEW

An effective learning strategy has been defined as a set of processes or
steps that can be used by an individual to facilitate the acquisition, storage,
and/or utilization of information (Dansereau, 1980). In this chapter, selected
theories of information processing were briefly reviewed as a prelude to
describing spatial learning techniques. Because these theories are directly
oriented toward explaining how individuals encode, store, and retrieve information, they offer a number of important heuristics to guide the developer of
a learning strategy.

First, the technique should be targeted toward semantic rather than episodic memory. While episodic strategies should not be ignored, it is semantic memory that is commonly associated with *meaningful* learning (cf. Ausubel, 1963).

Second, the technique should be concerned with facilitating the coherent representation of new information in semantic memory. Artificial intelligence research has demonstrated the critical role of representation in comprehension (e.g., Newell & Simon, 1972; Quillian, 1968).

Third, the technique must be designed to capitalize on such notions as depth and elaboration of processing, top-down/bottom-up processing, and reorganization. Abstract spatial learning strategies, as they have been developed, have the potential of meeting all three of these requirements.

While the three preceding heuristics are concerned with theoretical foundations for spatial learning strategies, a fourth important heuristic concerns the practicalities involved in their application. In this regard, Anderson (1979) has suggested that mapping may not be desirable for larger bodies of material (e.g., textbook chapters) because students find the technique too cumbersome, and Holley *et al.* (1979) have suggested that insensitivity to students' existing learning strategies may create an interfering situation that impedes performance. The domain of practical considerations includes the general categories of (1) selection and development of strategies, (2) training in the strategies, and (3) evaluating the effectiveness of the strategies. (See Dansereau, 1980, for a discussion of these issues.)

This book is concerned with both theory and application. The next two chapters in Part I develop specific theoretical underpinnings for spatial learning strategies. Part II contains reports on specific learner-oriented techniques that have been developed to improve the text processing performances of students. Part III presents reports on specific techniques that have been developed and applied to other types of processing tasks (e.g., test taking, problem solving) or to teacher–author communication (e.g., text analysis, instructional strategies). Finally, Part IV provides critiques of the preceding chapters' suggestions regarding educational implications and applications.

REFERENCES

Anderson, J. R., & Bower, G. H. (1973). *Human associative memory*. New York: Winston.
Anderson, R. C., Spiro, R. J., & Montague, W. E. (Eds.). (1977). *Schooling and the acquisition of knowledge*. Hillsdale, NJ: Erlbaum.
Anderson, T. H. (1979). Study skills and learning strategies. In H. F. O'Neil, Jr. & C. D. Spielberger (Eds.), *Cognitive and affective learning strategies*. New York: Academic Press.
Anderson, T. H., & Armbruster, B. B. (1981). Studying. In P. D. Pearson (Ed.), *Handbook on reading research*. New York: Longman.

Armbruster, B. B. (1979). *An investigation of the effectiveness of "mapping" text as a studying strategy for middle school students.* Unpublished doctoral dissertation, University of Illinois.

Armbruster, B. B., & Anderson, T. H. (1980). *The effect of mapping on the free recall of expository text* (Tech. Rep. 160). Champaign, IL: Center for the Study of Reading, University of Illinois.

Armbruster, B. B., & Schallert, D. L. (1980, December). *Understanding text through mapping.* Paper presented at the Annual Meeting of the National Reading Conference, San Diego, CA.

Ausubel, D. P. (1963). *The psychology of meaningful verbal learning.* New York: Grune & Stratton.

Baddeley, A. D. (1976). *The psychology of memory.* New York: Basic Books.

Balser, E. (1972). The free recall and category clustering of factual material presented in complex sentences. *Psychonomic Science, 27,* 327–328.

Bartlett, F. C. (1932). *Remembering.* Cambridge, England: The Cambridge University Press.

Bobrow, D., & Fraser, B. (1969). An augmented state transition network analysis procedure. In D. Walker and L. Norton (Eds.), *Proceedings of the international joint conference on artificial intelligence.* Washington, DC.

Bourne, L. E., Jr., Dominowski, R. L., & Loftus, E. F. (1979). *Cognitive processes.* Englewood Cliffs, NJ: Prentice-Hall.

Bousfield, W. A. (1953). The occurrence of clustering in the recall of randomly arranged associates. *Journal of General Psychology, 49,* 229–240.

Bower, G. H. (1972). Stimulus-sampling theory of encoding variability. In A. W. Melton & E. Martin (Eds.), *Coding processes in human memory.* Washington, DC: Winston.

Bower, G. H. (1974). Selective facilitation and interference in retention of prose. *Journal of Educational Psychology, 66,* 1–8.

Bower, G. H., Clark, M. C., Lesgold, A. M., & Winzenz, D. (1969). Hierarchical retrieval schemes in recall of categorized word lists. *Journal of Verbal Learning and Verbal Behavior, 8,* 323–343.

Bransford, J. D., & McCarrell, N. S. (1974). A sketch of a cognitive approach to comprehension. In W. Weimer & D. S. Palermo (Eds.), *Cognition and the symbolic processes.* Hillsdale, NJ: Erlbaum.

Breuker, J. A. (1979, January). *Theoretical foundations of schematizations: From macrostructures to conceptual frames.* Paper presented at the EARDHE International Conference, Klagenfurt, Austria.

Breuker, J. A. (1980). *In kaart brengen van leerstof.* Utrecht/Antwerpen: Uitgeverij Het Spectrum.

Camstra, B. (1979, January). *Empirical research with "learning by schematizing".* Paper presented at the EARDHE International Conference, Klangenfurt, Austria.

Camstra, B., Metten, A., & Mirande, M. (1979). *Effectonderzoek van enn studievaardigheidscursus.* Unpublished manuscript, Center for Research into Higher Education (COWO), University of Amsterdam, Amsterdam, the Netherlands.

Cofer, C. N. (1965). On some factors in the organizational characteristics of free recall. *American Psychologist, 20,* 261–272.

Collins, K. W., Dansereau, D. F., Holley, C. D., Garland, J. C., & McDonald, B. A. (1981). Control of concentration during academic tasks. *Journal of Educational Psychology, 73,* 122–128.

Conrad, C. (1972). Cognitive economy in semantic memory. *Journal of Experimental Psychology, 92,* 149–154.

Craik, F. I. M., & Jacoby, L. L. (1975). A process view of short-term retention. In F. Restle, R. M. Shiffrin, J. J. Castellan, M. R. Lindman, & D. B. Pisoni (Eds.), *Cognitive theory* (Vol. 1). Hillsdale, NJ: Erlbaum.

Craik, F. I. M., & Lockhart, R. S. (1972). Levels of processing: A framework for memory research. *Journal of Verbal Learning and Verbal Behavior, 11,* 671–684.

Craik, F. I. M., & Tulving, E. (1975). Depth of processing and the retention of words in episodic memory. *Journal of Experimental Psychology: General, 104,* 268–294.

Craik, F. I. M., & Watkins, M. J. (1973). The role of rehearsal in short-term memory. *Journal of Verbal Learning and Verbal Behavior, 12,* 599–607.

Dansereau, D. F. (1978). The development of a learning strategies curriculum. In H. F. O'Neal, Jr. (Ed.), *Learning strategies.* New York: Academic Press.

Dansereau, D. F. (1980). Learning strategy research. *Proceedings of the NIE-LRDC conference on thinking and learning skills.* Washington, DC: National Institute of Education.

Dansereau, D. F., Collins, K. W., McDonald, B. A., Holley, C. D., Garland, J. C., Diekhoff, G., & Evans, S. H. (1979). Development and evaluation of a learning strategy training program. *Journal of Educational Psychology, 71,* 64–73.

Dansereau, D. F., & Holley, C. D. (1982). Development and evaluation of a text mapping strategy. In A. Flammer & W. Kintsch (Eds.), *Discourse processing.* Amsterdam: North-Holland.

Dansereau, D. F., Holley, C. D., Collins, K. W., Brooks, L. W., McDonald, B. A., & Larson, D. (1980, April). *Validity of learning strategies/skills training.* AFHRL-TR-79-84. Air Force Systems Command, Brooks AFB, Texas. (ADA 085-659).

Dansereau, D. F., Long, G. L. McDonald, B. A., Actkinson, T. R., Collins, K. W., Evans, S. H., Ellis, A. M., & Williams, S. (1975, June). *Learning strategy training programs: Visual imagery for effective learning.* AFHRL-TR-75-47. Technical Training Division, Lowry AFB, Colorado. (ADA 014 724).

Dansereau, D. F., McDonald, B. A., Collins, K. W., Garland, J. C., Holley, C. D., Diekhoff, G. M., & Evans, S. H. (1977, December). *Development and evaluation of an interactive learning strategy system.* Invited paper, Learning Strategies Measures and Modules Seminar, Carmel, CA.

Dansereau, D. F., McDonald, B. A., Collins, K. W., Garland, J. C., Holley, C. D., Diekhoff, G. M. & Evans, S. H. (1979). Evaluation of a learning strategy system. In H. F. O'Neil, Jr., & C. D. Spielberger (Eds.), *Cognitive and affective learning strategies.* New York: Academic Press.

DiVesta, F. J., Schultz, C. B., & Dangel, I. R. (1973). Passage organization and imposed learning strategies in comprehension and recall of connected discourse. *Memory and Cognition, 6,* 471–476.

Dwyer, F. M. (1973a). Effect of method in presenting visualized instruction. *AV Communication Review, 21,* 437–451.

Dwyer, F. M. (1973b). The relative effectiveness of two methods of presenting visualized instruction. *Journal of Psychology, 85,* 297–300.

Dwyer, F. M. (1978). *Strategies for improving visual learning.* State College, PA: Learning Services.

Ellis, H. C. (1978). *Fundamentals of human learning, memory, and cognition* (2nd ed.). Dubuque, IA: Brown.

Frase, L. T. (1969a). Cybernetic control of memory while reading connected discourse. *Journal of Educational Psychology, 60,* 49–55.

Frase, L. T. (1969b). Paragraph organization of written materials: The influence of conceptual clustering upon the level and organization of recall. *Journal of Educational Psychology, 60,* 394–401.

Friedman, M. P., & Greitzer, F. L. (1972). Organization and study time in learning from reading. *Journal of Educational Psychology, 1972, 63,* 609–616.

Frijda, N. H. (1972). Simulation of human long-term memory. *Psychological Bulletin, 77,* 1–31.

Hauf, M. B. (1971). Mapping: A technique for translating reading into thinking. *Journal of Reading, 14,* 225–230.

Holley, C. D., Dansereau, D. F., McDonald, B. A., Garland, J. C., & Collins, K. W. (1978). *Networking as an information processing approach to classroom performance.* Paper presented at the Southwestern Educational Research Association Annual Meeting, Austin, TX.

Holley, C. D., Dansereau, D. F., McDonald, B. A., Garland, J. C., & Collins, K. W. (1979). Evaluation of a hierarchical mapping technique as an aid to prose processing. *Contemporary Educational Psychology, 4,* 227–237.

Jacoby, L. L., & Craik, F. I. M. (1979). Effects of elaboration of processing at encoding and retrieval: Trace distinctiveness and recovery of initial context. In L. S. Cermak and F. I. M. Craik (Eds.), *Levels of processing in human memory.* Hillsdale, NJ: Erlbaum.

Kaplan, R. M. (1972). Augmented transition networks as psychological models of sentence comprehension. *Artificial Intelligence, 3,* 77–100.

Kaplan, R. M. (1973). A general syntactic processor. In R. Rustin (Ed.), *Natural language processing.* New York: Algorithmics Press.

Kaplan, R. M. (1974). *Transient processing load in relative clauses.* Unpublished doctoral dissertation, Harvard University.

Kintsch, W., & van Dijk, T. A. (1978). Toward a model of text comprehension and production. *Psychological Review, 85,* 363–394.

Kulhavy, R. W., & Swenson, I. (1975). Imagery instructions and the comprehension of text. *British Journal of Educational Psychology, 45,* 47–51.

Landauer, T. K., & Freedman, J. L. (1968). Information retrieval from long-term memory. *Journal of Verbal Learning and Verbal Behavior, 7,* 291–295.

Landauer, T. K., & Meyer, D. E. (1972). Category size and semantic-memory retrieval. *Journal of Verbal Learning and Verbal Behavior, 11,* 539–549.

Levin, J. R., & Divine-Hawkins, P. (1974). Visual imagery as a prose-learning process. *Journal of Reading Behavior, 6,* 23–30.

Lindsay, P. H., & Norman, D. A. (1977). *Human information processing: An introduction to psychology* (2nd ed.). New York: Academic Press.

Lockhart, R. S., Craik, F. I. M., & Jacoby, L. L. (1976). Depth of processing, recognition and recall: Some aspects of a general memory system. In J. Brown (Ed.), *Recall and recognition.* London: Wiley.

Mandler, G. (1967). Organization and memory. In K. W. Spence & J. T. Spence (Eds.), *Advances in the psychology of learning and motivation* (Vol. 1). New York: Academic Press.

Mandler, G., & Worden, P. E. (1973). Semantic processing without permanent storage. *Journal of Experimental Psychology, 100,* 277–283.

Martin, E. (1968). Stimulus meaningfulness and paired-associated transfer: An encoding variability hypothesis. *Psychological Review, 75,* 421–441.

Melton, A. W. (1967). Repetition and retrieval from memory. *Science, 158,* 532.

Melton, A. W., & Martin, E. (1972). *Coding processes in human memory.* Washington, D.C.: Winston.

Merritt, J., Prior, D., Grugeon, E., & Grugeon, D. (1977). *Developing independence in reading.* Milton Keynes: Open University Press.

Mirande, M. J. A. (1979, January). *Schematizing: Techniques and applications.* Paper presented at the EARDHE International Conference, Klagenfurt, Austria.

Mirande, M. J. A. (1981). *Studeren door schematiseren.* Utrecht/Antwerpen: Uitgeveij Het Spectrum.

Milner, B. (1968). Visual recognition and recall after right temporal-lobe excision in man. *Neuropsychologia, 6,* 191–209.

Munro, A., & Rigney, J. W. (1977). *A schema theory account of some cognitive processes in complex learning* (Tech. Rep. 81). Los Angeles: University of Southern California, Behavioral Technology Laboratories.

Musgrave, B. S., & Cohen, J. C. (1966, May). *Relationships between prose and list learning.* Paper presented at the Verbal Learning and Written Instructional Materials Conference. Office of Naval Research.

Musgrave, B. S., & Cohen, J. C. (1971). Relationships between prose and list learning. In E. Z. Rothkopfe & P. E. Johnson (Eds.), *Verbal learning research and the technology of written instruction.* New York: Teachers College Press.

Myers, J. L. (1974). *Memory for prose material.* Amherst, Mass.: University of Massachusetts. (ERIC Document Reproduction Service No. ED 094 360)

Newell, A., & Simon, H. A. (1972). *Human problem solving.* Englewood Cliffs, NJ: Prentice-Hall.

Norman, D. A., Rumelhart, D. E., & LNR Research Group. (1975). *Explorations in cognition.* San Francisco: Freeman.

O'Neil, H. F., Jr. (Ed.). (1978). *Learning strategies.* New York: Academic Press.

O'Neil, H. F., Jr., & Spielberger, C. D. (1979). *Cognitive and affective learning strategies.* New York: Academic Press.

Palmer, S. E. (1975). Visual perception and world knowledge: Notes on a model of sensory cognitive interaction. In D. A. Norman, D. E. Rumelhart, & LNR Research Group (Eds.), *Explorations in cognition.* San Francisco: Freeman.

Perlmutter, J., & Royer, J. M. (1973). Organization of prose materials: Stimulus, storage and retrieval. *Canadian Journal of Psychology, 27,* 200–209.

Quillian, M. R. (1968). Semantic meaning. In M. Minsky (Ed.), *Semantic information processing.* Cambridge, MA: MIT Press.

Quillan, M. R. (1969). The teachable language comprehender. *Communications of the Association for Computing Machinery, 12,* 459–475.

Rasco, R. W., Tennyson, R. P., & Boutwell, R. C. (1975). Imagery instructions and drawings in learning prose. *Journal of Educational Research, 67,* 188–192.

Reddy, D. R. (Ed.). (1975). *Speech recognition.* New York: Academic Press.

Rigney, J. W., & Munro, A. (1977, March). *On cognitive strategies for processing text* (Tech. Rep. 80). Los Angeles: University of Southern California, Behavioral Technology Laboratories.

Rumelhart, D. E. (1977). *Introduction to human information processing.* New York: Wiley.

Rumelhart, D. E., Lindsay, P. H., & Norman, D. A. (1972). A process model for long-term memory. In E. Tulving & W. Donaldson (Eds.), *Organization of memory.* New York: Academic Press.

Rumelhart, D. E., & Ortony, A. (1977). The representation of knowledge in memory. In R. C. Anderson, R. J. Spiro, & W. E. Montague (Eds.), *Schooling and the acquisition of knowledge.* Hillsdale, NJ: Erlbaum.

Schaeffer, B., & Wallace, R. (1969). Semantic similarity and the comparison of word meanings. *Journal of Experimental Psychology, 82,* 343–346.

Schultz, C. B., & DiVesta, F. J. (1972). Effects of passage organization and note taking on the selection of clustering strategies and on recall of textual materials. *Journal of Educational Psychology, 63,* 244–252.

Shallice, T., & Warrington, E. K. (1970). Independent functioning of verbal memory stores: A neuropsychological study. *Quarterly Journal of Experimental Psychology, 22,* 261–273.

Shimmerlick, S. M. (1978). Organization theory and memory for prose: A review of the literature. *Review of Educational Research, 48,* 103–120.

Stevens, A. L., & Rumelhart, D. E. (1975). Errors in reading: Analyses using an augmented network model of grammar. In D. A. Norman, D. E. Rumelhart, & LNR Research Group (Eds.), *Explorations in cognition.* San Francisco: Freeman.

Thomson, D. M., & Tulving, E. (1970). Associative encoding and retrieval: Weak and strong cues. *Journal of Experimental Psychology, 22*, 261–273.

Thorne, J., Bratley, P., & Dewar, H. (1968). The syntactic analysis of English by machine. In D. Michie (Ed.), *Machine intelligence* (Vol. 3). New York: American Elsevier.

Tulving, E. (1968). Theoretical issues in free recall. In T. R. Dixon & D. L. Horton (Eds.), *Verbal behavior and general behavior theory*. Englewood Cliffs: Prentice-Hall.

Tulving, E. (1972). Episodic and semantic memory. In E. Tulving & W. Donaldson (Eds.), *Organization of memory*. New York: Academic Press.

Tulving, E. (1978). Relation between encoding specificity and levels of processing. In L. S. Cermak & F. I. M. Craik (Eds.), *Levels of processing and human memory*. Hillsdale, NJ: Erlbaum.

Tulving, E., & Madigan, S. A. (1970). Memory and verbal learning. *Annual Review of Psychology, 21*, 437–484.

van Bruggen, J. M. (1980). *Vaardig leren studeren; een literatuuronderzoek naar de effecten van studievaardigheidskursussen*. COWO-rapport, University of Amsterdam.

van Dijk, T. A. (1977). Semantic macro-structures and knowledge frames in discourse comprehension. In M. A. Just and P. A. Carpenter (Eds.), *Cognitive processes in comprehension*. Hillsdale, NJ: Erlbaum.

Voss, J. F. (1972). On the relationship of associates and organizational processes. In E. Tulving & W. Donaldson (Eds.), *Organization of memory*. New York: Academic Press.

Wanner, E., & Maratsos, M. M. (1974). *On understanding relative clauses*. Unpublished manuscript, Harvard University, Department of Psychology and Social Relations.

Warrington, E. K., & Shallice, T. (1969). The selective impairment of auditory verbal short-term memory. *Brain, 92*, 885–896.

Wertheimer, M. (1970). *A brief history of psychology*. New York: Holt.

Wilkins, A. J. (1971). Conjoint frequency, category size, and categorization time. *Journal of Verbal Learning and Verbal Behavior, 10*, 382–385.

Winograd, T. (1972). *Understanding natural language*. Edinburgh: Edinburgh University Press.

Winograd, T. (1975). Frame representations and the declarative-procedure controversy. In D. A. Bobrow & A. M. Collins (Eds.), *Representation and understanding*. New York: Academic Press.

Winston, P. (1977). *Artificial intelligence*. Philippines: Addison-Wesley.

Wood, G. (1969). Retrieval cues and the accessibility of higher order memory units in multi-trial free recall. *Journal of Verbal Learning and Verbal Behavior, 8*, 782–789.

Woods, W. A. (1970). Transition network grammars for natural language analysis. *Communications of the ACM, 13*, 501–606.

Woodward, A. E., Bjork, R. A. & Jongeward, R. H., Jr. (1973). Recall and recognition as a function of primary rehearsal. *Journal of Verbal Learning and Verbal Behavior, 12*, 608–617.

Yin, R. (1969). Looking at upside-down faces. *Journal of Experimental Psychology, 81*, 141–145.

CHAPTER 2

A Theoretical Framework for Spatial Learning Strategies

JOOST A. BREUKER

WHAT IS SPECIAL ABOUT SPATIAL?

Doing ordinary arithmetic with paper and pencil is a good illustration of the potentials of spatial learning strategies. Although there are some obvious limits to the analogy, spatial learning strategies facilitate text understanding in the same way that pencil-and-paper arithmetic simplifies mental arithmetic. As far as the use of spatial representations is concerned, there are some strong parallels. The use of paper-and-pencil visualizations in arithmetic and in spatial learning strategies has an obvious function: to provide for an almost unlimited external memory. In text understanding, this function is also implicit in such practices as note-taking, outlining, underlining, and summarizing (for reviews on these study aids, see T. H. Anderson, 1980, and Mc-Conkie, 1977). However, in arithmetic the spatial arrangement of the written numbers is almost essential to performing the arithmetic operations; for example, compare the following problem statements:

Seventy-two thousand, four hundred and fifty-two minus sixty-seven thousand five hundred and fifty-seven. According to Dutch or German grammar, this problem

SPATIAL LEARNING STRATEGIES
Techniques, Applications, and Related Issues

would be expressed as two and seventy thousand four hundred two and fifty minus seven and sixty thousand five hundred seven and fifty. In either case, the problem may be expressed spatially as:

$$72452 - 67557$$

or

$$72452$$
$$-67557$$

The spatial arrangement makes information explicit that otherwise has to be abstracted from the sequential problem statements, particularly if the statements are not coded into numbers and the sequence of number words does not correspond one-to-one with the structure (order) that is required for the arithmetic operations—that is, the word order is "left to right" whereas the order of operations is right to left. In a similar way, text can hide information and the sequence of words requires complex transformations to fit mental operations.

Spatial learning strategies are aimed at coding and transforming text information into spatial representations that preserve and make explicit the structural information that can be abstracted from a text. These spatial representations are not arbitrary with respect to the mental operations that produce them and that permit them to be read. In arithmetic the spatial arrangements are directly related to the mental operations that produce them and that permit them to be read (cf. Young & O'Shea, 1981). (Also, diagrams that aid problem solving in physics [e.g., mechanics problems], use an implicit "grammar" that permits knowledge about physics to be applied [Hayes & Simon, 1976; Larkin, 1982].) Specifically, the spatial arrangement and the external memory permit the problem-solver to use a relatively small store of basic factual knowledge (e.g., the multiplication tables) and to split up the arithmetic procedures into successively applicable subprocedures, thereby attenuating the demands on processing capacity.

So far the analogy between paper-and-pencil arithmetic and spatial representations of the conceptualizations in a study text still holds—both employ external memory, explicit structures, and decomposition of procedures into simple steps. However, the grammars in spatial representations of text are tailored to specific domains of knowledge and strategies associated with task performance. In this respect, the analogy between paper-and-pencil arithmetic and spatial learning strategies breaks down. The skills involved in doing arithmetic and text understanding are quite different. Specifically, the knowledge required in arithmetic is very restricted; the procedures are completely algorithmic; the problems are well-defined. In text understanding the opposite is the case.

Spatial representations of text are specifically related to skills in text understanding. The aim of this chapter is to explicate these relations. There are two principal types of relationships to be clarified: products and processes.

First, the correspondence between the *products* of text understanding and spatial learning strategies is discussed: In what respect does a spatial representation reflect the knowledge that is intended by the text? and can this representation be read by a student? In instructional terminology, what can be expected from spatial representations as adjunct study aids in understanding study texts? These issues are discussed in the next section.

Producing spatial representations of a study text requires some major adjustments in the strategies used in traditional studying of texts. Therefore relationships between the *processes* of text understanding and spatial learning strategies appear to be more important: How can spatial learning strategies interact with and facilitate text understanding? In other words, what improvements in understanding can be expected from applying spatial learning strategies as specific study skills? This issue is addressed in the final section, after a review of competencies and processes involved in understanding difficult texts.

KNOWLEDGE AND SPATIAL REPRESENTATION

Text understanding can be conceived of as the transformation of sequences of words, sentences, and paragraphs into a coherent conceptual structure: synthesized knowledge. What is knowledge, or rather, what model of knowledge can be proposed? In all theories, two major categories are distinguished as the building material for human knowledge: concepts and relationships (cf. Brachman, 1979; Frijda, 1972; Woods, 1975). The category *concept* is difficult to define, but entails a wide variety of entities such as ideas, objects, images, notions, conceptions, beliefs, events, features, properties, and states. A concept represents anything that can be recognized, that is, that can be attributed identity. This description strongly suggests some circularity: the availability of a concept is a necessary requirement for identification (cf. Fodor & Pylyshyn, 1981). For instance, if the human mind contained only five concepts, only five "things" could be identified. This number of identifiable things is extended by combining old concepts to create new concepts. Such combinations cannot be done arbitrarily. They are related by meaningful associations or *relations*.

Relations can also be thought of as concepts (Frijda, 1972), but of a particular nature. Specifically, a relation is a function that indicates the role of a concept toward one or more other concepts. The meaning of a relation is

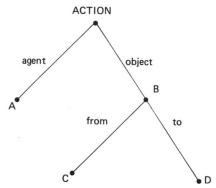

FIGURE 1. A structured list and its graphic representations: ACTION ((agent A)(object B (from C) (to D))).

less context dependent, more general, invariant and "empty" than that of other concepts. In knowledge representation systems, the set of (primitive) relationships is often relatively limited, while there appear to be no restrictions on the number of (other) concepts (e.g., Quillian, 1968; Schank, 1972; Woods, 1975).

There are several ways to represent this conception of human knowledge. The weakest method is a set-theoretic model: concepts simply consist of sets of features, where features can be thought of as concepts (Smith, Shoben, & Rips, 1974)—in a pseudoalgebraic formulation, A(B, C, D . . .), where A, B, C, and so on are concepts. Propositional or list-structure models can be symbolized as A(r, B), or A(r(B)), where r stands for a relation. A network representation can be symbolized as (A, r, B). These elementary building blocks can be further combined by embedding into more complex structures. Some structures function as units and are called *schemas* (cf. next section). An example of a basic schema is a conceptual role schema for transport action: ACTION ((agent A) (object B (from C) (to D))) (Schank, 1972). (See graphic representation, Figure 1.)

Formally, different representation models can be logically equivalent, for instance, network and set-theoretic models (Hollan, 1975). But this does not mean that they are therefore the same. Minor differences between representational formats can have drastic consequences for the processing of these data structures. In network models the relations (r) are an explicit part of the data, while in set theoretic models relations between concepts have to be derived (computed) from the combinations of sets (Breuker, 1981; Smith, 1978). More detailed examples of the key role of the way representations are cast in conceptual processing are presented by Winston (1977). Logical equivalence does not mean that identical operations can be applied.

I have raised this point for the following reason. Network models are at present the most widely used format for representing knowledge (see Findler, 1979). In applying spatial learning strategies as aids for understanding study texts, the student often produces a network-like representation. Therefore, it is tempting to refer to network models for knowledge representation as a theoretical foundation for the use of spatial learning strategies (Breuker, 1979; Dansereau, *et al.*, 1979). In a nutshell the argument is as follows. If network representations are the most adequate model of human knowledge available, then presenting information in the form of a network will be the most adequate parallel to the knowledge intended by the text. In other words, fewer transformations are required to process a network presentation into a conceptual structure than to process sequentially organized presentations like texts. There is some flaw in this reasoning. If implemented in a computer, networks have the form of a structured list. A structured list in network models is analogous to a text in spatial learning strategies: both are partially structured by the order of symbols (words). A structured list and a graphic representation can be logically equivalent (see Figure 1), but that does not mean that they are equivalent with respect to processing characteristics. For computer input, structured lists are used in accordance with the computer's serial processing characteristics. However, for convenience to the human reader, such structured lists are often presented as graphs in publications. List structures are difficult to read for humans. Therefore, it may be true that in spatial learning strategies, notions like concept and relation are adopted from models of knowledge representation, but further correspondence with respect to *graphic* representation is accidental, or rather theoretically unfounded. Network models do not explain why humans appear to recognize a structure in a two-dimensional arrangement so much more easily than in a one-dimensional structured list. Graphic representations of networks are based on the same intuition regarding ease of processing as spatial learning strategies are.

Can this intuition be made more explicit? One can speculate at least. In a serial representation of data, like a text, the structure of the data has to be abstracted (see the next section); in a spatial representation the structure is given. However, this spatial representation cannot be read by humans in one gaze: there is a succession of fixations. In other words, the spatial structure has to be broken down to some extent in order to be understood. This extent is determined by the familiarity and Gestalt-like properties of configuration, besides the content for which the spatial representation stands. Therefore, facilitation of processing from the preservation of structure is probably mainly restricted to spatial representations that exhibit a "good figure" and familiar patterns (Minsky, 1975). In spatial learning strategies the use of familiar structures like hierarchies is strongly recommended and the schematizing technique, for example, contains explicit instructions to produce "good figures."

Besides "being easily grasped," familiar spatial arrangements may also have a second advantage. They can be used as mnemonic frames, in a manner similar to the use of images of well-known locations as memory aids (e.g., Galton's Walk; see Yates, 1966). Research on the use of images as mnemonic techniques for text shows equivocal results, but in general the results are positive (for a short review, see McConkie, 1977). Another potentially beneficial effect from reading spatial representations, compared to reading a text, is that inspection of a graphic presentation provides more focus-of-attention control to the reader, while maintaining a structured background.

While graphic representations can support text comprehension, a large number of studies have shown no improvement in comprehension or even negative results (cf. McDonald-Ross, 1977; Schallert, 1980). There is little empirical evidence on the effectiveness of spatial representations of the conceptual structure of a text on understanding and remembering the gist of the text. Van Oostendorp (1980) found that a schematization (see Chapter 7, present volume) of the main theme of a study text improved recall, but the improvement was similar to that for providing a verbal summary. In spatial learning strategies, the process may be more valued than the product because in applying these strategies, the normal course of (incomplete) text comprehension is drastically changed, as I argue in the next sections.

TASK ANALYSIS: A COMPETENCE MODEL

I discuss two complementary approaches to describe the process of text understanding. The first is an idealized task analysis: an abstract description of the competencies involved in text understanding. A *competence model* serves no other purpose than to clarify the problems one faces in transforming a text into a *text base:* a new structure of knowledge (Kintsch & van Dijk, 1978). The second approach is a description of processing components as they can be abstracted from literature on understanding text, that is, a *performance model*. The two approaches complement one another because the first one provides a heuristic to identify the functions that the components in the second model have to perform.

In the task analysis, two characteristics of language will be taken as basic assumptions. The first is that language is a serial expression of a multidimensional knowledge structure. The second is that only a small part of the intended text-base is explicitly expressed in a text; much information is implicit and has to be inferred by the reader.

The projection of a multidimensional structure onto a one-dimensional sequence necessarily requires repetition of (symbols for) nodes of the structure (see Figure 2). Or to phrase it in a paper-and-pencil metaphor, one can

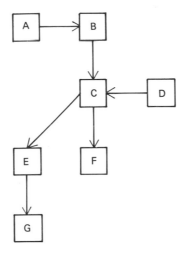

FIGURE 2. Two examples of a linearization of a network: (a) A → B, B → C, C → E, E → G, C → D, C → F; (b) C ← B, C ← D, C → E, C → F, A → B, E → G.

only trace a network without lifting one's pencil by once in a while retracing one's steps. One can use many strategies for these projections. For instance, first express all nodes and then fill in the gaps (Figure 2, caption (a)); or express everything that is said of one node and then go to the next node, leaving out what has already been said (Figure 2, caption (b)).

Levelt (1981) has argued that the linearization strategy people use can be very strongly content dependent, but constraints are imposed, based on human processing limitations. A first constraint is that the number of jumps should be minimized. This means that in texts the most recent topic is also the most probable next topic. A *topic* is an instantiated concept about which the text asserts something. For example, the word *horse* is interpreted as a specific instantiation of the concept HORSE; if the text tells something about the horse, this interpretation is called a topic. In Figure 2,(a), the successive topics are A, B, C, E, C, C. A second constraint is to keep jumps as short as possible. The processing principles formulated by Levelt (1981) are somewhat more complicated and avoid the potential conflicts between these constraints.

In text, a jump back to a previous topic (node) is infrequently expressed by explicit repetition of words or expressions. Language has many devices to identify whether an expression refers to some new topic or is anaphoric. The most obvious devices to indicate the latter situation are definite determiners and pronouns. Mere repetition is often "forbidden" because it can lead to ambiguity, as (1) shows:

(1) John thought that John would meet John's wife.

If not "forbidden," the use of repetitions can lead to stylistically bad, unreadable texts. It is still unclear what psychological mechanism elicits this effect, for instance:

(2) Mary's husband, John, thought he could have his way with other women.

(3a) Mary's husband had to pay dearly.

(3b) John had to pay dearly.

(3c) He had to pay dearly.

(3d) The fool had to pay dearly.

(3e) Fools have to pay dearly.

The acceptability (or stylistic force) of the continuations (3, a–e) of (2) seems to be better the less there is resemblance between referent and antecedent. Note that in (3d) anaphoric reference is made by description (cf. Garrod & Sanford, 1977). In (3e) any explicit indication of anaphoric reference is absent; there is not even correspondence in number (see Webber & Reiter, 1977).

In sum, the competence involved in constructing a multidimensional text-base from a one-dimensional text can be stated as follows:

1. Determine whether a word or expression refers to an old or to a new topic.

2. If the word or expression is anaphoric, then the referent has to be found.

This competence, topic identification, is by no means a trivial one, as is illustrated by (3e); nor is it only a subordinate aspect of text understanding. One of the most prevailing theories of text processing (Kintsch & van Dijk, 1978) is almost exclusively based on anaphoric references, called *argument repetition*.

The necessity to repeat topics makes the use of language relatively cumbersome. This is compensated by a second characteristic of language: leave unsaid what the reader can infer from prior knowledge. This characteristic is succinctly formulated by Grice (1975) as the first of three global rules of pragmatics: *be informative*—do not tell old news that can be inferred by the reader. Telling some story in a very detailed way, where all *whys*, *whos*, and *whats*, are explicitly stated, would probably result in a loss of interest by the listener; if escape by the listener were impolite, most probably suspicion and confusion would arise. There are some conclusions to be drawn from these arguments. First, complete explicitness is uninteresting and boring; den Uyl (1980) even argues that implicitness is a main source of interest because it adds to the novelty of a text (e.g., verbal jokes). Second, reading between the lines is the default mode of discourse processing; gaps are assumed and if one cannot find them—at least relevant ones—there must be some misunderstanding going on.

Competence at making such inferences is quite important in transforming a text into a text-base. The goal of making inferences is to establish coherence in the text-base. Coherence, an overall quality of a knowledge structure, is related to the accessibility of concepts. The more coherent a structure (i.e., the more dense a network) the more ways concepts can be accessed. Locally, the coherence of a structure may vary; it is not necessary that a knowledge structure should be uniformly coherent. If the most important, embedding concepts form a coherent, global structure, subordinate or supporting concepts can be accessed from them. This economic notion on the distribution of coherence is at the base of theories of macrostructures in text-bases (van Dijk, 1980) and, generally, hierarchical structures (e.g., Quillian, 1968) of which taxonomies are a specific instance (Collins & Loftus, 1975; Frijda, 1972).

If the reader cannot make sense of a text, this means that the coherence of the text-base (at least the most recent part) is below some criterion. Coherence can be enhanced by making inferences, which serve two purposes. The first purpose is to reduce the number of topics. This can be achieved by cognizing that two topics are the same (e.g., "John" and "the fool" in (3)), or that one topic entails another topic, for example, by embedding. Inference for this purpose also supports the competence of topic identification. The second purpose is to produce new relationships between topics: the more relations in a network the greater the coherence.

Two of the prevailing models of text understanding differ in the way priority is given to these two purposes of inferences. According to Kintsch and van Dijk's (1978) theory, a text-base is organized by identification of topics or *arguments;* that is, all propositions with the same argument are collected under the same node. Text understanding is driven by recognizing argument repetition. Inferences are first made to recognize identity with previously processed topics, for instance, by inferring the antecedent of a pronoun or some other anaphoric expression (see 3c, d, and e). Any topic has to have at least one relation with another topic, so supplementary inferences can be made to establish relations. This topic-centered, structure-building strategy is also part of many other text understanding models (e.g., Just & Carpenter, 1980; Kieras, 1981a,b).

In Schank's theory (1975; Schank & Abelson, 1977; Schank & Riesbeck, 1981) the focus is on achieving coherence by constructing relations. Knowledge abstracted from a text is not organized around topics, but as causal chains. Text understanding is *event driven,* and understanding means that events and their preconditions are causally related to other events, which can be part of hierarchical structures.

The contrast between the two theoretical approaches can be demonstrated as follows:

(4) John wanted to go to Amsterdam.
(5) The car did not start easily.

According to the Kintsch and van Dijk (1978) model, the reader would try to connect or embed the topics from (4) and (5), and a plausible inference would be

(6) John had a car.

In the Schank and Abelson (1977) model, the inference would be an instrumental one, for example,

(7) John intended to use a car as a means of transportation.

In both models, inferences are made to construct relations and to identify topics. The difference between the models is the priority given to each kind of inference. Different priorities lead to different organizations of the text base: topic-centered vis-à-vis chain-centered. Both organizations are plausible, and the appropriateness of a particular organization depends on the nature of the text. For instance, in an introductory study text, organization by topic is likely to be preferred; in a story, causal chaining appears to be a more appropriate organization principle.

Therefore, the two models describe different prototypical strategies, each representing a particular perspective. For example, in reading a story, both the perspectives of characters (topics) and chains of events can be (alternatingly) present. There may be many more types of perspectives: in reasoning and talking about mechanical devices, people freely switch from a structural to a functional perspective (Williams, Hollan, & Stevens, 1983; also de Kleer & Brown, 1981).

Multiple perspectives are hard to combine in one single spatial representation. In our laboratory, we have observed that students using the schematization technique can have great difficulties when the study text interweaves several perspectives (e.g., the text alternates between teleologic and causal arguments, proofs, theories, descriptions of objects, processes, and functions) about one global topic. It is not clear whether these problems that the students experience in schematizing are due to limitations of spatial representations, or to problems in understanding. Experts in a domain of knowledge have less problems with making spatial representations, probably because they possess some underlying unifying notions (see de Kleer & Brown, 1981).

In addition to competencies for topic identification and making inferences, a third competence is the availability of several types of knowledge.

The first type of knowledge that is necessary for text understanding is knowledge of words. Concepts can be accessed either by name or by description. The latter method is typical for making inferences or for thinking. If words are unknown to the reader, which occurs rather frequently in study text, then complicated inferences are required to abstract their meaning from the context (Elshout-Mohr & van Daalen-Kapteijns, 1981).

Another type of knowledge that is necessary for text understanding is syntactic knowledge. However, the role of syntax is subordinate to that of content knowledge (Schank & Birnbaum, in press) and there are no indications that syntax is a source of problems for students reading a text.

Of crucial importance is knowledge that is required for making inferences. Some inferences can be based on very specific information that bridges a gap (Clark & Havilland, 1977), but in general, inferences are not that isolated. The specific information to be applied is generally part of some larger context of knowledge and can consist of complex schemas that can be instantiated into the text-base. This context can have a very powerful function, because it can serve as a target structure that is, the text is interpreted in terms of a more general structure of prior knowledge, which provides a *control structure* for understanding. This function is particularly emphasized in recent constructivist or schema-theoretic conceptions (e.g., Collins, Brown, & Larkin, 1980; Spiro, 1980). A text is not simply the visible tip of a knowledge iceberg, but is a complex condition for applying, combining, elaborating and/or modifying an individual's prior knowledge. In this sense, text-bases are schemas-with-corrections (Woodworth, 1938).

The notion of schema as a tightly organized "package" of knowledge is not new (e.g., Bartlett, 1932), but has recently received new attention and new specifications; particularly in work in artificial intelligence, where it developed in the mid-1970s under such names as beta-structures (Moore & Newell, 1974), frames (Minsky, 1975), scripts (Schank, 1975; Schank & Abelson, 1977) and schemata (Norman, *et al.,* 1975; Rumelhart & Ortony, 1977). In network terms, schemas are the logical consequence of the fact that there coherence in a network is not necessarily uniformly distributed. For whatever reason, particularly "experience," the network of knowledge can be locally very dense and tight, and this is a schema. Obviously, the notion of schema is somewhat fuzzy but this does not mean that schemas and their use are holistic concepts (see Abelson, 1980). If schemas are considered to be the relatively highly coherent areas in a knowledge network, then there is the question: where does one schema end and another one start? Is eating at a hamburger joint an instance of eating in a restaurant? and is eating in a French three-star restaurant covered by the same schema?

It has been shown that prototypical instances of schemas facilitate text understanding (e.g., Bower, Black, & Turner, 1979; den Uyl & van Oostendorp, 1980). Fuzzy boundaries and prototypical instances are typical for concepts in general (Wittgenstein, 1953; Rosch, 1978), and schemas specify what is a prototypical sense of a concept. What schema theory contributes to conceptions of cognitive processing are descriptions of structural categories for knowledge representation and of their use.

Besides the competence to apply relevant knowledge in understanding a text, there is the competence to integrate what is understood—the text-base or parts of this structure—into prior knowledge (Collins, Brown, & Larkin, 1980). Texts may differ widely in the amount to which they are intended to rely on this competence. In reading a novel, the emphasis is on understanding a unique series of events and the roles of the main characters. Novels focus on constructing an episodic text-base (Tulving, 1972); as a side effect, the reader may learn about physical and psychological worlds. In study texts, this integration into prior conceptual knowledge is the intended main effect; as a side-effect, episodic information may be remembered as well.

Integration differs from applying knowledge. *Application* means that a text-base is constructed according to the "grammar" of prior knowledge; *integration* means that specific relations are constructed between the text-base and prior knowledge. Both competencies are part of a continuum that is called depth of understanding. In reading a text, applying knowledge can be sufficient, but in studying a text, integration is also required. Integration can have levels similar to applying knowledge. For instance, bridging gaps in the text-base is equivalent to elaborations with prior knowledge. Integration at higher levels may particularly occur if there is a discrepancy between a target structure and information in the text, which may call for more-or-less drastic accommodations. Integration enhances access to the text-base to such an extent that there is no longer a distinction between prior knowledge and the text-base, that is, between old and new information.

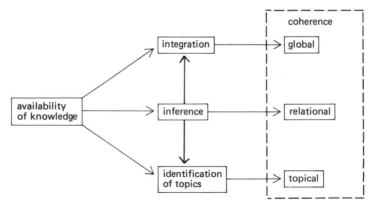

FIGURE 3. Schematization of competences in constructing a coherent text base.

In sum, I have described four types of competencies in text understanding. Three of these are aimed at achieving a coherent text-base: topic identification, integration, and making inferences. The last is implied in the first two. A fourth competence, availability of prior knowledge, is conditional or supportive to the first three, and does not so much refer to a process as to a state of mind. Topic identification and making inferences complement the fact that texts are serial and incomplete. Integration is a condition for future use of the text information. What type of integration is achieved is therefore dependent on how the student thinks this knowledge is to be used. In other words, task requirements may have large effects on these competencies; the type of text particularly affects the first competence. This is illustrated schematically in Figure 3.

PROCESS OF TEXT UNDERSTANDING

A processing model consists of a configuration of components that perform the task of transforming a text into a text-base, thereby achieving the competencies described in the previous section. A component is an input—output device. If the internal processing cannot be described, it is a black box, characterized by its input—output. Components can make up a complex assembly, but here I present its simplest form: a succession of components that represents bottom-up processing. Each component receives two types of input: the output of a preceding component and specific prior knowledge. The model is intended to indicate potential bottlenecks. The series of components can be described as follows:

1. A first component accomplishes recognition of words: a letterstring is decoded into an access code to the mental lexicon. The nature of the access code is still disputed, as well as whether the lexicon is accessible by different types of codes (cf. Hudson, 1981; La Berge & Samuels, 1977). A plausible code is a phonological one, but direct access in the form of a graphic code appears to be possible as well. Both routes can be taken, but the phonological route takes longer in reading, and is available longer, than the graphic one (Baron, 1977). Recently Hudson (1981) has proposed that both graphic and phonological codes may project on a morphemic analysis system that gives access to the lexicon by some mapping procedure (cf. Forster, 1978; Morton, 1979).

2. The lexical entry is the key to the knowledge network. Whether the lexical entry itself is part of this knowledge of the world or of a separate lexicon is not important here. Access to the network evokes the meaning of a word concept, probably by a process of spreading activation (Collins &

Loftus, 1975). The activated meaning of a concept can be quite extensive and not appropriate to the context in many respects. A specific meaning has to be selected or constructed. Selection may be partly due to spreading activation from related concepts that are processed quite recently; however, these priming effects appear to be rather restricted (e.g., Breuker, 1981; Myers & Lorch, 1980).

Therefore, it is plausible that the selection and, particularly, the construction of meanings is guided by specific inferences (R. Anderson & Ortony, 1975; Tabossi & Johnson-Laird, 1980). Data from Yates (1978) suggests that activation is followed by more controlled inhibition. Yates found that both meanings of an ambiguous word are activated for up to a half-second; after this half-second only the meaning that suits the context is available. A meaning is more than a selection or construction from the "full" meaning of a concept. It is also a unique instantiation of a concept, for example, a topic (see Brachman, 1979).

3. The selected meanings are combined in structures of propositions, which represent states and actions. In many theories, this low-level integration consists of mapping some kind of "conceptual role schema" onto sets of word meanings with more-or-less the scope of a clause. A conceptual role schema (Figure 1) defines role relations between entities (e.g., actors, objects, locations, instruments) which participate in an action (e.g., Kintsch, 1974; Norman *et al.*, 1975; Schank, 1972). In general, the verb indicates the type of action or state. Which meaning fills which conceptual role slot in the schema is dependent on many factors such as syntactic relations, compatibility between slot and sense, and focus. Breuker (1981) found that the notion of conceptual role schemas, similar to those proposed by Schank (1972, 1975), was consistent with reaction times for identifying the referent of a pronoun.

4. These conceptual role schemas have to be related to the text-base under construction and/or to some other knowledge structure. In process models of text understanding, this activity is distinguished from that of constructing the conceptual role schemas (Just & Carpenter, 1980; Kieras, 1981a; Kintsch & van Dijk, 1978). It is conceivable that fitting meanings into slots and fitting instantiated conceptual role schemas into a knowledge structure are simply different structural levels on which the same process may operate. For instance, assigning the referent of a pronoun is aimed at filling a slot, but it requires search and inferences that go beyond the conceptual role schema under construction (Breuker, 1981; Clark & Sengul, 1979; Webber, 1978).

5. Kintsch and van Dijk (1978; see also van Dijk, 1980) propose a specific component in the form of *macro rules,* for deriving a macrostructure

from the text structure information. This would seem to be necessary, because a nonoptimally linearized text appears to be an important determiner of problems with abstracting a macrostructure (Circillo, 1981; Kieras, 1981b).

6. Finally, there is some executive control component that monitors and guides the processing. In some (bottom-up) processing models, this control is almost absent and locally distributed (e.g., Just & Carpenter, 1980); each component has its own set of goals and strategies. Executive control accomplishes two things. First, it determines whether the macrostructure and the recent part of the text-base are still in line with plans and target models (i.e., with a goal structure), which represent coherence criteria. Second, if goals are not met and not changed, a control component will try to redistribute

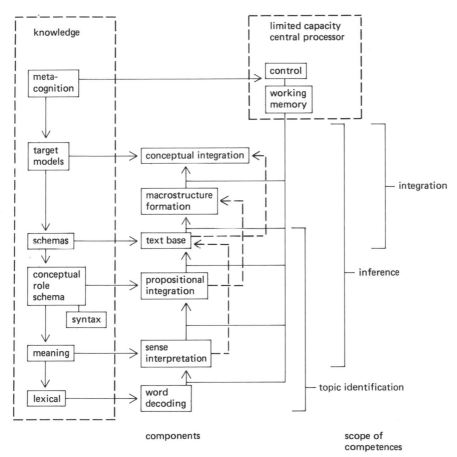

FIGURE 4. Schematization of knowledge and processing components in text comprehension.

resources and to get access to new data to improve performance (Norman & Bobrow, 1975). These resources are buffers between components, where codes can be parked temporarily if the speed of intake of the next component is too slow and/or if the next component has to wait for specific information before it can proceed. For instance, the "propositional integration component" (see Figure 4) generally has to delay processing until the verb-sense information is transferred.

Figure 4 presents a schematic representation of the processing model. The right-hand side indicates which series of components achieve which competencies. The availability-of-knowledge competence is symbolized by the "Knowledge" box in the figure.

A model of language processing as a succession of components—more or less monitored by a control component—not only lacks many details, but is structurally incomplete. Text understanding occurs not only from interpreting a succession of codes at successively higher levels by applying the relevant knowledge, but also from interpreting top-down information for contextual support in processing. In Figure 4, top-down processing is symbolized by arrows pointing to lower levels of knowledge. Levels are not absolute, but relative to the level of discourse of the text. Contextual support from higher levels of knowledge can vary from specific expectancies of what the input will be, to global restrictions on the set of possible interpretations. Top-down information facilitates and speeds up processing, and occurs at all levels of text understanding (e.g., Adams & Collins, 1979).

Processing can also be speeded up by becoming automated (Posner & Snyder, 1975; Schneider & Shiffrin, 1977). It is plausible that automation of a process is accompanied by information of adequate schemas (Baron, 1978). Automation then refers to schema application within a component, not to top-down transfer of information. Particularly in lower components processing is to a large extent automatic, probably because of less "news" at this level.

Buffers are crucially important for automated processing. There can be postulated as many buffers as there are types of codes; or, on the other extreme, only one, centrally controlled buffer that can retain various types of codes. The latter corresponds with the notion of limited capacity central processing, that is, with working memory. According to Baddeley and Lieberman (1980) working memory can contain an "articulatory loop," that is, a series of phonological codes and a "spatial scratch-pad." This spatial scratch-pad permits two-dimensional parking of codes, and it is assumed to be intermediary in facilitating memory retrieval by use of images and of spatial retrieval schemas or mnemonics.

INCOMPLETE UNDERSTANDING AND REASONING

Text processing is goal directed and in the previous sections, two types of goals were identified. The first was a form criterion of whether the text base is sufficiently coherent, and it defines the level of understanding the reader is seeking. The second type of goal was a content criterion, determining whether the text makes sense with respect to a "grammar" of world knowledge such as a target model or schema. Form and content goals can complement one another. Obviously, when a coherent target schema can be applied, both goals are satisfied by implication: the processing is then strongly top-down and the text contains relatively little new information. However, if the target schema is superficial, the reader has to comply with the coherence criterion by bottom-up processing.

Bottom-up processing also becomes necessary if the target schema that is applied does not correspond with the information from the text. For example, Collins, Brown, and Larkin (1980) presented subjects with short, difficult stories, which relied strongly on the competence to identify topics (Who is who?) and on availability of target models (What does all this mean?), and asked them to think aloud while reading. These protocols not only revealed how target schemas guided understanding, but also how they were revised via a variety of problem-solving strategies (for similar conclusions, see Olshavsky [1978] and Kavale & Schreiner [1979]).

While problem solving (or reasoning) and making inferences in everyday text understanding both go beyond the information given, they are completely different processes. Reasoning proceeds slowly and consciously. It allows for thinking aloud and requires all attention and efforts. On the other hand, making inferences in understanding everyday discourse appears to be an automatic and unattended process. Reasoning and making inferences can be viewed as different modes of processing, whereby "the reasoner and the inferencer do not talk much to each other," as Abelson (1975) has put it (see also Abelson, 1980).

If no detailed and applicable target models or plans are available, coherent structures can be built from scratch by reasoning. In reasoning, operations are successively applied to conceptualizations in working memory. These operations can come from some very global, formal system; for instance, logic in syllogistic reasoning. By these operations the conceptualizations become related; or the operations can transform the conceptualizations in some new representational format that is more coherent (Frijda, 1977). For instance, one can transform a verbally stated mechanics problem into a diagram. Larkin (1982) calls this "spatial reasoning."

Reasoning, and particularly abstract syllogistic reasoning that is typical for understanding difficult expository text, implies stepwise combining of small sets of concepts, whereby new arrangements of these concepts in working memory are required. In reasoning, previous steps have to be remembered; dead ends occur so that one has to be able to retrace. Therefore, one can easily run out of working memory space, particularly if resources have to be spent on keeping track of which occurrences of concepts refer to the same topic (topic identification competence). Reasoning is difficult, because it requires a systematic bookkeeping over insufficiently organized objects.

In long and difficult texts, like study texts, every paragraph or group of paragraphs can posit problems in retrieving, recognizing, revising, or designing appropriate target models (cf. Collins, Brown, & Larkin, 1980). An obstacle to higher-order integration is that working memory will overload. Digit-span tests, which may indicate an individual's working memory capacity, have low correlations with measures of text comprehension (Perfetti & Lesgold, 1977). Therefore, size of working memory by itself would not seem to be a bottleneck. A reading-span test, which consists of reading sentences and remembering the last words of these sentences, is a good predictor of text comprehension (Daneman & Carpenter, 1980); in this test, the working memory required for reading restricts the amount of "spare" capacity available for retaining the words. Because indicators of text comprehension are usually based on texts and tests of moderate difficulty, this may explain why good readers perform better than poor readers on tasks that are indicators of the amount of automated processing occurring at low levels, like speed of decoding (Perfetti & Lesgold, 1977), decoding span (Jackson & McClelland, 1975; Marcel, 1974), and factual verification of simple statements (Hanso, Schreiner, & Hummel, 1978). One would expect these correlations to diminish as text difficulty increases and the corresponding tests require deeper understanding.

While comprehension tests are generally highly intercorrelated (see Rosenshine, 1980), Felker and Dapra (1975) found a very low correlation between recall and insight performance over the same text. One would predict insight and understanding a difficult text to be rather correlated with reasoning skills. Frijda (1977) has argued that these skills may be identified as a general reasoning factor in intelligence, specifically as cognition of semantic systems (CMS) in Guilford's terminology (Guilford, 1967). (Also see Chapter 8, present volume.)

SPATIAL LEARNING STRATEGIES

I come now to the key question: Where do spatial learning strategies fit in this picture? I try to complete this picture by presenting spatial learning strategies, in particular schematizing (see Chapter 7, present volume; Breuker, 1980) as a succession of steps. The successive steps can be labeled as (1) selecting key concepts, (2) writing the key concepts, (3) making an attribute list, (4) relating key concepts into a spatial arrangement, (5) rearranging the spatial representation, and (6) comparing the representation with the text. Each of these steps is subsequently described.

In each step the student tries to accomplish some subgoal. This goal may be preparatory to a next step, and can be related to processing components, but some steps also imply passing a potential bottleneck. In that case, such a step is explicitly related to one of the competences discussed before. The procedures actually taught to students may not exactly correspond with the steps presented here, because a number of steps can be combined in one procedural unit. This splitting up of a complex problem into subproblems that can be solved step-by-step is typical for skilled problem-solving. The global power of spatial learning strategies should, therefore, be credited to an adequate analysis of a major problem, constructing coherence, into subproblems for which heuristics and recommendations (which can also facilitate solving the next subproblem) are specified.

STEP 1: SELECTING KEY CONCEPTS

The first step is to select the key concepts, key topics, or themes from a part of a text, which is often a few paragraphs, but can also be a section or a chapter, depending on the difficulty of the text. Several heuristics for selection can be used: (1) a topic-comment strategy (What is stated about what? What is this paragraph about?), (2) frequency of occurrence of a topic, (3) explicit signals in the text, and (4) global target models and metacognitions ("I do not know much about this topic.") Of course, the technique presupposes that students do not have problems at the level of integrating role schemas (see Figure 4). Selection of key concepts involves the following:

1. Recognition of concepts; relations play only a subordinate role (see 2).
2. Activating relevant knowledge (availability-of-knowledge competence)—low demands on inferences competency, because only decisions between key and nonkey concepts are required.
3. Topic identification—the several occurrences of the same topic are subsumed under one label.

The set of selected concepts is a provisional one. During subsequent steps, concepts can be added or removed because new information can become available.

STEP 2: WRITING THE KEY CONCEPTS

The second step seems trivial: to write down these concepts. This creates an external, almost unlimited, working memory. This external working memory can support further processing; however, it does not really extend the processing resources with orders of magnitudes. If that were the case, the study text is, in fact, the most informative external memory. What has been written down has to be internally captured as well. The main advantage in writing down is that reinstatement (i.e., retrieving concepts that are no longer in working memory) hardly requires the usual high demands on central processing (Breuker, 1981; Kintsch & van Dijk, 1978).

A second advantage of writing down the labels of key concepts is that a single, external referent is created for all occurrences of a topic. Because working memory can also contain spatial information, a few single referents may also be created internally (Baddeley & Lieberman, 1980), but this coding reduces the capacity of central processing (Phillips & Christie, 1977). Spatial working memory can be considered as an intermediary between external spatial representations and reasoning.

STEP 3: MAKING AN ATTRIBUTE LIST

In the schematizing technique the student also makes a list of relevant attributes of key concepts, besides the spatial representation. Optionally, the student can record relevant comments for each selected topic. In doing so, the student makes explicit in what sense the concepts are used in the text, and, in case of completely new word-concepts, retains relations with prior knowledge. Making an attribute list is a form of explicit elaboration coding, which may support higher order forms of integration.

STEP 4: RELATING KEY CONCEPTS INTO A SPATIAL ARRANGEMENT

The preceding steps are not spatial and are similar to note-taking, which appears to be beneficial to understanding a study text (e.g., Howe, 1974; van Oostendorp, 1980). Spatial learning techniques have something more to offer.

Step 4 consists of trying to find out how the selected concepts are related. In principle, for each combination of two concepts the student can ask the questions: "Are these concepts related?" and, if yes, "How?" One would easily run out of resources if this is performed mentally, because it is difficult to keep track of all combinations of concepts.

The text itself can be used as a first source of information about relationships. If a relationship is identified, this is indicated by drawing a line or arrow or some other relation symbol. The strategies in the present volume vary somewhat in the types of relationships that are distinguished and symbolized as relations (see Chapter 1, present volume). The two main categories are attributive and conditional relationships.

Identifying relationships (or the absence of relationships) often relies on whether they are not explicitly stated in the text, and are hidden by intermediary conceptualizations and specifications. In this case, necessary inferences can be made one-by-one and do not have to be cognized simultaneously within some coherent target model. The preceding is typical of expert problem-solving, but to the student a step-by-step approach may be the only way to come at least to partial solutions. However, if used too algorithmically the method may have a certain overkill, because relationships may be inferred uncritically and out of context. It is always possible to create a spurious relationship between two isolated concepts.

STEP 5: REARRANGING THE SPATIAL REPRESENTATIONS

The web of relations created in the preceding step has to be rearranged. The pattern may look very complicated, because the distances between the key concepts may not exhibit Gestalt-like properties. In the networking technique (see Chapter 4, present volume) some of these patterns—such as hierarchies, taxonomies, and chains—are explicitly part of the instruction. In schematizing, a number of rules are presented to rearrange spatial representations into "good figures." The aim of rearrangement is not an aesthetic one. Familiar, or simple patterns can exhibit by analogy or by implication information that is hard to abstract from badly arranged spatial representations. In particular, metacognitive categories can become manifest. For instance, the student can recognize in the pattern a hierarchy of concepts, and grasp immediately which concepts belong to the same level.

Another function of rearrangement is that a greater independence can be achieved from the particular succession of topics in the text. The new pattern may better correspond with the student's prior knowledge and better reflect the relatedness of concepts. In other words, this independence can facilitate achieving integration competence. If the complete structure cannot be apprehended in some target model, then at least some subparts can become integrated with already known schemas.

Not only the "good figure" quality of a rearrangement can facilitate integration, but particularly the activity itself can be very beneficial. Puzzling around with the key concepts is a way of spatial reasoning with fewer serial, working-memory constraints. Rearranging is both form-driven ("the pattern looks coherent"; "are there no loose ends?") and content-driven ("this concept is the theme of the text and should be a top node"; "what if I label this set of concepts 'means' and the other set 'goals'?").

Finally, even if no sufficient integration can be achieved (i.e., the accessibility of the new knowledge is still low), a good figure, particularly a hierarchical one, can provide a systematic retrieval schema or macrostructure (i.e., the availability can be enhanced, if necessary, by sheer spatial rehearsal).

STEP 6: COMPARING THE REPRESENTATION WITH THE TEXT

The last step consists of evaluation of the spatial representation against the information in the text. The text is scanned with specific questions to identify "bugs" in the spatial representation. Evaluation procedures are particularly relevant to examine relations that are inferred, but not necessarily implied by the text (see Step 4). The spatial representation can have become so independent of the text, that erroneous preconceptions of the student may have smuggled in (see Stevens, Collins, & Goldin, 1979), so that careful comparison with the text, or with spatial representations provided by the teacher, is no luxury, but a necessary step (Breuker, 1981). However, misconceptions are easier to diagnose in spatial representations than in essays produced by the students, because the essay formulation can hide the specific nature of relationships (Breuker & van de Roest, 1978).

SUMMARY

Spatial learning strategies break up the problems in understanding a difficult text into steps that correspond with text understanding. Only the supportive competence, availability of knowledge, is not explicitly tackled. It is implicit in Steps 1, 2, 3, 4, and 5. Spatial learning strategies cannot make up for lack of essential knowledge; only education can do that. However, the strategies do permit the student to make a more efficient use of this knowledge. The first step focuses on topic identification problems, the fourth step on making inferences and the fifth step on integration with prior knowledge and/or macrostructure reinforcement.

Some steps also imply the execution of components of text understanding (Step 1), but it should be noted that above the level of integration into a role schema, the strategies are rather problem-solving oriented. In Step 5 the spatial reasoning involved in rearrangement is completely different from usual text understanding processes and might, therefore, reveal perspectives that were previously hidden. One important implied perspective is that knowledge is not explicitly given by the text, which means that failing to immediately grasp the meaning in text is not a sure sign of incompetence to the student, but a cue for adapting one's strategy. Training study skills is not only aimed at extending the tactical repertoire of the student, but also at a flexible use of these means.

REFERENCES

Abelson, R. P. (1975). The reasoner and the inferencer don't talk much to each other. In R. C. Schank & B. L. Nash-Webber (Eds.), *Theoretical issues in natural language processing.* Cambridge, MA: MIT Press.

Abelson, R. P. (1980). *In defense of common sense representations of knowledge.* Cognitive Science Technical Report, no. 6. New Haven, CT: Yale University.

Adams, M. J. & Collins, A. (1979). A schema theoretic view of reading. In R. O. Freedle (Ed.), *New directions in discourse processing* (Vol. 2). Norwood, NJ: Ablex.

Anderson, R. C. & Ortony, A. (1975). On putting apples into bottles. *Cognitive Psychology, 7,* 167–180.

Anderson, T. H. (1980). Study strategies and adjunct aids. In R. J. Spiro, B. C. Bruce, & W. F. Brewer (Eds.), *Theoretical issues in reading comprehension.* Hillsdale, NJ: Erlbaum.

Baddeley, A. D., & Lieberman, K. (1980). Spatial working memory. In R. S. Nickerson (Ed.), *Attention and performance* (VIII). Hillsdale, NJ: Erlbaum.

Baron, J. (1978). The word-superiority effect: Perceptual learning from reading. In W. K. Estes (Ed.), *Handbook of learning and cognitive processes* (Vol. 6). Hillsdale, NJ: Erlbaum.

Bartlett, F. C. (1932). *Remembering.* London: Cambridge University Press.

Bower, G. H., Black, J. B., & Turner, T. J. (1979). Scripts in memory for text. *Cognitive Psychology, 11,* 177–220.

Brachman, R. J. (1979). On the epistemological status of semantic networks. In N. V. Findler (Ed.), *Associative networks: Representation and use of knowledge by computers.* New York: Academic Press.

Breuker, J. A. (1979). A schematic view on the acquisition of knowledge from text. In M. Borillo (Ed.), *Representation des connaissances et raisonnement dans les sciences de l'homme et de la societé.* Marseille: IRIA-LISH.

Breuker, J. A. (1980). *In kaart brengen van leerstof.* Utrecht/Antwerpen: Spectrum, [Schematizing subject matter].

Breuker, J. A. (1981). *Availability of knowledge.* Doctoral dissertation, Report 82-02, COWO-University of Amsterdam, Amsterdam.

Breuker, J. A., & van der Roest, W. (1978). Conceptual structure of texts: A study in the validity of scoring essay examinations. *Tijdschrift voor Onderwijsresearch, 3,* 10–21.

Cirillo, R. K. (1981). Referential coherence and text structure in story comprehension. *Journal of Verbal Learning and Verbal Behavior, 20,* 358–367.

Clark, H. H., & Havilland, S. E. (1977). Comprehension and the given-new contract. In R. O. Freedle (Ed.), *Discourse processes.* Norwood, NJ: Ablex.

Clark, H. H., & Sengul, C. J. (1979). In search for referents for pronouns. *Memory & Cognition, 7,* 35–41.

Collins, A., Brown, J. S., & Larkin, K. M. (1980). Inferences in text understanding. In R. J. Spiro, B. C. Brown, & W. F. Brewer (Eds.), *Theoretical issues in reading comprehension.* Hillsdale, NJ: Erlbaum.

Collins, A. M., & Loftus, E. F. (1975). A Spreading activation theory of semantic processing. *Psychological Review, 82,* 407–428.

Daneman, J., & Carpenter, P. A. (1980). Individual differences in working memory and reading. *Journal of Verbal Learning and Verbal Behavior, 19,* 450–466.

Dansereau, D. F., McDonald, B. A., Collins, K. W., Garland, J., Holley, C. D., Diekhoff, G. M., & Evans, S. M. (1979). Evaluation of a learning strategy system. In H. F. O'Neill, Jr., & C. D. Spielberger (Eds.), *Cognitive and affective learning strategies.* New York: Academic Press.

de Kleer, J. & Brown, J. S. (1981). Mental models of physical mechanisms and their acquisition. In J. R. Anderson (eds.). *Cognitive Skills and their acquisition,* Hillsdale, N.J., Erlbaum.

Dijk, T. A. van (1980). *Macrostructures.* Hillsdale, NJ: Erlbaum.

Elshout-Mohr, M., & Daalen-Kapteijns, M. M. van. (1981). The acquisition of word meanings as a cognitive learning process. *Journal of Verbal Learning and Verbal Behavior, 4,* 386–399.

Felker, D. B., & Dapra, R. A. (1975). Effects of question type and question placement on problem solving ability from prose material. *Journal of Educational Psychology, 67,* 380–384.

Findler, N. V. (Ed.) (1979). *Associative networks: Representation and use of knowledge by computers.* New York: Academic Press.

Fodor, J. A., & Pylyshyn, Z. W. (1981). How direct is visual perception? Some reflections on Gibson's "Ecological Approach." *Cognition, 9,* 139–196.

Forster, K. I. (1978). Levels of processing and the structure of the language processor. In W. E. Cooper & E. C. T. Walker (Eds.), *Sentence processing.* Hillsdale, NJ: Erlbaum.

Frijda, N. H. (1972). The simulation of long term memory. *Psychological Bulletin, 77,* 1–31.

Frijda, N. H. (1977). Memory processes and instruction. In A. M. Lesgold, J. W. Pellegrino, S. D. Fokkema, & R. Glaser (Eds.), *Cognitive psychology and instruction.* New York: Plenum.

Garrod, S., & Sanford, A. (1977). Interpreting anaphoric relations: The integration of semantic information while reading. *Journal of Verbal Learning and Verbal Behavior, 16,* 77–90.

Grice, P. (1975). Logic and conversation. In P. Cole & J. Morgan, (Eds.), *Syntax and semantics* (Vol. III): *Speech acts.* New York: Academic Press.

Guilford, J. P. (1967). *The nature of human intelligence.* New York: Academic Press.

Hanson, K. R., Schreiner, R., & Hummel, T. (1978). The relationship between reading ability and semantic verification tasks. In P. O. Pearson & J. Hansen (Eds.), *27th Yearbook of the National Reading Conference.* Clemson: NRC.

Hayes, J. R., & Simon, H. A. (1976). The understanding process: Problem isomorphs. *Cognitive Psychology, 8,* 165–190.

Hollan, J. D. (1975). Features and semantic memory: Set theoretic or network model? *Psychological Review, 82,* 154–155.

Howe, M. J. A. (1974). The utility of taking notes as an aid to learning. *Educational Research, 16,* 222–227.

Hudson, P. T. W. (1981). Psycholinguistic approaches to the mental lexicon. In J. F. Matter (Ed.), *Toegepaste taalwetenschappen in artikelen.* Amsterdam: A.N.E.L.A.

Jackson, M. D., & McClelland, J. L. (1975). Sensory and cognitive determinants of reading speed. *Journal of Verbal Learning and Verbal Behavior, 14,* 565–574.

Just, M. A., & Carpenter, P. A. (1980). A theory of reading: From eye fixations to comprehension. *Psychological Review, 87,* 329–354.

Kavale, K., & Schreiner, R. (1979). The reading processes of above average and average readers. *Reading Research Quarterly, 15,* 102–128.

Kieras, D. E. (1981a). Component processes in the comprehension of simple prose. *Journal of Verbal Learning and Verbal Behavior, 20,* 1–23.

Kieras, D. E. (1981b). The role of major referents and sentence topics in the construction of passage macrostructure. *Discourse Processes, 4,* 1–15.

Kintsch, W. (1974). *The representation of meaning in memory.* Hillsdale, NJ: Erlbaum.

Kintsch, W., & van Dijk, T. A. (1978). Toward a model of text comprehension and production. *Psychological Review, 85,* 363–394.

La Berge, D., & Samuels, S. J. (Eds.) (1977). *Basic processes in reading.* Hillsdale, NJ: Erlbaum, 1977.

Larkin, J. H. (1982). *Spatial reasoning in solving physics problems* (C.I.P., No. 434). Pittsburgh: Carnegie-Mellon University.

Levelt, W. J. M. (1981). The speakers linearization problem. *Philosophical Transactions of the Royal Society London, B295,* 305–315.

Marcel, T. (1974). The effective visual field and the use of context in fast and slow readers of two ages. *British Journal of Educational Psychology, 65,* 479–492.

McConkie, C. W. (1977). Learning from text. In L. S. Shylman (Ed.), *Review of research in education* (Vol. 5). Itahca, IL: Peacock.

McDonald-Ross, J. (1977). Graphics in texts. In L. S. Shylman (Ed.), *Review of research in education* (Vol. 5). Itahca, IL: Peacock.

Minsky, M. (1975). A framework for representing knowledge. In P. H. Winston (Ed.), *The psychology of computer vision.* New York: McGraw-Hill.

Moore, J., & Newell, A. (1974). How can MERLIN understand? In L. Gregg (Ed.) *Knowledge and cognition.* Potomac, NJ: Erlbaum.

Morton, J. (1979). Word recognition. In J. C. Marshall & J. Morton (Eds.), *Psycholinguistics.* London: Elek.

Myers, J. L., & Lorch, R. F. (1980). Interferences and facilitation effects of primes upon verification processes. *Memory & Cognition, 8,* 405–414.

Norman, D. A., & Bobrow, D. G. (1975). On data-limited and resource-limited processes. *Cognitive Psychology, 7,* 44–64.

Norman, D. A., Rumelhart, D., & The LNR Research Group. (1975). *Explorations in cognition.* San Francisco: Freeman.

Olshavsky, J. (1978). Comprehension profiles of good and poor readers across materials of increasing difficulty. In P. D. Pearson & J. Hansen (Eds.), *27th Yearbook of the National Reading Conference.* Clemson: NRC.

Oostendorp, H. van. (1980). De invloed van aantekeningen maken en schema's op het be-studeren van teksten. *Tijdschrift voor Taalbeheersing, 2,* 17–30.

Perfetti, C. A., & Lesgold, A. M. (1977). Discourse comprehension and sources of individual differences. In M. A. Just & P. A. Carpenter (Eds.), *Cognitive processes in comprehension.* Hillsdale, NJ: Erlbaum.

Phillips, W. K., & Christie, W. F. M. (1977). Interference with visualization, *Quarterly Journal of Experimental Psychology, 29,* 637–650.

Posner, M. I., & Snyder, C. R. R. (1975). Facilitation and inhibition in the processing of signals. In P. M. S. Rabitt & S. Dornic (Eds.). *Attention and Performance V,* New York: Academic Press.

Quillian, M. R. (1968). Semantic memory. In M. Minsky (Ed.), *Semantic information processing.* Cambridge, MA: MIT Press.

Rosenshine, B. V. (1980). Skill hierarchies in reading comprehension. In R. J. Spiro, B. C. Bruce, & W. F. Brewer (Eds.), *Theoretical issues in reading comprehension.* Hillsdale, NJ: Erlbaum.

Rosch, E. (1978). Principles of categorization. In E. Rosch & B. B. Lloyd (Eds.), *Cognition and categorization.* Hillsdale, NJ: Erlbaum.

Rumelhart, D. E., & Ortony, A. (1977). The representation of knowledge in memory. In R. C.

Anderson, R. J. Spiro, & W. E. Montague (Eds.), *Schooling and the acquisition of knowledge.* Hillsdale, NJ: Erlbaum.

Schallert, D. L. (1980). The role of illustrations in reading comprehension. In R. J. Spiro, B. C. Bruce, & W. F. Brewer (Eds.), *Theoretical issues in reading comprehension.* Hillsdale, NJ: Erlbaum.

Schank, R. C. (1972). Conceptual dependency: A theory of natural language understanding. *Cognitive Psychology, 3,* 552–631.

Schank, R. C. (1975). *Conceptual information processing.* Amsterdam: North Holland.

Schank, R. C., & Abelson, R. P. (1977). *Scripts, plans, goals and understanding.* Hillsdale, NJ: Erlbaum.

Schank, R. C., & Birnbaum, L. (in press). Memory, meaning and syntax. In T. Bever & L. Miller (Eds.), *Cognitive philosophical computational foundations of language.* Hillsdale, NJ.

Schank, R. C., & Riesbeck, C. (1981). *Inside computer understanding.* Hillsdale, NJ: Erlbaum.

Schneider, W., & Shiffrin, R. M. (1977). Automatic and controlled information processing in vision. In D. LaBerge & S. J. Samuels (Eds.) *Basic Processes in Reading,* Hillsdale, NJ: Erlbaum.

Smith, E. E. (1978). Theories of semantic memory. In W. K. Estes (Ed.), *Handbook of learning and cognitive processes.* Hillsdale, NJ: Erlbaum.

Smith, E. E., Shoben, E. J., & Rips, L. J. (1974). Structure and process in semantic memory. *Psychological Review, 81,* 214–241.

Spiro, R. J. (1980). Constructive processes in prose comprehension and recall. In R. J. Spiro, B. C. Bruce, & W. F. Brewer (Eds.), *Theoretical issues in reading comprehension.* Hillsdale, NJ: Erlbaum.

Stevens, A., Collins, A., & Goldin, S. E. (1979). Misconceptions in student's understanding. *International Journal of Man-Machine Studies, 11,* 145–156.

Tabossi, P., & Johnson-Laird, P. N. (1980). Linguistic context and the priming of semantic information. *Quarterly Journal of Experimental Psychology, 32,* 595–603.

Tulving, E. (1972). Episodic and semantic memory. In E. Tulving & W. Donaldson (Eds.), *Organization of memory.* New York: Academic Press.

Uyl, M. J. den. (1980). *Controlling inferences by semantic cohesion.* Paper presented at the Second Annual Cognitive Science Conference, New Haven, CT, Yale University.

Uyl, M. J. den, & van Oostendorp, H. (1980). The use of scripts in text comprehension. *Poetics, 9,* 275–294.

Webber, B. (1978). Inference in an approach to discourse anaphora (Tech. Rep. No. 77). Urbana: Center for the Study of Reading, University of Illinois.

Webber, B., & Reiter, R. (1977). *Anaphora and logical form: A formal meaning representation for natural language.* (Tech. Rep. No. 36). Urbana: Center For the Study of Reading, University of Illinois.

Williams, M. D., Hollan, J. D., & Stevens, A. L. (1983). Human reasoning about a simple physical system. In D. Gentner & A. S. Stevens (Eds.), *Mental models.* Hillsdale, NJ: Erlbaum.

Winston, P. M. (1977). *Artificial intelligence.* Philippines: Addison-Wesley.

Wittgenstein, L. (1953). *Philosophical investigations.* New York: MacMillan.

Woods, W. A. (1975). What's in a link?: Foundations for semantic networks. In D. G. Bobrow & M. Collins (Eds.), *Representation and understanding.* New York: Academic Press.

Woodworth, R. (1938). *Experimental psychology.* New York: Holt.

Yates, F. A. (1966). *The art of memory.* London: Routledge & Kegan Paul.

Yates, J. (1978). Priming dominant and unusual senses of ambiguous words. *Memory and Cognition, 6,* 636–643.

Young, R. M., & O'Shea, T. (1981). Errors in children's subtraction. *Cognitive Science, 5,* 153–177.

CHAPTER 3

The Role of Spatial Strategies in Processing and Remembering Text: A Cognitive—Information-Processing Analysis

Ernest T. Goetz

STUDYING TEXT: HISTORICAL PERSPECTIVE ON THE READER AND RESEARCH

Success in school has long been dependent on the ability to deal successfully with written text. Enter any grade school classroom and the sheer number of books of all shapes and sizes serves as a graphic reminder of the central place of written material in the classroom. A casual perusal of a college course syllabus makes the same point. As students progress through school, they are expected to derive an ever greater portion of the intended knowledge and benefits of their educations through reading and studying books. The importance of the ability to comprehend, to remember, and to apply what one reads does not stop with the end of schooling; as anyone who has struggled with tax forms, assembly instructions, office memos, or any of the other vital reading demanded of us by our highly complex and literate society can attest. Although each of us reads for many purposes, in school it is reading to accomplish some instructional objective—that is, studying—that

47

is most important (Anderson, 1980; Anderson & Armbruster, 1982). Studying is the focus of this chapter.

While it is obvious and beyond dispute that the ability to read and study texts is crucial to success in our schools and our society, the point is reiterated here to emphasize some rather conspicuous and disturbing failures of our schools, and of educational and psychological research. Our schools have neither been very successful nor even very active in training their students to derive information from text (Durkin, 1978/1979; Weinstein, 1978). Schools may require that students become effective studiers, but they typically provide little direct instruction or guidance that would help them with their task.

Psychological theory and research have also failed the students. Although verbal learning has been an important and active area of experimental psychology since the time of Ebbinghaus (1885/1913), practical applications of this research that assist the student in becoming a more effective studier are as yet very limited. Additionally, applied educational research has, for the most part, failed to reveal effective study methods which could be imparted to the students. Educational psychologists have evaluated the effectiveness of study strategies for at least the past 50 years (e.g., Barton, 1930), but the results of these studies have been conflicting and inconclusive (see Anderson, [1980], Anderson & Armbruster [1982], and Dansereau, Actkinson, Long, & McDonald [1974] for reviews).

Although these failings are regrettable, they are not incomprehensible. Teachers have perhaps thought that the ability to learn effectively from reading was either innate or an ability that would naturally emerge as the student progresses through school (Weinstein, 1978). Or perhaps teachers have been too busy attempting to control behaviors that disrupt instruction, or attempting to convey the content of the instruction, to devote sufficient time and energy to this vital aspect of the learning–instruction process. Perhaps, too, teachers have simply been at a loss about how to teach students to become effective studiers because no one ever taught them.

The problem with the research can probably be traced to traditions. One of the traditions that has hindered useful research has been the sharp separation between basic research, applied research, and educational practice. Within each of these isolated strands, individual traditions have hindered progress. In basic research on verbal learning, tradition—again, since Ebbinghaus—has emphasized the study of the rote memorization of simple and artificial verbal stimuli (e.g., nonsense syllables, word lists, paired associates). The emphasis on nonsense syllables and memorization reflected the dominant S–R and associationist theoretical orientation of the field, and was intended to permit the observation of the formation of associations uncontaminated by prior knowledge. From our point of view, however, the major effect of this emphasis was to isolate the research from legitimate concerns of applied educational researchers, teachers, and students. The S–R framework and paired-associate research can easily be applied to the learning of state capitals or the facts of simple addition, but the implications for learning from text are by no means straightforward.

In applied educational research, the tradition has been that one or more study strategies are trotted out and tested against one another and the ubiquitous control group in "race horse" studies. One problem with these studies is that they have failed to produce any consistent winners. Such obvious favorites as note-taking, underlining, and outlining simply have not fared all that well in these tests. A secondary deficiency in this area of research results from the traditional method of data collection. Typically, the researcher collects his or her data in one or two sorties into the classroom. Little or no instruction is provided in the study strategy to be applied. Those few studies in which students have been provided with extensive training in a study strategy have produced more favorable results (e.g., Barton, 1930). Further, usually no attempt is made to analyze what the students actually *did* when they were instructed to outline the text (or take notes, etc.). It is simply assumed that the participating students are skilled and sophisticated studiers who will produce adequate outlines (notes, etc.) when told to do so. As this assumption is highly suspect, the interpretation of the success or failure of a particular strategy in a particular study is problematic, and the inconsistent results across studies are not surprising.

Within educational practice, the tradition has been to underrepresent or ignore study strategies in the classroom. About the only guidance available to students and teachers has come from works that present studying systems prescriptively, telling the student what he or she should do (e.g., Pauk, 1962; Robinson, 1970). Although the advice may often have been sound, the effectiveness of these study systems has seldom been empirically documented. For example, Adams, Carnine, and Gersten (1982), who recently reported a test of training based on SQ3R (Survey–Question–Read–Recite–Review) (Robinson, 1941), were able to locate only six previous studies of the technique. Moreover, recent examinations of students' reported study methods have revealed that even among presumably sophisticated college students, few employ SQ3R or any of the other widely prescribed study methods (Anderson, 1980; Dansereau, Long, McDonald, & Actkinson, 1975; Weinstein, 1978).

In summary, the traditional separation of basic research, applied research, and educational practice—coupled with traditions within each of these strands of inquiry—have led to the failure to provide students with effective study methods. Nevertheless, recent developments suggest that things may be changing. In basic research, there is an increasing emphasis on studying how people learn from complex verbal stimuli (e.g., text) and how knowledge is acquired and represented. In applied research, investigators have begun to carefully examine what students do when they underline or take notes (e.g., Brown & Smiley, 1977). Perhaps most encouraging of all, efforts are now underway to bring together basic research, applied research, and educational practice. For example, Dansereau (e.g., Dansereau, 1978; Dansereau, et al., 1979) and Weinstein (e.g., Weinstein, 1978, 1982; Weinstein, Underwood, Wicker, & Cubberly, 1979) and their colleagues have established study strategy training projects in which strategies taught (i.e., the educational practice) are based upon findings from basic research, and are constantly being studied and refined (i.e., ongoing applied research). This trend is exemplified by the topic of this volume. Spatial learning strategies were designed as an attempt to apply what has been learned in basic research (e.g., notions of the structure of knowledge, the memorial advantage of pictures and mental images) as a practical tool for students.

The change that has brought formerly separate areas of research and instructional practice closer together, and that has made these recent attempts at synthesis possible, is a reconceptualization of the learner and of the learning process. Within the past 20–30 years, the cognitive–information-processing view of learning has emerged and researchers are forging a consensus in this area. From this perspective, the learner is the central and active agent, rather than the passive recipient, of learning. Learning is seen as the product of complex, interrelated cognitive operations which greatly transform the information being processed, rather than as the simple reception of stimuli, production of responses, or formation of associations.

The purpose of this chapter is to examine the extent to which spatial learning strategies are consistent with what we have learned about how written information should be processed in order to promote comprehension and memory. Although spatial strategies have been employed for other purposes, such as curriculum development, problem solving, and text analysis (see Part IV, present volume), in this chapter we consider only their use as study strategies; that is, the use by students of spatial learning strategies to improve their understanding of and memory for the text being studied. The remainder of the chapter is organized into four sections. First, recent cognitive–information-processing theory and research on learning from verbal material is reviewed, highlighting those findings with clear implications for effective study strategies. Second, the cognitive processing involved in the use of spatial learning strategies is analyzed. Third, the efficacy of spatial learning strategies for studying is evaluated based on the earlier review and analysis. Finally, directions for future research and development are considered.

COMPREHENDING AND REMEMBERING TEXT: A SELECTIVE REVIEW

With the emergence of the cognitive–information-processing approach has come an explosion of journal articles and books dealing with how people learn from and remember written information. Given the limitations of this chapter, no pretense is made at presenting a review of this vast literature that is comprehensive or even truly representative. More extensive reviews are available from numerous sources (e.g., Carroll, 1971; Goetz & Armbruster, 1980; McConkie, 1977; Reder, 1978, 1980). Rather, attention is focused on those areas which (1) represent major findings or themes in the literature, and (2) have clear implications for any effective study strategy. Studies of prose learning are highlighted, but results of studies employing other forms of verbal material (e.g., sentences, word lists) are also reported where appropriate. The review is organized under several subheadings that depict the types of processing that will improve a studier's comprehension and memory for text. The areas described under these subheadings are not mutually exclusive—indeed, they are highly interrelated—rather, they are intended to convey emphasis and facilitate exposition. It should be noted that the ordering of the subheadings is not intended to reflect relative importance.

With all that said, let me assert that a growing body of literature within the cognitive–information processing literature suggests that studiers will learn and remember more from text when they:

1. Study the text in a deep, meaningful fashion
2. Form mental images
3. Construct an organized, interrelated representation
4. Bring to bear appropriate prior knowledge and incorporate the new information with what they already know
5. Process the material initially in a manner compatible with testing conditions
6. Actively plan, monitor, and regulate their studying processes.

STUDYING TEXT IN A DEEP, MEANINGFUL FASHION

The idea that people can process information in a variety of ways, and that this processing determines what is learned and how well it is remembered, is central to the information-processing description of learning. When applied to verbal material, this principle has led to the description of qualitatively different levels at which processing may occur. Assuming visual presentation of verbal material, the "shallowest" processing deals with the physical properties of the stimulus, such as the lines or angles in the letters or the overall shape and size of the words. The "deepest" processing entails the construction of a meaningful, semantic representation.

The levels of processing analysis is so intuitively attractive and well-suited to the description of learning from verbal material that it sprang up nearly simultaneously (and apparently independently) out of both the basic and applied literatures. Craik and Lockhart (1972), in a landmark paper, reviewed the literature developed around multistore models of memory (e.g., Atkinson & Shiffrin, 1968; Waugh & Norman, 1965) and proposed levels of processing as an alternative framework for interpreting the results. This proposed framework shifted the emphasis from the description of the properties of separate stores in multistore models to an analysis of how verbal material is processed and the consequences of that processing for retention. Since deeper processing led to better memory for the material being processed, Craik and Lockhart stressed that effective learning requires that material be processed semantically and elaboratively, rather than merely being recycled via rote rehearsal

Anderson (1970, 1972) suggested a similar analysis for the applied literature of learning from text. Reflecting upon several unexpected findings from the study of programmed instruction and related instructional techniques, Anderson (1970) noted that students: (1) learned less with programmed texts which were heavily prompted to ensure correct responding than with less heavily prompted texts (e.g., Anderson, Faust, & Roderick, 1968), (2) learned no more when required to write the answer to the questions in the program than when instructed to think of the answers (see Kemp & Holland [1966] for a review), and (3) profitted as much from a programmed text presented in a scrambled order as from the same program in its carefully sequenced order (e.g., Levine & Baker, 1963). He proposed that these findings reflected the fact that heavily cued, highly redundant, sequenced programs permitted the students to correctly answer the questions based upon only a superficial search of the text. Anderson argued that since students are inclined to expend the least effort (i.e., employ the shallowest processing) possible when embarked on an academic task, effective instruction results only when the task requires that the student engage in deep, meaningful processing.

To be sure, the original formulations of Craik and Lockhart and of Anderson have not been treated as if they were etched in stone. The levels of processing notion has been refined (e.g., Craik, 1973), reformulated (e.g., Craik & Tulving, 1975; Jacoby & Craik, 1979; Jacoby, Craik, & Begg, 1979), and repeatedly challenged (e.g., Baddeley, 1978; Morris, Bransford, & Franks, 1977; Nelson, Walling, & McEvoy, 1979; Nelson, 1977). It remains, however, a powerful heuristic. Numerous studies have demonstrated that when people are required to semantically process verbal material, they remember it better than when shallower processing is required (e.g., Bobrow & Bower, 1969; Craik, 1973; Hyde & Jenkins, 1969; Mistler-Lachman, 1972, 1974; Schallert, 1976; Walsh & Jenkins, 1973). Educational applications have also been plentiful. For example, Anderson (1972) applied the levels of processing analysis to the design of comprehension questions and concluded that such questions must at least paraphrase the original text, becuase if they were verbatim copies of the text students could respond correctly without comprehension by matching surface features. When such paraphrased questions are presented with the text, they can be particularly helpful in promoting comprehension and memory (e.g., Andre, 1981). Because paraphrasing requires semantic processing, simply having readers paraphrase material can improve memory (e.g., Dansereau et al., 1976). The elaboration skills—including use of imagery, analogy, comparison, and various forms of verbal elaboration—that form the focus of Weinstein's (1978, 1982; Weinstein et al., 1979) program of research and development are clearly the sort of activities that require deep processing of the material being studied (see Weinstein [1978] for a review of related research).

Reformulation of levels of processing in terms of distinctiveness of encoding (Jacoby & Craik, 1979; Jacoby et al., 1979) brings the concept closely in line with the notion of cognitive effort (e.g., Tyler, Hertel, McCallum, & Ellis, 1979). Jacoby, Craik, and Begg (1979) argued that "difficult initial processing implies more extensive or elaborate analysis, and that this more extensive analysis is reflected in a richer, more distinctive memory record of the event. The distinctive record, in turn, is highly discriminable from other memory traces and is retrieved with relative ease" (p. 596). Glover and his colleagues have recently reported several studies supporting the facilitative effect of encoding distinctiveness or effort. For example, students who read texts that were made more difficult by scrambling the topic sentences recalled more than students who read the unaltered text (Glover, Bruning, & Plake, 1982). Also, when given instructional objectives and asked to classify them according to Bloom's taxonomy (Bloom, Englehart, Furst, Hill, & Krathwohl, 1956), students encountered more difficulty classifying higher-level objectives (e.g., analysis and synthesis) and subsequently recalled them better than the lower-level objectives (e.g., knowledge and comprehension) (Glover, Plake, & Zimmer, 1982). Although the notion of distinctiveness of encoding or cognitive effort may not entirely supplant the notion of levels of processing (indeed, Tyler et al. [1979] demonstrated independent effects for depth and effort), the emphasis of these accounts is very much in line with

Anderson's (1970) initial argument that students are unlikely to learn very much unless they devote sufficient attention and effort to their instructional material and tasks.

FORMING MENTAL IMAGES

One way to ensure deep, meaningful, elaborative processing is to form a mental image of objects referred to, or events described, in verbal material. The powerful effect of imagery instructions on memory for word lists has been extensively documented by Paivio (1971). Bower (1970a) demonstrated that forming interactive images that united the words in a paired-associate learning task nearly doubled recall over rote-learning or independent-image instructions. The use of imagery is an integral aspect of such powerful mnemonics as the peg word method (in which one forms an image that integrates the peg word with the to-be-remembered information) and the method of loci (in which one images a familiar location and then images the to-be-learned information being deposited there). (See Belezza [1981] for a review.)

Use of imagery has been found to enhance recall of text in both adults (e.g., Anderson & Kulhavy, 1972; Kulhavy & Swenson, 1975) and children (e.g., Guttman, Levin, & Pressley, 1977; Levin, 1973). Training in the use of imagery in text comprehension has been shown to improve children's memory for text (e.g., Lesgold, McCormick, & Golinkoff, 1975; Pressley, 1976) and is one of the bases of Weinstein's elaboration strategy training (e.g., Weinstein, 1978, 1982; Weinstein et al., 1979).

CONSTRUCTING AN ORGANIZED,
INTERRELATED REPRESENTATION

Although it may have been "apparent for over 2000 years that human thought flows in organized sequences" (Puff, 1979, p. 3), and Gestalt psychologists focused on organizational processes in perception, systematic investigation of the role of organization in the learning and memory of verbal material awaited the coming of the cognitive–information-processing "revolution." Contemporary research on organization was marked by the appearance of influential papers by Mandler (1967) and Bower (1970b) and the publication of *Organization of Memory,* edited by Tulving and Donaldson (1972).

Concepts and definitions of organization have varied, but in this chapter I treat it as a process (see, e.g., Pellegrino & Ingram, 1979)—a process that leads to the formation in memory of a highly structured, interrelated representation. The importance of organization is due in large part to the need to access stored information. It is difficult to conceive how human memory, or any large information storage and retrieval system, could function without organization. For example, a library that simply heaped its books in a large pile in the center of the floor and kept no record of new acquisitions or books being checked out would not stay in business long.

Contemporary study of organization in human memory began with investigations of the role of organization in free recall of word lists. Bousfield (1953) observed that when subjects studied a list of words drawn from a small number of conceptual categories (e.g., animals, vegetables) they tended to recall words from the same category together, even though the list had been scrambled to separate category members. Subsequent research revealed that as organization increased—from unrelated word lists to scrambled categorical lists to categorical lists ordered by categories—recall improved (see Bower [1970b], Mandler [1967], and Pellegrino & Ingram [1979] for reviews). However, even with randomly ordered lists of unrelated words, subjects sought to impose order, and their efforts were reflected by the appearance of "subjective organization" in recall (Tulving, 1962). The ability of interactive mental images (Bower, 1970a) and mnemonics (see, e.g., Belezza, 1981), such as the method of loci and peg word technique, to improve recall is based in large part on the organization they supply. In describing human memory, Bartlett (1932) wrote of an "effort after meaning," but it may be that an "effort after organization" is equally pervasive and essential. Recently, an elaborative encoding theory in which the development of a highly redundant, interconnected representation leads to better memory has been proposed as an alternative to the levels of processing account (Anderson & Reder, 1979; Bradshaw & Anderson, 1982).

In the study of learning from text, early research demonstrated that intact text was much easier to learn and remember than scrambled text or unrelated lists of words or sentences (see Goetz [1975] and Goetz & Armbruster, [1980] for reviews). Subsequent research has focused on attempts to describe how memory for text is organized or structured, often in terms of story grammars (e.g., Mandler & Johnson, 1977; Rumelhart, 1975; Stein & Glenn, 1978; Thorndyke, 1977) and hierarchical network or propositional representations (e.g., Frederiksen, 1975; Kintsch, 1974; Meyer, 1975). Meyer, Brandt, and Bluth (1980) focused on the upper-level rhetorical structure of texts and found that students whose recalls reflected that structure recalled more of the passage. Recent descriptions of the organization of knowledge have typically developed around schemata (e.g., Anderson, 1977; Rumelhart & Ortony, 1977; Schallert, 1982; Schank & Abelson, 1977) and related constructs (e.g., frames, scripts), which stress how information is organized into structures that code the relationships between various components of familiar concepts and events. These structures not only keep previously acquired information organized, but guide the comprehension of text and the acquisition of new knowledge.

USING PRIOR KNOWLEDGE
AND INCORPORATING NEW INFORMATION

In his analysis of meaningful verbal learning, in his development of subsumption theory and the notion of ideational scaffolding, and in his research on advance organizers, Ausubel (e.g., 1960, 1962, 1963, 1968) has stressed that meaningful learning will only occur if the new information is related to what is already known. Although research on advance organizers has produced some controversy (see Ausubel, 1978; Barnes & Clawson, 1975; Hartley & Davies, 1976; Mayer, 1979), Ausubel's notion of the crucial role of prior knowledge in learning now seems beyond dispute. Mayer's assimilation encoding theory (1975, 1979) and Wittrock's (1974) generative process theory stress this same point. Bartlett's (1932) "effort after meaning" referred to the need to relate new information to existing knowledge structures.

The recent development of schema-theoretic descriptions of knowledge structure was motivated in large part by the desire to further articulate how existing knowledge guides learning. For example, Johnson (1973) demonstrated that those elements of a text that are most closely related to the reader's existing knowledge are best remembered, a finding replicated by Bower, Black, and Turner (1979). Whereas Johnson defined the relationship to prior knowledge by using "meaningfulness" ratings, the latter researchers employed a detailed analysis of the relevant schema.

Some of the most dramatic demonstrations of this role of prior knowledge have come from Bransford and his colleagues. For example, Bransford and Johnson (1972) demonstrated that simple passages, made up of familiar words in grammatically simple sentences, were either almost impossible or quite easy to understand and remember, depending upon whether a picture or title preceded them. The effect of the picture or title, they argued, was to permit the comprehenders to construct a sensible interpretation of the text, based on their prior knowledge. As one of the passages described a perfectly mundane matter well within the prior knowledge base of most people (washing clothes), the problem was not that the people who read the passage without the title lacked the appropriate knowledge, but rather that they could not apply it without the contextual support provided by the title. Similarly, Pichert and Anderson (1977) demonstrated that students who had been told to think of themselves as burglars when reading a passage about two boys playing hookey at one of their homes recalled more of the information relevant to the burglar perspective. Those told to think of themselves as homebuyers remembered more information relevant to that perspective.

Failure to appropriately utilize prior knowledge can also result from shortcomings in that knowledge. Chiesi, Spilich, and Voss (1979) investigated memory for verbal descriptions of baseball games and found that comprehension and memory of those readers with expert knowledge of baseball games as both quantitatively superior to and qualitatively different than those with less knowledge of the sport. Steffenson, Joag-Dev, and Anderson (1979) showed that people in India and the United States each recalled more from text consistent with the customs of their own cultures. If students lack the appropriate prior knowledge, then they must be supplied with it, as Gagne (1965) and Merill (1965) have stressed.

Making Initial Processing Compatible with Test Conditions

Tulving and Thomson (1973) proposed that "specific encoding operations performed on what is perceived determine what is stored, and what is stored determines what retrieval cues are effective in providing access to what is stored" (p. 39). This proposal, the *encoding specificity principle*, clearly has two parts. The first part embodies the cognitive–information-processing emphasis on the crucial role of the learner and how he or she processes the information in determining what is learned, and echoes the Gestalt position that the organizational processes of perception determine what gets into memory. At a general level, therefore, the first part of the encoding specificity principle is similar to levels of processing analysis. The emphasis, however, has been on the second part of the principle: For information in memory to be retrieved, the initial processing of the material must be compatible with the way it will later be tested.

The encoding specificity principle has stirred up a good deal of controversy, primarily related to its implications for models of recognition memory (e.g., Light, Kimble, & Pelligrino, 1975; Watkins & Tulving, 1975). The validity of the crucial second part of the principle, however, is now well documented. For example, Tulving and Thomson (1973) and Thomson and Tulving (1970) presented subjects with word pairs in which one of the words was designated the target (to-be-remembered) word and presented in capital letters (e.g., *glue* - *CHAIR*). Later, when tested for cued recall, close associates of the target words which were not present during encoding (e.g., *table*) proved ineffective at aiding recall, but the words that had accompanied the targets (e.g., *glue*) were quite effective. Presumably, the close associates failed to aid recall because they were inconsistent with the way the target words had initially been encoded.

It should be noted, however, that in order to be effective, a retrieval cue need not have been present at the time of encoding. Rather, it must be consistent with the way the information was encoded. For sentences and texts, the central aspect of the way in which the information is encoded is the meaning which the reader or listener constructs from the words. Two strikingly similar, yet independently conducted, sets of experiments by Barclay, Bransford, Franks, McCarrell, and Nitsch (1974) and by Anderson and Ortony (1975) illustrate this point. For example, in the latter study, subjects read the sentence *The container held the apples,* and then received a cued recall test in which both *basket* and *bottle* appeared as cues. *Basket* proved far more effective at aiding recall. For subjects who had read *The container held the cola,* however, *bottle* proved more effective. In fact, a retrieval cue that was not present at encoding can produce better recall than a word that was a part of the original sentence, provided that the retrieval cue is closer to the meaning the reader has constructed (Anderson *et al.,* 1976). For example, after reading *The woman was outstanding in the theater,* recall was better when cued with *actress* than with *woman.*

Recently, transfer-appropriate processing has been proposed as an alternative framework for reinterpreting results which were previously interpreted to support the levels of processing account (Bransford, Franks, Morris, & Stein, 1979; Morris *et al.,* 1977). The concept of transfer-appropriate processing is quite similar to the encoding specificity principle in stressing that memory will only be as good as the match between initial processing and test conditions (cf. Bransford *et al.,* 1979; Tulving, 1979). In the transfer-appropriate-processing framework, previous studies are viewed as having shown deep, semantic processing to be superior because that is the type of processing most appropriate to the typical recognition and recall tests. When memory for rhymes (Morris *et al.,* 1977) or letter cases (i.e., upper vs. lower case; Stein, 1978) is tested, however, supposedly superficial processing that was directed at the sound or sight of the words was superior to semantic processing. The transfer-appropriate-processing account rejects the claim that semantic processing is always better. From an educational perspective, however, in view of the fact that students are typically expected to remember the meaning of discourse, the emphasis on semantic processing within the levels of processing account seems well placed.

PLANNING, MONITORING, AND REGULATING PROCESSING

If, as we have just argued, (1) readers can process text material in a variety of fashions, (2) some types of processing lead to better memory than others, and (3) the type of processing that is appropriate and beneficial depends in part on the reader's goal and the task requirements, then it is unlikely that the studier will be successful without a sophisticated "executive function" to plan, orchestrate, and monitor cognitive processes. Recently, a good deal of attention has been directed toward the description and investigation of this executive function, under the rubric of metacognition (see Brown, 1978, 1980).

According to Flavell (1976), "*Metacognition* refers to one's knowledge concerning one's own cognitive processes and products or anything related to them. . . . *Metacognition* refers, among other things, to the active monitoring and consequent regulation and orchestration of the processes . . . usually in the service of some concrete goal or objective" [italics added; p. 232]. A metacognitive analysis of studying stresses the active role of the studier in constructing a sensible, coherent representation of the meaning of the text. The studier must be flexible and adaptive, modifying the study process to fit both the purpose for studying and the characteristics of the text. Comprehensive monitoring, the conscious assessment of the adequacy of one's own understanding, is a crucial process. Recent research suggests that poor comprehension monitoring may be a common source of comprehension problems (see Baker & Brown [in press] for a review).

If comprehension monitoring is to be beneficial, then the studier must have methods or strategies for dealing with comprehension failure, once detected. "Fix-up" strategies for remediating detected comprehension failures might include: (1) rereading a portion of the text that presents information crucial to understanding; (2) skimming ahead in the text or reading on in search of information that will clear up the current confusion; (3) employing a study strategy, such as paraphrasing a sentence or outlining a section, that ensures deep, semantic processing of the text; or (4) seeking an outside resource such as another text, another student, or a teacher (Alessi, Anderson, & Goetz, 1979). Myers and Paris (1978) interviewed 8- and 12-year-old children and found that the older children exhibited greater knowledge of fix-up strategies. Several investigators have argued that encountering the blank left by word deletion in a *cloze* test is analogous to detecting that a word has not been comprehended while reading, and that the knowledge and strategies needed to successfully fill in the blank may be similar to the fix-up skill needed during normal reading (e.g., DiVesta, Hayward, & Orlando, 1979; Goetz & Dixon, 1979; Neville & Pugh, 1976/1977). They have reported that good readers are more flexible and effective in their inspection and use of passage context in cloze tests than are poor readers.

The potential of metacognitive training for improving study skills seems great, and preliminary investigations appear promising (e.g., Brown, Campione, & Day, 1981; Brown & Palincsar, 1982; Meichenbaum & Asarnow, 1979).

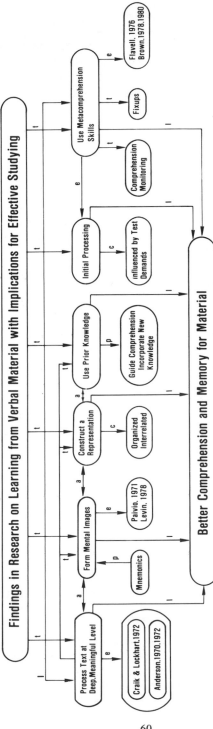

FIGURE 1. Partial network representation of the literature review. This network represents each of the six subheadings in the review as a node in the center level of the network. The network is intended to graphically represent that the types of processing described under the subheadings: (1) may be viewed both as representative of the literature on learning from verbal material and as leading to better learning of the material studied, (2) are very similar, (3) may all be viewed as applications of metacognitive skill, and (4) are described in some detail (not fully represented here) in the text. Key: a = analogous or similar, c = characteristic, e = evidence, l = leads to, p = part, t = type or example.

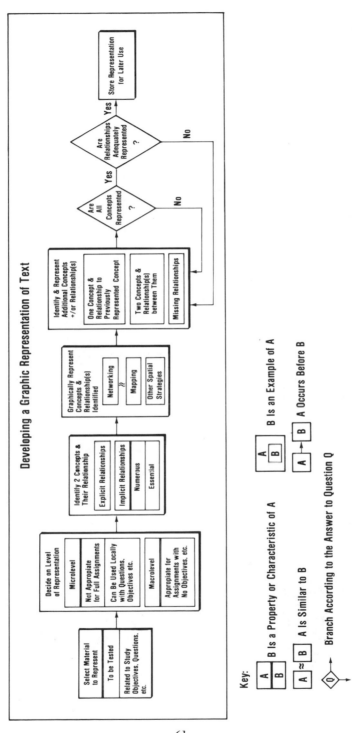

FIGURE 2. Map of the process of using a spatial learning strategy for studying. This map shows the sequence of operations involved in graphically representing text and illustrates some of the details of individual operations.

61

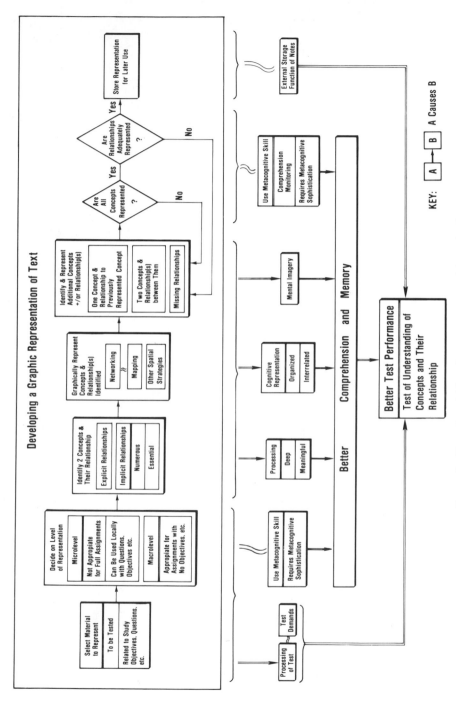

FIGURE 3. Map of spatial learning strategy use and its evaluation.

ANALYSIS OF THE PROCESSING PROMOTED
OR REQUIRED BY SPATIAL STRATEGIES

Just what does the studier do when, during the course of studying a text, he or she employs a spatial learning strategy to produce a graphic representation such as that presented in Figure 1, of the material being studied? In attempting to answer this question, I present an analysis of how the studier constructs the representation, focusing on the cognitive processes involved. This analysis is directed primarily toward the use of mapping (Armbruster & Anderson, Chapter 9, present volume) and networking (Holley & Dansereau, Chapter 4; Holley, Dansereau, McDonald, Garland, & Collins, 1979), but it is more or less representative of the process of applying other spatial strategies such as concept structuring (Vaughan, Chapter 6) and schematizing (Mirande, Chapter 7; Camstra & van Bruggen, Chapter 8) that are intended to graphically represent the relationships between concepts in a text. A similar analysis aimed specifically at the process of schematizing is presented by Breuker (Chapter 2). Examples of the types of graphic representations a studier might produce upon applying networking or mapping to portions of this text are presented in Figures 1, 2, and 3.

The analysis presented here lists eight steps (operations in sequential order), noting those operations which are applied recursively. Although the analysis does not represent the only possible set or sequence of operations, it is a reasonable account of how most studiers apply spatial strategies in most instances. The process is presented graphically in Figure 2.

When using a spatial strategy to construct a graphic representation of the text, the studier will (or should):

1. *Select the material to be represented.* In order to apply a spatial learning strategy—or any other study strategy—profitably, it is crucial that it be applied to appropriate material. Because spatial strategies require considerable time and effort, learners cannot (and certainly will not) go about mapping or networking everything they read. The material must be appropriate in the obvious sense that it is the material for which the learner will be held responsible and tested. Reading assignments are the primary determinants of this sense of appropriateness—along with objective statements, question topics, and the like (see Anderson *et al.,* 1979; Anderson & Armbruster, 1982).

The material should also be appropriate in the sense that it *requires* intensive study. If the material presents information that is already well known to the studier or is trivial or easily assimilated to the studier's existing knowledge structures, no such time- and effort-consuming activities are warranted or required.

Finally, the material should be appropriate in terms of being suited for the use of the particular study strategy to be used. Because networking and mapping were designed to represent the semantic relationships—such as temporal and causal sequence, and similarity or contrast—between concepts in a text, they should prove especially well-suited to text intended to convey information about such relationships. Because most informative, content-area texts the studier will encounter are intended to convey information of this type, networking and mapping should usually be appropriate for the material.

2. *Decide the level at which to represent the text.* Because the concepts that become related in mapping and networking are written in natural language, and since the same semantic relationships appear to characterize relationships in text at both the micro and macro level, it is possible to map or network sentences or paragraphs minutely. On the other hand, with a map or network of about the same size and complexity, the relationships between key concepts and events in an entire chapter or larger text unit can be represented. Schallert, Ulerick, and Tierney (Chapter 12) describe a procedure for developing an exhaustive microstructure account of a text. While such detailed description may be appropriate for text analysis, it is certainly too exhaustive and exhausting for most studiers with most reading assignments. As in the preceding Step 1 information such as the reading assignment and any objectives or questions should guide the micro–macro level decision. If the studier has a large reading assignment and no objectives or questions, a macro level representation of the relationships between major concepts and events seems most appropriate. If a large assignment is accompanied by objectives or questions, local microlevel representations of the information related to each could be developed.

3. *Identify at least two concepts and the relationship between them.* This step could have been subdivided into three components (i.e., identify one concept, identify a second concept, identify one or more relationships between them), but to do so would be to miss the point. The essence of networking and mapping is the representation of the *relationships between concepts.* You cannot have relationships between concepts with fewer than two concepts. It should be noted that important relationships will often not be explicitly stated in the text and will have to be inferred (see Shallert, Ulerick, & Tierney, Chapter 12).

4. *Graphically represent the concepts and relationship identified.* The form of representations for mapping and networking are presented, respectively, by Armbruster and Anderson (Chapter 9) and Holley and Dansereau (Chapter 4). Assuming that the studier is familiar with the formalisms, the operation is straightforward.

5. *Identify and graphically represent at least* (1) one new concept and its relationship to an already represented concept, or (2) two new concepts and the relationship between them.

6. *Repeat Step 5 until all of the concepts have been represented.* Specifically, until all of the concepts in the text unit identified in Step 1 are represented at the level decided upon in Step 2. The studier must match concepts in the representation against concepts in the text to test whether all of the concepts in the set of concepts-to-be-represented have actually been represented. Because the set of all concepts-to-be-represented is not explicitly marked for the studier in the text and will almost never be the same as the set of all concepts in the text, and because the development of a map or network will make the spatial relationships between concepts appear quite different than in the text, knowing when "all" of the concepts have been represented is not a straightforward matter.

7. *Check the graphic representation to verify that the relationships represented match those expressed in the text.* As in the previous steps, selection of the unit of text to be represented and the level of representation (Steps 1 and 2) will greatly influence this process. As in Step 6, because (1) it will almost never be the case that all of the relationships in the text will be represented, (2) those that are to be represented will not have been marked for the studier, and (3) in any case, relationships look quite different in networks and maps than in texts, this matching operation will not be trivial. Further, as noted in Step 3, many of the relationships needed to construct an adequate representation of the text will not be directly stated in the text. These inferred relationships must be indirectly verified against information presented in the text. It should be noted that this operation could be performed recursively after Steps 4 and 5. The size of the text unit to be represented may determine whether continuous monitoring or a final check is best, since if a lot of the text is to be represented, waiting until completion of the representation to check it may lead to a lot of wasted time and effort, particularly if improper representational decisions are made early on.

8. *Store the graphic representation so that it can be amended when new information is acquired and retrieved for later review.*

EVALUATION OF SPATIAL STRATEGIES FOR STUDYING TEXT

The preceding section outlines an analysis of what the studier does when developing a graphic representation from text. As that analysis suggests, and as several of the other chapters in this volume explicitly state, development of a graphic representation can be difficult and time-consuming. (However, Vaughan, Chapter 6, presents some data indicating that students who used his spatial strategy did not invest more than the normal amount of time.) The question then becomes Is all this time and effort justified? The ultimate answer to this question would require an extended validation process involving extensive laboratory studies, field research, and widespread implementation and evaluation. Whether such a process will occur remains to be seen. If spatial strategies are difficult and time-consuming to employ, they are also difficult and time-consuming to train and to research. In any case, this validation process has only just begun. Existing direct empirical evidence is reviewed elsewhere in this volume, but as Holley and Dansereau (Chapter 1) point out, it is as yet somewhat sketchy and preliminary. Therefore, rather than attempting an ultimate answer to an ultimate question, I would like to consider two preliminary questions.

1. *Is the processing involved in the construction of a graphic representation for text consistent with that which has been found to improve comprehension and memory for verbal material?* To address this question, the *steps* of spatial learning strategies, given in the immediately preceding analysis, are considered in relation to the *points* discussed earlier in the second section of this chapter, which summarize research and theory on comprehending and remembering text. If what the studier must do when using a spatial strategy to represent text is to engage in the sort of cognitive–information-processing activities that have been found to improve comprehension and recall, then the time and effort will probably be well spent. Steps 1 and 2 reflect decisions about the unit of text to be represented and the level at which to represent it. To the extent that studiers make use of available information about the instructional task (e.g., reading assignments, objective statements, study questions), processing of the text material should be more compatible with test demands (Point 5), and test performance should improve. Further, these decisions represent the type of planning activities advocated by the metacognitive analysis of reading and study skills previously outlined (Point 6).

Steps 3 to 5 reflect the identification of the concepts and relations to be represented and the development of the graphic representation. Searching the text to find the important concepts and relations should ensure deep, meaningful processing of information in the text (Point 1). Since the essence of a networking or mapping representation of text is the relationship between concepts, the process of developing the representation entails the sort of organizational processing that has been shown to improve memory (Point 3). Further, because many of the relationships will not be explicitly stated in the text, elaborative semantic processing is once again indicated, and the studier will be forced to bring prior knowledge to bear on the task (Point 4). It is possible that the studier must produce a mental image of a relationship before producing its graphic representation. Perhaps the graphic representation, once created, can be stored and retrieved as a mental image by the studier. Such speculation, however, has not yet been supported, and in any case, the imagery process for abstract graphic representations may be quite different from that for the images of concrete objects which have proven so beneficial (Point 2).

In Steps 6 and 7, the studier checks the graphic representation against the text to see whether all of the important concepts have been represented and whether the relationships expressed in the two representations correspond. To the extent that a map or network represents the studier's understanding of the intended meaning of the text, checking the graphic representation against the text can serve as a form of comprehension monitoring (Point 6).

Finally, if the studier does put the network or map away and later gets it out and reviews it prior to taking a test, performance may be improved (Step 8). Although not reviewed here previously, a number of investigators have reported that students who take notes on a text and review them prior to a delayed test remember more than those who only read the text or take notes without a review (e.g., Rickards & Friedman, 1978).

Based on this examination of the processing required to generate a graphic representation of text via mapping or networking, it appears that most of the processing the studier will employ in this endeavor is the sort of processing that has been shown to improve memory for verbal material. It would seem then that the studier's time would be well spent.

Nevertheless, one might still insistently ask: "Is it *really worth* all the time and effort? Will the performance gains justify their increased costs?" This is a question that individual studiers must answer for themselves, with guidance from educational researchers. We must be careful, however, about how we address this question. Faw and Waller (1976), in a review of research on study strategies and adjunct aids, argued that

> it is absurd to think that psychologists and educators can be content with improving subjects' learning and retention of textual materials if the altered performance is simply a function of augmented study time. This would be analogous to attributing the increased length of a skier's jump to superior coaching when, in fact, the coach had simply provided a steeper and longer hill from which the jump could be made [p. 703].

I assert, however, that this analogy is misleading. The educator who gets the student to learn and remember more through increased study time is more like the coach who elicits superior athletic performances by having his or her athletes better conditioned and better prepared through longer practice periods. Further, if the coach and athletes are to be successful, just putting in time going through the motions is not sufficient. To improve performance, the practice must be intensive and focused. Thus, if a study strategy (including spatial strategies) is to be successful in improving student performance, it must cause the student to spend study time more effectively, that is, in the types of processing that will improve comprehension and memory for verbal material.

Faw and Waller (1976) proposed that study strategies be evaluated in terms of their value on an "efficiency index." This value is calculated by finding a mean "efficiency score" (average test score divided by average study time) for the study strategy group and a read-only control group and then dividing the former group's mean efficiency score by that of the latter. As Reynolds, Standiford, and Anderson (1979) point out, however, this computational scheme is ill conceived because it is systematically biased against any study system that requires more time than simply reading the text. They argued that use of the efficiency index could also promote study systems in which students spend less than a nanosecond on a reading assignment, since, assuming that the students get *any* points on the test, their efficiency score and therefore their efficiency index would approach infinity. Instructors in our schools and colleges have long reported that many students employ this strategy.

Having answered the first question affirmatively, and having concluded, therefore, that the use of spatial strategies may improve comprehension and memory of text, I proceed to the second question.

2. *Under what conditions will the use of spatial strategies to graphically represent text prove beneficial to the studier?* Assuming that the studier knows *how* to use a spatial strategy, the first of these conditions is as obvious as it is essential: Use of spatial strategies can only benefit studiers who actually *use* them. To return to our coaching analogy, suppose a coach worked the athletes so long and hard that they all broke down or quit the team. As previously noted, very few students report the use of SQ3R or study strategies that require more of them than simply reading the text. Student perceptions of the amount of time, effort, or expertise required by a study strategy may prove a powerful mediator of strategy use. If the use of spatial strategies is viewed as too difficult or time-consuming, potential users will be hard to find. Although it might be argued that because networking and mapping stress the semantic relationships between concepts, students trained in these techniques will benefit even on reading assignments that they do not graphically represent, such positive transfer has not yet been demonstrated.

A second condition is that the use of spatial strategies will only benefit a studier who knows when to use them, when to stop using them, and when not to use them at all. As argued earlier, because an exhaustive graphic representation of every word in every reading assignment is not possible within the lifetime of mortal studiers, objective statements and study questions should be used to guide the selection of text to be represented. The studier who faces a long text passage with no such guides should attempt to represent the relationships between only the most important concepts and events. Further, the studier would be well advised to focus on that information which he or she does not already know and which is somewhat difficult to understand and remember. To be able to identify important information, to accurately assess what one knows and does not know, and to decide when further processing is needed requires a level of metacognitive sophistication that recent research suggests many studiers lack (see Baker & Brown, in press; Brown, 1978, 1980). For the process of checking an already developed network or map against the text to serve as a form of comprehension monitoring (see the preceding section), similar metacognitive skills would seem to be required.

Finally, if benefits to the studier are measured in terms of a score on a test, then for the use of a spatial strategy to be beneficial, the test should assess understanding of the concepts and the relationships between them (see Surber, Chapter 10). Despite the concerns of Spiro (1977), we assume this will typically be the case. If, however, the test measures verbatim recall of definitions, the studier might better concentrate on rote memorization or employ a key-word mnemonic (e.g., Levin, 1981).

DIRECTIONS FOR THE FUTURE

It should be clear from the discussion in the preceding section that I feel that the use of spatial learning strategies to graphically represent text holds considerable promise. How then is this promise to be realized? I address three directions in which we might proceed.

The first direction is the development of effective instruction in spatial strategy use. Networking seems to be the most advanced in this regard, but further development is still needed. Holley et al. (1979) showed that 5½ hours of training in networking improved college students' comprehension and recall of an experimental passage. It is doubtful, however, that many of those students continued to use the technique after the study was completed. To expect college students, whose existing study (or nonstudy) habits are entrenched by 12 or more years of prior schooling, to change the way they study with so little exposure to the technique is probably unrealistic (see Camstra & van Bruggen, Chapter 8). Incorporation of spatial strategies training into an extensive, semester-long study skills course such as those reported by Weinstein (e.g., 1978), Dansereau (e.g., Dansereau et al., 1979), and

Mirande (Chapter 7) seems more promising. In such a context, the training might address the concerns raised in the previous section about the conditions necessary for profitable use of study strategies.

A potential difficulty with the instructional material developed for mapping (Anderson *et al.,* 1979) and some of the early networking materials is that they presented the instruction in a "building block" fashion (Dansereau, in press), beginning with examples and practice at the proposition or sentence level for each of the relationships in turn. From there, students progressed to short paragraphs or passages which again tended to present just one type of relationship. It is possible that such instruction might bias students to attempt to apply spatial strategies in a strictly bottom-up fashion (see Armbruster & Anderson, Chapter 9; Dansereau, in press). Dansereau (in press) reports that this approach has since been abandoned with the networking strategy.

A second potential difficulty with spatial strategy instruction is the use of examples and practice on sentences or short texts that occur out of context, and may appear artificial to the student. This may cause students to perceive the instruction as isolated drill and to fail to see the possible utility of the technique in their academic courses. Having the students apply the techniques to their actual reading assignments from their other courses would seem to be helpful. Perhaps spatial strategies should be taught in the content areas themselves rather than in, or in addition to, special study skills courses. (However, Camstra and van Bruggen in Chapter 8 report some pitfalls with this approach.) This approach would make possible a potentially beneficial "immersion" in the strategy (see Vaughan, Chapter 6). If a content area instructor used spatial strategies to develop teacher-provided graphic aids to accompany instruction, students could be provided with considerable exposure to the representation system before having to generate representations themselves. Whether students would learn spatial strategy use more easily or effectively if the reception mode preceded the production mode remains to be seen.

The second direction is the improvement of the spatial strategies themselves. One apparent shortcoming of spatial strategies at present is that the development of a graphic representation of the text may be excessively text-bound. The studier may need to infer relations from the text, but if the studier focuses on representing the text, the activity may not require or foster sufficient integration of new information with the studier's existing knowledge structures. In order to address this problem, activities might be developed in which studiers would elaborate a graphic representation of the text with information from their prior knowledge. If the text presents examples of a concept or causes of an event, studiers might be encouraged to generate other examples (or close nonexamples) or other causes (or effects) of their own to add to the representation.

A second approach would be to use the spatial strategy to structure information presented to the students that they could use to incorporate information from subsequent reading assignments. Dansereau (in press) has advocated the development of content-dependent strategies in which studiers are provided with schemata which are useful for assimilating information about a certain topic area. He presented one such example, DICEOX (*Description, Inventor—History, Consequences, Evidence, Other theories, X-tra information*), for structuring information about scientific theories. Spatial learning strategies could be used to present such structures to the student. Armbruster and Anderson (Chapter 9) provide several related examples in their discussion of text frames.

The final direction for the future is to develop a program of process-oriented research (see Belmont & Butterfield, 1977; Ryan, 1981) on spatial strategy use. We do not need another study strategy literature in which sometimes the strategy works and sometimes it does not and there is no way to make sense of the hodgepodge of conflicting results. When spatial strategies are shown to improve performance, we need to know *how* they were effective. When spatial strategies do not improve performance, we need to know *why* they failed. We need to delineate the conditions under which spatial strategy use will be effective in terms of learner, text, and task dimensions. The chapters in this volume make a hopeful beginning in that direction.

ACKNOWLEDGMENTS

I would like to thank Diane Schallert, Pat Alexander, Charles D. Holley, and Claire Weinstein for their comments on earlier drafts of this chapter.

REFERENCES

Adams, A., Carnine, D., & Gersten, R. (1982). Instructional strategies for studying content area texts in the intermediate grades. *Reading Research Quarterly, 18,* 27–55.

Alessi, S. M., Anderson, T. H., & Goetz, E. T. (1979). An investigation of lookbacks during studying. *Discourse Processes, 2,* 197–212.

Anderson, J. R., & Reder, L. M. (1979). An elaborative processing explanation of depth of processing. In L. Cermak & F. Craik (Eds.), *Levels of processing in human memory.* Hillsdale, NJ: Erlbaum.

Anderson, R. C. (1970). Control of student mediating processes during verbal learning and instruction. *Review of Educational Research, 40,* 349–369.

Anderson, R. C. (1972). How to construct achievement tests to assess comprehension. *Review of Educational Research, 42,* 145–170.

Anderson, R. C. (1977). The notion of schemata and the educational enterprise. In R. C. Anderson, R. J. Spiro, & W. E. Montague (Eds.), *Schooling and the acquisition of knowledge.* Hillsdale, NJ: Erlbaum.

Anderson, R. C., Faust, G. W., & Roderick, M. C. (1968). Over prompting in programmed instruction. *Journal of Educational Psychology, 59,* 88–93.

Anderson, R. C., & Kulhavy, R. W. (1972). Imagery and prose learning. *Journal of Educational Psychology, 63,* 242–243.

Anderson, R. C., & Ortony, A. (1975). On putting apples into bottles: A problem of polysemy. *Cognitive Psychology, 7,* 167–180.

Anderson, R. C., Pichert, J. W., Goetz, E. T., Shallert, D. L., Stevens, K. V., & Trollip, S. R. (1976). Instantiation of general terms. *Journal of Verbal Learning and Verbal Behavior, 15,* 667–679.

Anderson, T. H. (1980). Study strategies and adjunct aids. In R. J. Spiro, B. C. Bruce, & W. F. Brewer (Eds.), *Theoretical issues in reading comprehension: Perspectives from cognitive psychology, artificial intelligence, linguistics, and education.* Hillsdale, NJ: Erlbaum.

Anderson, T. H., Alessi, S., Armbruster, B., Baker, L., Camp, M., Dixon, K., Goetz, E., Davis, A., Miller, C., Schallert, D., Siepart, G., & Walker, C. (1979). *Techniques for studying textbook materials in preparation for taking an exam.* Final Report to the Advanced Research Projects Agency for Contract No. N00123-77-C-0622. Champaign, IL.: Center for the Study of Reading, University of Illinois.

Anderson, T. H., & Armbruster, B. B. (1982). Reader and text—studying strategies. In W. Otto & S. White (Eds.), *Reading expository materials.* New York: Academic Press.

Andre, T. (1981). The role of paraphrased adjunct questions in facilitating learning from prose. *Contemporary Educational Psychology, 6,* 22–27.

Atkinson, R. C., & Shiffrin, R. M. (1968). Human memory: A proposed system and its control processes. In K. W. Spence & J. T. Spence (Eds.), *The psychology of learning and motivation: Advances in research and theory* (Vol. II). New York: Academic Press.

Ausubel, D. P. (1960). The use of advance organizers in the learning and retention of verbal material. *Journal of Educational Psychology, 51,* 267–272.

Ausubel, D. P. (1962). A subsumption theory of meaningful verbal learning and retention. *Journal of General Psychology, 66,* 213–224.

Ausubel, D. P. (1963). *The psychology of meaningful verbal learning.* New York: Grune & Stratton.

Ausubel, D. P. (1968). *Educational psychology: A cognitive view.* New York: Holt.

Ausubel, D. P. (1978). In defense of advance organizers: A reply to the critics. *Review of Educational Research, 48,* 251–257.

Baddeley, A. D. (1978). The trouble with levels: A reexamination of Craik and Lockhart's framework for memory research. *Psychological Review, 85,* 139–152.

Baker, L., & Brown, A. L. (in press). Cognitive monitoring in reading. In J. Flood (Ed.), *Understanding reading comprehension.* Newark, DE: International Reading Association.

Barclay, J. R., Bransford, J. D., Franks, J. J., McCarrell, N. S., & Nitsch, K. (1974). Comprehension and semantic flexibility. *Journal of Verbal Learning and Verbal Behavior, 13,* 471–481.

Barnes, B. R., & Clawson, E. V. (1975). Do advance organizers facilitate learning? Recommendations for further research based on an analysis of 32 studies. *Review of Educational Research, 45,* 637–659.

Bartlett, F. C. (1932). *Remembering: A study in experimental and social psychology*. London: Cambridge University Press.

Barton, W. A. (1930). *Outlining as a study procedure*. New York: Teachers College, Columbia University.

Belezza, F. S. (1981). Mnemonic devices: Classification, characteristics, and criteria. *Review of Educational Research, 5,* 247–275.

Belmont, J. M., & Butterfield, E. C. (1977). The instructional approach to developmental & cognitive research. In R. V. Kail, Jr. & J. Hagen (Eds.), *Perspectives on the development of memory and cognition*. Hillsdale, NJ.: Erlbaum.

Bloom, B. S., Englehart, M. D., Furst, E. J., Hill, W. H., & Krathwohl, D. R. (1956). *Taxonomy of educational objectives handbook I: Cognitive domain*. New York: McKay.

Bobrow, S. A., & Bower, G. H. (1969). Comprehension and recall of sentences. *Journal of Experimental Psychology, 80,* 455–461.

Bousfield, W. A. (1953). The occurrence of clustering in the recall of randomly arranged associates. *Journal of General Psychology, 49,* 229–240.

Bower, G. H. (1970a). Imagery as a relational organizer in associative learning. *Journal of Verbal Learning and Verbal Behavior, 9,* 529–533.

Bower, G. H. (1970b). Organizational factors in memory. *Cognitive Psychology, 1,* 18–46.

Bower, G. H., Black, J. B., & Turner, T. J. (1979). Scripts in memory for texts. *Cognitive Psychology, 11,* 177–220.

Bradshaw, G. L., & Anderson, J. R. (1982). Elaborative encoding as an explanation of levels of processing. *Journal of Verbal Learning and Verbal Behavior, 21,* 165–174.

Bransford, J. D., Franks, J. J., Morris, C. D., & Stein, B. S. (1979). Some general constraints on learning and memory research. In L. S. Cermak & F. I. M. Craik (Eds.), *Levels of processing in human memory*. Hillsdale, NJ: Erlbaum.

Bransford, J. D., & Johnson, M. K. (1972). Contextual prerequisites for understanding: Some investigations of comprehension and recall. *Journal of Verbal Learning and Verbal Behavior, 11,* 717–726.

Brown, A. L. (1978). Knowing when, where, and how to remember: A problem of metacognition. In R. Glaser (Ed.), *Advances in instructional psychology* (Vol. 1). Hillsdale, NJ: Erlbaum.

Brown, A. L. (1980). Metacognitive development and reading. In R. J. Spiro, B. C. Bruce, & W. F. Brewer (Eds.), *Theoretical issues in reading comprehension: Perspectives from cognitive psychology, linguistics, artificial intelligence, and education*. Hillsdale, NJ: Erlbaum.

Brown, A. L., Campione, J. C., & Day, J. D. (1981). Learning to learn: On training students to learn from texts. *Educational Researcher, 10,* 14–21.

Brown, A. L., & Palincsar, A. S. (1982). Inducing strategic learning from texts by means of informed, self-control training. *Topics in Learning and Learning Disabilities, 1982, 2,* 1–17.

Brown, A. L., & Smiley, S. S. (1977). The development of strategies for studying text. *Child Development, 48,* 1–8.

Carroll, J. B. (1971). *Learning from verbal discourse in educational media: A review of the literature.* U.S. Office of Education, Final Report for Project No. 7-1069, Contract No. 1-7-071069-4243. Princeton: Educational Testing Service.

Chiesi, H. L., Spilich, G. J., & Voss, J. F. (1979). Acquisition of domain related information in relation to high and low domain knowledge. *Journal of Verbal Learning and Verbal Behavior, 18,* 257–273.

Craik, F. I. M. (1973). A "levels of analysis" view of memory. In P. Pliner, L. Kramer, & T. Alloway (Eds.), *Communication and affect: Language and thought*. New York: Academic Press.

Craik, F. I. M., & Lockhart, R. S. (1972). Levels of processing: A framework for memory research. *Journal of Verbal Learning and Verbal Behavior, 11,* 671–684.

Craik, F. I. M., & Tulving, E. (1975). Depth of processing and the retention of words in episodic memory. *Journal of Experimental Psychology: General, 104,* 268–294.

Dansereau, D. F. (1978). The development of a learning strategies curriculum. In H. F. O'Neil (Ed.), *Learning strategies.* New York: Academic Press.

Dansereau, D. F. (in press). Learning strategy research. In J. Segal, S. Chipman, & R. Glaser (Eds.), *Thinking and learning skills: Relating instruction to basic research.* Hillsdale, NJ: Erlbaum.

Dansereau, D. F., Actkinson, T. R., Long, G. L., & McDonald, B. A. (1974). *Learning strategies: A review and synthesis of the current literature* (AFHRL-TR-74-70). Lowry Air Force Base, CO: Technical Training Division. (NTIS No. AD-A007 722)

Dansereau, D. F., Long, G. L., McDonald, B. A., & Actkinson, T. R. (1975). *Learning strategy inventory development and assessment* (AFHRL-TR-75-40). Lowry Air Force Base, CO: Technical Training Division. (NTIS No. AD-A014 721)

Dansereau, D. F., Long, G. L., McDonald, B. A., Actkinson, T. R., Ellis, A. M., Collins, K., Williams, S., & Evans, S. H. (1976). Effective learning strategy training program: Development and assessment. *Catalog of Selected Documents in Psychology, 6,* 19.

Dansereau, D. F., McDonald, B. A., Collins, K. W., Garland, J., Holley, C. D., Diekhoff, G. M., & Evans, S. H. (1979). Evaluation of a learning strategy system. In H. F. O'Neil, Jr. & C. D. Spielberger (Eds.), *Cognitive and affective learning strategies.* New York: Academic Press.

DiVesta, F. J., Hayward, K. G., & Orlando, V. P. (1979). Developmental trends in monitoring text for comprehension. *Child Development, 50,* 97–105.

Durkin, D. (1978/1979). What classroom observations reveal about reading comprehension instruction. *Reading Research Quarterly, 14,* 481–533.

Ebbinghaus, H. (1913). *Uber das gedachtnis* (H. Ruger & C. E. Bussenius, trans.). New York: Columbia Teachers College. (Original work published 1885)

Faw, H. W., & Waller, T. G. (1976). Mathemagenic behaviors and efficiency in learning from prose. *Review of Educational Research, 46,* 691–722.

Flavell, J. H. (1976). Metacognitive aspects of problem solving. In L. B. Resnick (Ed.), *The nature of intelligence.* Hillsdale, NJ: Erlbaum.

Frederiksen, C. H. (1975). Representing logical and semantic structure of knowledge acquired from discourse. *Cognitive Psychology, 7,* 371–458.

Gagné, R. M. (1965). *The conditions of learning.* New York: Holt.

Glover, J. A., Bruning, R. H., & Plake, B. S. (1982). Distinctiveness of encoding and recall of text material. *Journal of Educational Psychology, 74,* 522–534.

Glover, J. A., Plake, B. S., & Zimmer, J. W. (1982). Distinctiveness of encoding and memory for learning tasks. *Journal of Educational Psychology, 74,* 189–198.

Goetz, E. T. (1975, November). *Sentences in lists and in connected discourse* (Tech. Rep. No. 3). Champaign, IL: University of Illinois, Center for the Study of Reading. (ERIC Document Reproduction Service No. ED 134 927)

Goetz, E. T., & Armbruster, B. B. (1980). Psychological correlates of text structure. In R. J. Spiro, B. C. Bruce, & W. F. Brewer (Eds.), *Theoretical issues in reading comprehension: Perspectives from cognitive psychology, linguistics, artificial intelligence, and education.* Hillsdale, NJ: Erlbaum.

Goetz, E. T., & Dixon, K. M. (1979, November). *The use of context by good and poor readers in a cloze test.* Champaign, IL: Center for the Study of Reading, University of Illinois. (ERIC Document Reproduction Service No. ED 185 527)

Guttman, J., Levin, J. R., & Pressley, M. (1977). Pictures, partial pictures, and young children's oral prose learning. *Journal of Educational Psychology, 69,* 473–480.

Hartley, J., & Davies, I. K. (1976). Preinstructional strategies: The role of pretests, behavioral objectives, overviews, and advance organizers. *Review of Educational Research, 46,* 239–265.

Holley, C. D., Dansereau, D. F., McDonald, B. A., Garland, J. C., & Collins, K. W. (1979). Evaluation of a hierarchical mapping technique as an aid to prose processing. *Contemporary Educational Psychology, 4,* 227–237.

Hyde, T. S., & Jenkins, J. J. (1969). Differential effects of incidental tasks on the organization of recall of a list of highly associated words. *Journal of Experimental Psychology, 82,* 472–481.

Jacoby, L. L., & Craik, F. I. M. (1979). Effects of elaboration of processing at encoding and retrieval: Trace distinctiveness and recovery of initial context. In L. S. Cermak & F. I. M. Craik (Eds.), *Levels of processing in human memory.* Hillsdale, NJ: Erlbaum.

Jacoby, L. L., Craik, F. I. M., & Begg, I. (1979). Effects of decision difficulty in recognition and recall. *Journal of Verbal Learning and Verbal Behavior, 18,* 585–600.

Johnson, R. E. (1973). Meaningfulness and the recall of textual pose. *American Educational Research Journal, 10,* 49–58.

Kemp, F. D., & Holland, J. G. (1966). Blackout rates and overt responses in programmed instruction: Resolution of disparate results. *Journal of Educational Psychology, 57,* 109–114.

Kintsch, W. (1974). *The representation of meaning in memory.* Hillsdale, NJ: Erlbaum.

Kulhavy, R. W., & Swenson, I. (1975). Imagery instruction and the comprehension of text. *British Journal of Edcational Psychology, 45,* 47–51.

Lesgold, A. M., McCormick, C., & Golinkoff, R. M. (1975). Imagery training and children's prose learning. *Journal of Educational Psychology, 67,* 663–667.

Levin, J. R. (1973). Inducing comprehension in poor readers: A test of a recent model. *Journal of Educational Psychology, 65,* 19–24.

Levin, J. R. (1981). The mnemonic '80's: Keywords in the classroom. *Educational Psychologist, 16,* 65–82.

Levine, G. A., & Baker, B. L. (1963). Item scrambling in a self-instructional package. *Journal of Educational Psychology, 54,* 138–143.

Light, L. L., Kimble, G. A., & Pelligrino, J. W. (1975). Comments on episodic memory: When recognition fails, by Watkins and Tulving. *Journal of Experimental Psychology: General, 104,* 30–36.

McConkie, G. W. (1977). Learning from text. In L. S. Shulman (Ed.), *Review of research in education* (Vol. 5). Itasca, IL: Peacock.

Mandler, G. (1967). Organization and memory. In K. W. Spence & J. T. Spence (Eds.), *The psychology of learning and motivation* (Vol. 1). New York: Academic Press.

Mandler, J. M., & Johnson, N. S. (1977). Remembrance of things parsed: Story structure and recall. *Cognitive Psychology, 9,* 111–151.

Mayer, R. E. (1975). Information processing variables in learning to solve problems. *Review of Educational Research, 45,* 525–541.

Mayer, R. E. (1979). Can advance organizers influence meaningful learning? *Review of Educational Research, 49,* 371–383.

Meichenbaum, D., & Asarnow, J. (1979). Cognitive-behavioral modification and metacognitive development: Implications for the classroom. In P. C. Kendall, & S. D. Hollen (Eds.), *Cognitive-behavioral interventions: Theory, research, and procedures.* New York: Academic Press.

Merill, M. D. (1965). Correction and review on successive parts in learning a hierarchical task. *Journal of Educational Psychology, 56,* 225–234.

Meyer, B. J. F. (1975). *The organization of prose and its effects on memory.* Amsterdam: North Holland.

Meyer, B. J. F., Brandt, P. M., & Bluth, G. J. (1980). Use of top-level structure in text: Key for reading comprehension in ninth-grade students. *Reading Research Quarterly, 16,* 72–103.

Mistler-Lachman, J. L. (1972). Levels of comprehension in processing of normal and ambiguous sentences. *Journal of Verbal Learning and Verbal Behavior, 11,* 614–623.

Mistler-Lachman, J. L. (1974). Comprehension depth and sentence memory. *Journal of Verbal Learning and Verbal Behavior, 12,* 98–106.

Morris, C. D., Bransford, J. D., & Franks, J. F. (1977). Levels of processing versus transfer appropriate processing. *Journal of Verbal Learning and Verbal Behavior, 16,* 519–533.

Myers, M., & Paris, S. G. (1978). Children's metacognitive knowledge about reading. *Journal of Educational Psychology, 70,* 680–690.

Nelson, D. L., Walling, J. R., & McEvoy, C. L. (1979). Doubts about depth. *Journal of Experimental Psychology: Human Learning and Memory, 5,* 24–44.

Nelson, T. O. (1977). Repetition and depth of processing. *Journal of Verbal Learning and Verbal Behavior, 16,* 151–171.

Neville, M. H., & Pugh, A. K. (1976/1977). Context in reading and listening: Variations in approach to cloze tasks. *Reading Research Quarterly, 2,* 13–31.

Paivio, A. (1971). *Imagery and verbal processes.* New York: Holt.

Pauk, W. (1962). *How to study in college.* Boston: Houghton Mifflin.

Pelligrino, J. W., & Ingram, A. L. (1979). Processes, products, and measures of memory organization. In C. R. Puff (Ed.), *Memory organization and structure.* New York: Academic Press.

Pichert, J. W., & Anderson, R. C. (1977). Taking different perspectives on a story. *Journal of Educational Psychology, 69,* 309–315.

Pressley, G. M. (1976). Mental imagery helps eight-year-olds remember what they read. *Journal of Educational Psychology, 68,* 355–369.

Puff, C. R. (1979). Memory organization research and theory: The state of the art. In C. R. Puff (Ed.), *Memory organization and structure.* New York: Academic Press.

Reder, L. M. (1978, November). *Comprehension and retention of prose: A literature review* (Tech. Rep. No. 108). Champaign, IL: University of Illinois, Center for the Study of Reading. (ERIC Document Reproduction Service No. ED 165 114)

Reder, L. M. (1980). The role of elaboration in the comprehension and retention of prose: A critical review. *Reading Research Quarterly, 50,* 5–53.

Reynolds, R. E., Standiford, S. N., & Anderson, R. C. (1979). Distribution of reading time when questions are asked about a restricted category of text information. *Journal of Educational Psychology, 71,* 183–190.

Rickards, J. P., & Friedman, F. (1978). The encoding versus the external storage hypothesis in note taking. *Contemporary Educational Psychology, 3,* 136–143.

Robinson, F. P. (1941). *Diagnostic and remedial techniques for effective study.* New York: Harper & Brothers.

Robinson, F. P. (1970). *Effective study* (4th Ed.). New York: Harper & Row.

Rumelhart, D. E. (1975). Notes on a schema for stories. In D. G. Brown & A. Collins (Eds.), *Representation and understanding: Studies in cognitive science.* New York: Academic Press.

Rumelhart, D. E., & Ortony, A. (1977). The representation of knowledge in memory. In R. C. Anderson, R. J. Spiro, & W. E. Montague (Eds.), *Schooling and the acquisition of knowledge.* Hillsdale, NJ: Erlbaum.

Ryan, E. B. (1981). Identifying and remediating failures in reading comprehension: Toward an instructional approach for poor comprehenders. In G. E. Mackinnon & T. G. Waller (Eds.), *Reading research: Advances in theory and practice* (Vol. 3). New York: Academic Press.

Schallert, D. L. (1976). Improving memory for prose: The relationship between depth of processing and context. *Journal of Verbal Learning and Verbal Behavior. 15,* 621–632.

Schallert, D. L. (1982). The significance of knowledge: A synthesis of research related to schema theory. In W. Otto & S. White (Eds.), *Reading expository material*. New York: Academic Press.

Schank, R. C., & Abelson, R. P. (1977). *Scripts, plans, goals, and understanding*. Hillsdale, NJ: Erlbaum.

Spiro, R. J. (1977). Remembering information from text: Theoretical and empirical issues concerning the "State of Schema" reconstruction hypothesis. In R. C. Anderson, R. J. Spiro, & W. E. Montague (Eds.), *Schooling and the acquisition of knowledge*. Hillsdale, NJ: Erlbaum.

Steffenson, M. S., Joag-Dev, C., & Anderson, R. C. (1979). A cross-cultural perspective on reading comprehension. *Reading Research Quarterly, 15,* 10–29.

Stein, B. S. (1978). Depth of processing reexamined: The effects of precision of encoding and text appropriateness. *Journal of Verbal Learning and Verbal Behavior, 17,* 707–714.

Stein, N. L., & Glenn, C. G. (1978). An analysis of story comprehension in elementary school children. In R. Freedle (Ed.), *Discourse processing: Multidisciplinary perspectives*. Hillsdale, NJ: Erlbaum.

Thomson, D. M., & Tulving, E. (1970). Associative encoding and retrieval: Weak and strong cues. *Journal of Experimental Psychology, 86,* 255–262.

Thorndyke, P. W. (1977). Cognitive structures in comprehension and memory of narrative discourse. *Cognitive Psychology, 9,* 77–110.

Tulving, E. (1962). Subjective organization in free recall of "unrelated words." *Psychological Review, 69,* 344–354.

Tulving, E. (1979). Relation between encoding specificity and levels of processing. In L. S. Cermak & F. I. M. Craik (Eds.), *Levels of processing in human memory*. Hillsdale, NJ: Erlbaum.

Tulving, E., & Donaldson, W. (Eds.). (1972). *Organization of memory*. New York: Academic Press.

Tulving, E., & Thomson, D. M. (1973). Encoding specificity and retrieval processes in episodic memory. *Psychological Review, 80,* 352–373.

Tyler, S. W., Hertel, P. T., McCallum, M. C., & Ellis, H. C. (1979). Cognitive effort and memory. *Journal of Experimental Psychology: Human Learning and Memory, 5,* 607–617.

Walsh, D. C., & Jenkins, J. J. (1973). Effects of orienting task on free recall in incidental learning: "Difficulty," "effort," and "process" explanations. *Journal of Verbal Learning and Verbal Behavior, 12,* 481–488.

Watkins, M. J., & Tulving, E. (1975). Episodic memory: When recognition fails. *Journal of Experimental Psychology: General, 104,* 5–29.

Waugh, M. C., & Norman, D. A. (1965). Primary memory. *Psychological Review, 72,* 89–104.

Weinstein, C. E. (1978). Elaboration skills as a learning strategy. In H. F. O'Neil, Jr. (Ed.), *Learning strategies*. New York: Academic Press.

Weinstein, C. E. (1982). Training students to use elaboration learning strategies. *Contemporary Educational Psychology, 7,* 301–311.

Weinstein, C. E., Underwood, V. L., Wicker, F. W., & Cubberly, W. E. (1979). Cognitive learning strategies: Verbal and imaginal learning. In H. F. O'Neil, Jr., & C. D. Spielberger (Eds.), *Cognitive and affective learning strategies*. New York: Academic Press.

Wittrock, M. C. (1974). Learning as a generative process. *Educational Psychologist, 11,* 87–95.

PART   II

Spatial Strategies: Techniques and Evidence

CHAPTER 4

Networking: The Technique and the Empirical Evidence

Charles D. Holley   *Donald F. Dansereau*

NODE–ARC REPRESENTATIONS OF LONG-TERM MEMORY

In Chapter 1, we briefly described the mapping strategy (called networking) developed at Texas Christian University (T.C.U.). The present chapter explains the technique in greater depth. Specifically, the chapter discusses node–arc representations of human memory as a theoretical basis for the strategy, gives details on the technique, describes training methods, reviews several of the empirical studies underlying the strategy, describes related applications and associated techniques, and discusses future directions for the technique and related research.

Since Quillian's (1968, 1969) original formulations of node–arc representations of long-term memory, these notions have become quite popular among cognitive psychologists. Frijda (1972), in the context of computer simulation of human memory, argued that constructing a memory system with the necessary characteristics for such a simulation required the following components:

81

SPATIAL LEARNING STRATEGIES
Techniques, Applications, and Related Issues

1. An information store, with specified principles of information representation and of properties of organization;
2. Recognition mechanisms, which assure the communication between input and the memory store;
3. Input transformation mechanisms, which convert incoming information into internal representations;
4. Acquisition mechanisms, which imply storage rules;
5. Basic retrieval mechanisms;
6. Utilization procedures;
7. Output construction mechanisms [pp. 2–3].

The popularity of network representations may be based on their ability to satisfy, in a reasonably precise manner, these criteria.

The key feature of network representational schemes, aside from the fact that they are spatial or graphic, is the use of *nodes* to represent concepts and *lines* or *arcs* to represent relationships between concepts. Although a variety of such schemes have been proposed, two models of particular importance are those of Collins and Quillian (1969—based on Quillian, 1968, 1969) and Norman, Rumelhart, and the Lindsay, Norman, & Rumelhart (LNR) Research Group (1975). The former model is important because of its originality, and the latter model is important because of its greater breadth and precision. Together, these two models present the essence of network representational schemes.

Collins and Quillian's (1969) network representation of a three-level memory structure is shown in Figure 1. In this representation the hierarchical concepts are expressed via the "isa" relationship (e.g., a canary is a bird) and the attributes associated with each node are expressed via the unlabelled arcs. Such a representational scheme has a number of logical advantages. For example, the attributes associated with a higher-level node also apply to subordinate nodes. Thus, only unique attributes are stored with the subordinate nodes. Because response would be a function of the number of links one has to traverse to produce a response, the model is testable, and early experimental evidence provided support for the model (e.g., Collins & Quillian, 1969).

However, subsequent studies indicated that the model was too simple. For example, canary and ostrich are both birds, yet the response times are greater for ostrich, thereby suggesting that a canary is more of a bird (Conrad, 1972; Rosch, 1973; Smith, Shoben, & Rips, 1974). Kintsch (1974) argued that the greatest flaw in this particular model is that it is far too logical to be an accurate representation of human memory.

Expanding on the foregoing network scheme, Rumelhart, Lindsay, and Norman (1972) and Norman *et al,* (1975) developed a complex system, which demonstrated consistency with experimental results and also incorpo-

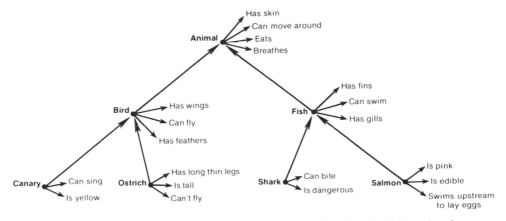

FIGURE 1. Illustration of a hypothetical memory structure for a three-level hierarchy (from Collins & Quillian, 1969).

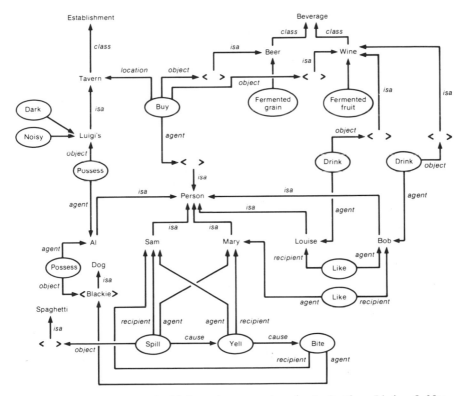

FIGURE 2. Network of intermixed information, semantic and episodic (from Lindsay & Norman, 1977).

rated episodic memory, or representation of specific events, into the network. Figure 2 provides an example of one such network. This figure shows both *definitions of terms* (semantic memory), such as a tavern being a class of or type of establishment, and *specific events* (episodic memory) such as Blackie, the dog, biting Sam.

Lindsay and Norman (1977) argued that such a scheme constituted a basic design for the data base underlying human memory, and that memory retrieval was analogous to running a maze. The memory system is an organized collection of pathways that specify possible routes through the maze (data base). Because all information is interconnected, it is theoretically possible to start at any node in the maze and, by making the right series of turns, end up at any other node. (For a detailed discussion, see Lindsay and Norman [1977], pp. 386–411.)

NETWORKING AS A LEARNING STRATEGY

Based on the foregoing models, a long-term project was undertaken at T.C.U. to develop a networking technique that could be used by learners to process information in a manner compatable with such representational schemes. A major obstacle to such an approach is finding an appropriate middle ground on a simplicity–complexity continuum. Specifically, such a strategy has to be simple enough for students to use; yet is has to be sufficiently complex to encompass the range of relationships a student might encounter. For example, Quillian's (1968, 1969) model is readily shown to be too simple for such an objective, yet Rumelhart, Lindsay and Norman's (1972) model is far too complex to have practical utility.

As an initial step in the development of an appropriate strategy, the domain of information was restricted to prototypical textual material that undergraduate college students could be expected to encounter. Within this domain, a set of 13 relationships (links) was identified that could accurately describe a variety of information contained in textual material. Experimental testing, subsequently described, indicated that the set of 13 experimenter-provided links was too unwieldly for students to remember and use. Several of these relationships were collapsed to create a four-link system, but this method lacked sufficient specificity to adequately describe some textual relationships. The final version of the networking method employed six experimenter-provided links, which seemed to be an appropriate compromise between specificity and utility.

During the transition from 13 to 6 links, the networking method concomitantly evolved an underlying hierarchical structure. The fact that authors

Structure	Link	Description	Key Words
	Part (of) (hand) ↓ p (finger) 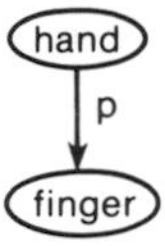	The content in a lower node is part of the object, idea, process or concept contained in a higher node.	part of segment of portion of
Hierarchy	Type (of)– Example (of) 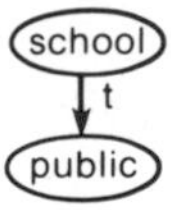 (school) ↓ t (public)	The content in a lower node is a member or example of the class or category of processes, ideas, concepts, or objects contained in a higher node.	type of category example of kind of Three "x" are
Chain	Leads to  (practice) ↓ l (perfection)	The object, process, concept, or idea in one node leads to or results in the object, process, idea, or concept in another node.	leads to results in causes is a tool of produces
	Analogy 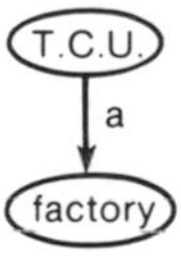 (T.C.U.) ↓ a (factory)	The object, idea, process, or concept in one node is analogous to, similar to, corresponds to, or is like the object, idea, process or concept in another node.	similar analogous to like corresponds to
Cluster	Character- istic 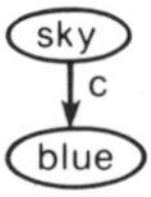 (sky) ↓ c (blue)	The object, idea, process, or concept in one node is a trait, aspect, quality, feature, attribute, detail or characteristic of the object, process, concept, or idea in another node.	has characterized feature property trait aspect attribute
	Evidence 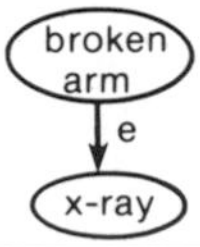 (broken arm) ↓ e (x-ray)	The object, idea, process, or concept in one node provides evidence, facts, data, support, proof, documentation, or confirmation for the object, idea, process, or concept in another node.	indicates illustrates demonstrates supports documents proof of confirms evidence of

FIGURE 3. Link types and structure types employed with the networking technique (from Holley et al., 1979).

typically use a hierarchical outline or hierarchically embedded headings with their textbook chapters, allowed the networking method to capitalize on processing advantages associated with the use of intact and embedded headings (see Brooks, Dansereau, Holley, & Spurlin, 1983; Brooks, Dansereau, Spurlin, & Holley, 1983; Holley, 1979; Holley, Dansereau, Evans, Collins, Brooks, & Larson, 1981).

The networking strategy is designed to assist the student in spatially reorganizing passage information as part of the encoding process. The student is trained to convert prose into hierarchically organized node–link diagrams (networks) using the set of six experimenter-provided links. The nodes contain paraphrases and images–drawings of key ideas and concepts, and the links specify the relationships between these concepts. For structural organization, the networking process emphasizes the identification and representation of hierarchies (type–part), chains (lines of reasoning–temporal orderings–causal sequences), and clusters (characteristics–definitions–analogies). A schematic representation of these three types of structures and their associated links is presented in Figure 3.

Application of this technique results in the production of hierarchically

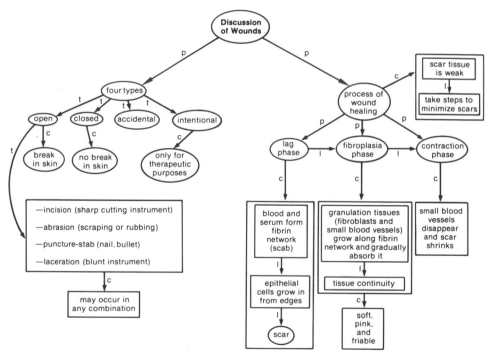

FIGURE 4. Example of a network of a chapter from a nursing textbook (from Holley et al., 1979).

structured two-dimensional maps. These maps provide the student with a spatial organization of the information contained in the passage. Figure 4 gives an example of a summary map of a nursing textbook chapter. In the next section, methods for training students on the technique are discussed.

TRAINING THE NETWORKING TECHNIQUE

Training in the networking method has typically been employed as a component of a learning strategy system (see Dansereau, Collins, McDonald, Holley; Garland, Diekhoff, & Evans, [1979a] and Dansereau, McDonald, Collins, Garland, Holley, Diekhoff, & Evans [1979b] for a description of this system), and we focus here on training in that context. (Specific training for experimental testing of the technique is presented in a subsequent section.) Two major issues are (1) sequence of training and (2) training methods.

SEQUENCE OF TRAINING

In sequencing the training within a particular strategy, such as networking, two possibilities have been explored. One of these is a building-block approach in which components of the strategy are first learned using simplified training materials and then later combined to form the overall strategy. For example, one approach to teaching concept–link networks is to have the learners apply parts of this strategy to single sentences, then paragraphs, and finally larger bodies of material. This approach is the most prevalent one appearing in the training literature and has been advocated by a number of educational theorists (e.g., Gagne, 1977).

Disadvantages to the building-block approach include the following:

1. Processes that are effective with the simplified materials used at the beginning of training may not be effective with the target materials (actual text). Consequently, the learner may have to eventually break habitual ways of dealing with information that he or she developed during the early stages of training.

2. The learner's motivation may suffer if the training materials and exercises are seen as too distant from the target task.

3. The learner may have a very difficult time acquiring the gestalt of the strategy through the building–block approach, another case of not seeing the forest for the trees. In general, our experience with the building-block approach to strategy training has not been very satisfactory, because many of the students never adequately acquire the terminal strategy.

An alternative to this approach is one that first communicates the gestalt of the strategy and then later adds detail and precision. For example, students are initially allowed to create networks identifying and laying out important concepts spatially without worrying about the precise relationships among concepts. As the students become more comfortable using this informal spatial strategy, further training is given to assist them in producing maps that more precisely represent the relationships among concepts. This approach has the advantage of allowing the students to practice on the target material almost from the beginning of training. We have found this training approach to be far more palatable to students than the building-block scenario, and therefore encourage the use of the gestalt approach whenever possible.

TRAINING METHODS

In our subjective experiences, one of the most potent methods of communicating learning strategies is modeling (i.e., demonstrations of correct strategy usage). However, due to the covert nature of learning, modeling demonstrations present a number of unique challenges. To date, we have had substantial success with the following modeling approaches:

1. Presentation of the products of correct strategy usage (e.g., a completed network) with annotations indicating how the products were created. Typically the learner is given a body of material with which to practice a particular strategy. Following the learner's attempt at processing the material, a model product with annotations is provided as feedback.

2. Real-time modeling by an expert. The expert provides a verbal protocol related to correct application of the strategy.

3. Interactive peer modeling. Typically, pairs of learners interact over a body of text material. One member of the pair attempts to process the material orally while the other member serves as a commentator or critic. The roles of the pair members are periodically reversed. McDonald, Dansereau, Garland, Holley, & Collins, (1979) have shown that this pair-learning procedure facilitates subsequent strategy usage in an individual study situation.

In conjunction with modeling, we have found it useful to provide specific feedback on the products representing the learner's attempts at strategy usage. The purpose is to assist the learner in identifying and remediating specific "bugs" that may inhibit effective application of the strategy.

Our experiences with traditional programmed instructional approaches have generally not been positive. Because these approaches to training are typically based on successive approximation, they implicitly encourage a building-block approach. As stated earlier, we have had very little success with a building-block model and recommend against an *exclusive* use of traditional programmed instruction as a learning strategy training tool.

EMPIRICAL STUDIES OF NETWORKING

EXPERIMENT 1

The earliest formal attempt in our laboratory to develop and experimentally test a networking learning strategy is reported by Long (1976). (Whereas this study actually contained two experiments, only the second is reported here, because the results were basically the same for both experiments.) In this study a primitive form of networking was employed which consisted of a three-link system. The three links were (1) *isa* (superset–subset), (2) *has* (concept–attribute), and (3) *t–e* (theme–evidence).

The experiment employed a four-group design with randomly assigned undergraduate college students. The passage stimuli were two 1000-word articles from *Scientific American* (counterbalanced for immediate and delayed testing), and both cued (multiple-choice) and uncued (essay) exams were employed as dependent measures. Students participated in three 2-hour sessions with a 1-week time lag between sessions. The dependent measures were administered immediately after studying the first passage and 1 week after studying the second passage.

The training procedure for the networking group consisted of the following steps:

1. The experimenter provided a brief overview and description of the technique.
2. Students read background information on the technique.
3. Students were given an algorithm for applying the technique.
4. Students practiced applying the technique to individual paragraphs and received written experimenter feedback.
5. Students practiced applying the technique to 1000-word articles from *Scientific American* and received written experimenter feedback.
6. Students applied the technique to the experimental passage.

Not surprisingly, the results were disappointing. Neither the strategy effect nor the interactions involving strategy type (each experimental group received a different strategy) were found to be significant. Long (1976) presented the following explanation for the results:

1. The networking technique may not have encouraged an active transformation of the material. Specifically, more training time is required for adequately learning and applying the strategy.

2. The control group may inadvertently have received a treatment, in the sense that the immediate test brought about an active review and rehearsal of the text material.
3. Most important, the set of links were *not* sufficiently comprehensive to encompass all of the relationships encountered in the experimental passages.
4. Individual differences in responsiveness to learning and applying the networking method were experientially observed, but no provision was made in the experimental design for considering such effects.

Based on subsequent studies, we would also add that *type* and *length* of passage seem to be important variables with the networking technique. Students are not typically used to, or interested in, reading articles from *Scientific American*. Textbook chapters seem to be more appealing, because the applicability of the strategy to "real material" is more apparent. Additionally, with longer passages (e.g., 2500 words) the networking method appears to assist the student with the extraction of a passage macrostructure, which is an aid to retrieval. With shorter passages, this macrostructure extraction may be unnecessary.

Although Long's (1976) study did not produce a networking technique that resulted in a significant difference between treatment and control groups, it did provide a substantial amount of useful information. This information was incorporated into subsequent development and testing of a networking learning strategy.

EXPERIMENT 2

The second experiment, conducted during fall, 1976, was designed to alleviate some of the potential problems uncovered in Experiment 1, in particular, the possibility of too little training time and the lack of a comprehensive set of named links. For this experiment a 13-link system was created and corresponding training materials developed. The training materials were administered to 22 undergraduates over an 8-hour period (four 2-hour evening sessions). In addition, these subjects were given a pre–post learning–study attitude test on three 700-word passages, and an intensive set of interviews. The data obtained were compared to data generated by a no-treatment control group (10 subjects). Although the results of the objective assessment tests indicated no significant differences, the networking technique was well received by the participating students. Their attitudes toward learning and studying improved considerably (pretest to posttest) in comparison to the control subjects. In addition, many of the treatment subjects indicated in subsequent interviews that they were using our strategy in their regular coursework.

Following their participation in the control group, the 10 subjects were given a "home study" version of the training. Subsequent interviews indicated that this nonguided approach to training was not nearly as successful as the "in class" training given to the previous group of subjects.

In both cases, the major complaint about the networking technique concerned the number of link types. The students felt the link system was too difficult to learn and too unwieldly to use efficiently. The individuals who continued to use the technique typically reported that they used a reduced set of links in their regular coursework. As a consequence, we modified the link system and reduced the number of link types to six (after some pilot work with a four-link system). The remaining experiments reported used the six-link system.

EXPERIMENT 3

During the spring of 1977, the final version of the six-link networking technique was implemented as a component strategy of a semester-long general learning strategies curriculum which 38 undergraduate students took for course credit (see Dansereau et al. [1979b] for a detailed discussion of this evaluation). The six links used in this version of networking are those presented in Figure 3.

In order to evaluate the effectiveness of the strategy system, two interlocking experiments were designed (see Figure 5). In one, the performances of differentially treated subgroups of the class were compared with each other and with a control group (the comprehension–retention controls—28 general psychology students). The bases of these comparisons were scores on a series of tests on textbook prose that had been studied one week earlier. These tests were given to the class members and the control group prior to the start of the course (the pretest), approximately halfway through the course (the midcourse test), and at the end of the course (the posttest). In the second experiment, the performance of the class members on a set of self-report measures was compared with a separate control group (the self-report controls—21 general psychology students) both before and after the course.

The dependent measures for the comprehension–retention experiment consisted of multiple-choice and short essay tests over three 3000-word passages (pretest, midcourse, and posttest passages). All students were given 1 hour to study the passage and then 1 week later were given 45 minutes to take the corresponding tests (essay followed by multiple-choice; see Battig

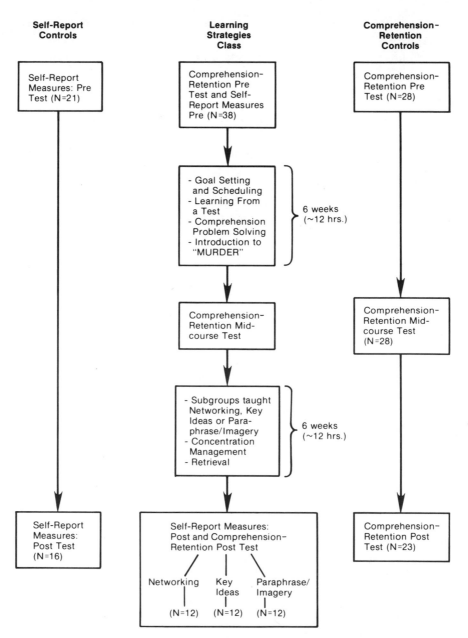

FIGURE 5. Training and assessment schedule for the learning strategies course (from Dansereau, McDonald, Collins, Garland, Holley, Diekhoff, & Evans, 1979b).

[1979] and Holley and Dansereau [1981] for a discussion of this testing sequence). The dependent measures for the self-report experiment, which were administered before and after the course, were (1) a 37-item test anxiety scale which was based on Sarason (1956), (2) the Brown–Holtzman Survey of Study Habits and Attitudes, (3) a 46-item questionnaire developed to assess concentration difficulties and coping skills, and (4) a 12-item learning attitude inventory designed to assess students' perceptions of their academic skills.

Training for the class members, following the pretest, consisted of 12 hours of training (2 hours per week) in goal setting and scheduling, learning from a test, comprehension and problem solving, and introduction to MURDER, which is an acronym for the six components of the strategy system (Mood, Understand, Recall, Digest, Expand, Review) (see Dansereau et al., 1979a, 1979b). The class then took the midcourse test. Following this measure, class members were subdivided into three groups (networking, paraphrase–imagery, and key ideas) and received an additional 12 hours of training (2 hours per week) on concentration management and retrieval (8 hours), and the particular strategy corresponding to group assignment (4 hours). Following this training period, students were administered the posttest.

The results for the self-report experiment indicated statistically significant differences ($p < .02$), favoring the class compared to the controls, on the Survey of Study Habits and Attitudes, the test anxiety scale, and the learning attitude inventory. The differences for the concentration questionnaire approached significance ($p < .12$) in the desired direction. Although these results were supportive of the program, caution should be exercised in attaching too much credence to self-report measures.

The results for the comprehensive–retention experiment indicated differences between the class members and the control group which were in the desired direction and approached significance with the change in total scores (essay plus multiple-choice) from pretest to midcourse test ($p < .07$), and from pretest to posttest ($p < .08$). With respect to subgroup performance within the class, only the networking group appeared to improve in performance between the midcourse exam and the posttest.

In a planned comparison of the networking students and the control students, the former group significantly outperformed the latter group (Holley, Dansereau, McDonald, Garland, & Collins, 1978). Although these data were supportive of the networking method, it is difficult to determine the specific impact of networking on these results. This is primarily due to its being embedded in a general learning strategies training program, with several potential sources of internal and external invalidity associated with the experimental design (Campbell & Stanley, 1966). In order to achieve a purer assessment of networking, the study reported in the next section was conducted.

Experiment 4

Based on the results from the previous study, the same six-link networking strategy was employed in this experiment, with the expectation that this technique would assist students in the assimilation and retention of prose material. (Details of this study are reported by Holley et al. [1979]). This study used a 3000-word passage as the prose stimulus and employed four dependent measures: (1) concept-cloze and essay exams to measure comprehension—retention of main ideas, and (2) short essay and multiple-choice exams to measure comprehension—retention of details.

Forty-four general psychology students were randomly assigned to treatment and control groups. The mean prior GPAs were slightly higher for the control group (2.88) than for the treatment group (2.81). The latter group received approximately 5 ½ hours of networking training as part of the following sequence of sessions:

Session 1. The students received a general introduction to the strategy, training on the links and structure names, practice on networking sentences, and an overview of networking as a general retrieval strategy.

Session 2. The students were introduced to the use of the hierarchical structure in developing a general-purpose organizing framework, and they were given practice on networking a series of 500—1000 word passages (experimenter-generated networks were provided as feedback for this exercise).

Session 3. The students were first given an additional practice passage exercise and then allowed to practice networking on their regular general psychology textbooks.

Session 4. The students continued to practice on their own materials. They were also given a short review lecture on the networking procedure.

Session 5. The students completed a short prestudy questionnaire and spent 1 hour studying a 3000-word passage extracted from an introductory geology textbook. (The content of this passage was unrelated to any of the practice materials used in prior sessions. See Holley [1979] and Holley et al. [1981] for details regarding technical aspects of passages.) The treatment group was required to make networks of the passage. These networks were collected for subsequent analysis.

Session 6. In this final session, which occurred 5 days after the previous session, the students were given 3 minutes to review their notes and then spent 14 minutes taking an essay exam over the entire passage. Following this, they spent a total of 35 minutes taking the following series of tests: (1) short essay (10 questions), (2) concept-cloze (7 questions), and (3) multiple-choice (18 questions).

The control group participated in two sessions identical to Sessions 5 and 6 just described. These students were instructed to use their normal methods in studying and test-taking (cf. Holley & Dansereau, 1981).

The results indicated that the networking group significantly out per-formed the control group on the "main ideas" dependent measures ($p < .03$), but not on the "details" dependent measures ($p < .90$). This suggested that the technique assists students in acquiring and organizing the main ideas in a passage but does not help in the retention of details.

With groups dichotomized into high-low GPA subgroups, additional analyses indicated that on the details measure, networking students with low GPAs substantially outperformed the control students with low GPAs, whereas the reverse held for students with high GPAs. The interaction effects on the main ideas measure indicated that the two networking groups were equivalent and both were superior to the control groups. These data suggested that the strategy may be more effective for low-GPA students, and that it can be deleterious to the performances of high-GPA students on some types of tests. It is likely that high-GPA students already have effective learn-ing strategies, particularly for dealing with multiple-choice exams, and that the new technique interfered with these existing strategies. The converse would seem to be true for low-GPA students.

EXPERIMENT 5

The focus of this experiment was threefold:

1. To examine networking training materials that were more instructor independent then those used previously
2. To determine the effectiveness of training modifications designed to focus the students' attention on details as well as main ideas; and
3. To assess the effectiveness of a less structured version of networking called annotation and mapping. With this technique the students read and annotated the text with their own words and images and then converted the main ideas into a node–link map. The major difference between this tech-nique and networking is that in annotation and mapping the students created their own links or relationships rather than attempting to identify and use a set of standard links (i.e., part, type, leads to, characteristic, analogy, evi-dence). It was hoped that this technique would be more easily internalized by the student and be more flexible in its use. Training on this technique also involved a set of self-instructional exercise booklets.

To test these techniques, 60 general psychology students were randomly assigned to one of three groups: networking, annotation and mapping, and delayed annotation and mapping (a control group for the original training). The treatment groups were given approximately 6 hours of training (over four sessions) followed by a comprehension–retention assessment. This assessment required the students to use the technique in studying a 3000-word passage extracted from a geology text. Five days later they took tests on the passage (assessing knowledge of main ideas and details). The delayed group had not received training prior to the testing and were instructed to use their typical strategies during the assessment phase.

Each group was divided into two subgroups based on their Delta vocabulary scores (this measure was administered during the first session of the experiment). Our basic approach to analyzing the data involved a series of 2 × 2 analyses of variance (ANOVAS) (treatment and Delta subgroup) comparing each of the treatment groups to the control (delayed) group on each of the dependent measures. The following results emerged from the analyses:

1. Networking performance on the details test was significantly better than control performance ($p < .04$). There was no interaction between treatment and high–low Delta subgrouping.

2. The overall difference between the annotation and mapping group and the controls did not reach significance on the details test, but the treatment by Delta subgroup interaction was significant ($p < .03$). Inspection of the means indicated that there was no difference between the low-Delta subgroups, but a substantial difference between the higher-Delta groups, with the annotation and mapping group outscoring the controls.

3. Although the mean differences were generally in the same direction as in the previous experiment across all measures, no other significant comparisons were found.

These results in conjunction with those of the previous experiments, suggest that the focus of the training (details vs. main ideas) directly influences students' performance on the outcome measures. It appears that greater amounts of training may be necessary to facilitate both detail and main idea performance simultaneously. In this regard, the next experiment reported incorporated slightly greater amounts of training and practice.

The annotation and mapping strategy appeared to be beneficial only to those students with high verbal aptitude. This finding, coupled with the apparent utility of the more structured networking technique for low-aptitude students (see previous experiment) provides a basis for differentially assigning strategies based on pretraining individual differences.

EXPERIMENT 6

This experiment was conducted in the context of a college learning strategy class during the fall of 1978. In addition to providing further evaluation of the networking strategy, the experiment was designed to examine the effects of strategy sequencing on various outcome measures (see Dansereau, Brooks, Holley, & Collins, 1983). Networking formed the basis of the "primary" strategies, while concentration management formed the basis of the "support" strategies.

The concentration management component, which is designed to help the student set and maintain constructive moods for studying and task performance, consists of a combination of elements from systematic desensitization (Jacobsen, 1938; Wolpe, 1969), rational behavior therapy (Ellis, 1963; Maultsby, 1971), and therapies based on positive self-talk (Meichenbaum & Goodman, 1971; Meichenbaum & Turk, 1975). The students are first given experiences and strategies designed to assist them in becoming aware of the negative and positive emotions, self-talk, and images they generate in facing a learning task. They are then instructed to evaluate the constructiveness of their internal dialogue and are given heuristics for making appropriate modifications. This approach to concentration management has been shown to lead to significantly better performance on text processing tasks in comparison to students using their own methods (Collins et al., 1981). These strategies have been supplemented by training on goal setting, scheduling, and monitoring to form the support component of the program (Dansereau, 1978).

To determine if the effectiveness of strategy training is influenced by the sequence of instruction, the participants in the learning strategies class were randomly assigned to two groups. One group of 28 students received primary strategy training during the first half of the semester and support training during the second half (P–S sequence). The other group of 29 students received the opposite instructional sequence (S–P). To provide an overall evaluation of the program, a control group of 42 students was recruited from general psychology classes. This group was not exposed to any treatments during the course of the experiment.

During the first four 1-hour sessions, all participants filled out the self-report measures (test anxiety scale, study methods utilization inventory, academic skills inventory, academic skills satisfaction scale) and the Delta Vocabulary Test, and studied and took tests (5 days after studying) on the premeasure passage. The class members were then randomly assigned to the two groups (P–S and S–P). The P–S group received approximately 7 hours (two 1-hour sessions per week) of distributed training and practice on the primary strategies while the S–P group received 7 hours of training and practice on the support strategies. Slightly modified versions of the self-instructional materials developed previously (Dansereau *et al.*, 1979a) formed the basis of this training. To increase motivation, the students were allowed to practice the strategies on material from their regular courses. (Students were not allowed to practice the techniques on material related to the dependent measure passages.)

Following this segment the P–S group received approximately 7 hours (two 1-hour sessions per week) of training and practice on the support strategies, while the S–P group received 7 hours of training and practice on the primary strategies. In both cases, the training materials and procedures were the same as those employed in the first segment of the study.

All participants were then given the posttraining assessment measures. The students studied and were tested (5 days later) on a 3000-word passage extracted from a basic science textbook. They were also asked to respond to the four self-report measures (Test Anxiety Scale, Study Methods Utilization Inventory, Academic Skills Inventory, Academic Skills Satisfaction Scale).

To provide a basis for an informal evalution of the long-term effects of the strategy training, a 10-item questionnaire was mailed to all participating class members 3 months after the conclusion of the course.

The results of a series of analyses of covariance on the four tests indicated significant differences on the combined score ($p < .01$), the short-answer test ($p < .05$), and the essay test ($p < .05$). There were no significant differences on the concept-cloze and multiple-choice tests. Tukey post hoc comparisons indicated that the P–S group significantly ($p < .05$) outperformed the control group on all three tests found significant via the analyses of covariance. All other post hoc comparisons were nonsignificant.

The results with the pre–post self-report measures indicated that both the P–S and S–P groups showed significantly greater gains than the control group. The long-term follow-up questionnaire indicated that the training had a moderate-to-strong positive effect on the academic behaviors and outcomes surveyed by the questionnaire. Further, the P–S group reported consistently more positive outcomes than the S–P group. This latter finding parallels the results with the text processing tasks.

The findings of this experiment suggest that giving networking training early in a strategy course leads to more positive outcomes than giving it late. This is probably due to the increased amount of time the students have to practice the technique. In this experiment the early networkers (P–S group) showed gains on both main idea and detail measures. Contrary to expectations, the late networkers (S–P group) did not show significant improvement in comparison to the control group, although the means were in the expected directions. The students in this group reported that one potential reason for this lack of effect was that by the time they were taught networking they were overloaded with other strategies, as well as pressures from other courses. As a consequence they felt that they did not adequately learn the technique.

We have subsequently administered the networking training in the context of this course during fall, 1979, 1980, and 1981. Although we have not conducted formal evaluations of the strategy, informal feedback suggests that the early training is effective and that the students continue to employ the strategy after the course is completed.

OTHER APPLICATIONS
AND ASSOCIATED TECHNIQUES

In this section we describe three alternative applications that have been explored with the networking strategy, although empirical evidence for their efficacy is lacking. Additionally, we describe three spin-off strategies from our networking method.

GRADUATE STATISTICS COURSE

Teacher-produced networks can be used to facilitate the teaching of college-level courses. Over the last 5 years Dansereau has used networking in the teaching of a graduate course in statistics. These networks have been used in two ways:

1. Chapter networks are projected on a screen to one side of the blackboard. The lecturer refers to a portion of the map (indicating to the students where they are in the "big picture"); then the lecturer goes to the board and explains what will be covered next. By using this process the lecturer is acting somewhat like a tour guide and is able to help the student keep the detailed information in perspective (i.e., provide a remedy for "not seeing the forest for the trees").

2. In addition, students are provided with copies of the instructor's chapter maps to help them review and integrate the material they have read.

Although not formally evaluated, feedback received to date on these two uses of network maps has been very positive. The students indicate that the maps help them see connections between ideas and help them remember the material by giving them an improved organization.

GRADUATE-LEVEL INDIVIDUAL STUDIES

While Holley was a student of Dansereau (1978), we applied the networking technique in the context of a graduate-level individual studies course. The specific procedures involved (1) selecting a textbook on the general topic of memory and cognition (i.e., Baddeley, 1976), (2) weekly networking of subsets of the textbook (e.g., chapters) by the student, and (3) weekly meetings between instructor and student to discuss the concepts and relationships in the networks.

Our observations are experiential, but a number of distinct advantages to this procedure were apparent:

1. Clarity and succinctness. The maps provided an unambiguous picture of what the student had comprehended from the material. Any perceived relationships that were either inaccurate or confusing to the instructor were quite explicit and provided a focal point for discussion.
2. Mathemagenic activity. Creating the maps, coupled with the explicit expression of the perceived relationships during the subsequent discussions, compelled the student to (1) strive for accuracy in the networks, and (2) ensure that he or she understood and could defend the relationships presented in the maps.
3. Instructional effectiveness. The networking procedure resulted in a greater quantity of material being processed by the student and a qualitatively better use of time for instructor–student interaction.

The use of networking in this context seemed to be an extremely beneficial learning strategy. Obviously, both instructor and student must be reasonably well-versed in the networking technique.

GENERAL PROBLEM-SOLVING

According to Gagne (1977), the process of problem solving (whether the problem is mathematical, logical, or even personal) consists of four stages: (1) defining the problem, that is, representing the essential features of the problem space; (2) searching for the appropriate methods of solution; (3) deciding on the appropriate method; and (4) verifying the solution. Problem-solving methods over the past 25 years have mainly focused on the last three stages of the process (cf. Newell & Simon, 1972). As a consequence, not much is known about the first stage of problem solving, the defining and representation of the problem.

For many problems, the difficulty of the solution lies in finding the appropriate representation. Once the problem is correctly understood and defined, the solution often becomes obvious (Greeno, 1980; Newell & Simon, 1972). One difficulty in defining the problem lies in awareness of the dimensions of the problem. An additional difficulty is communication (to oneself or to another) of the problem in a systematic way using an appropriate representational system. Although verbal language has been the most common method of representation, many researchers suggest that natural language is too ambiguous and too limited to properly describe complex problems (Newell & Simon, 1972). What is needed is a symbolic system that eliminates some of this ambiguity and provides a relatively unconstrained view of the problem.

Although the empirical results are somewhat ambiguous, some researchers and teachers have suggested that spatial representations, such as pictures, figures, and graphs, lead to increased understanding of the problem (Greeno, 1980; Larkin, 1980; Polya, 1957). Spatial representation presumably helps problem solvers understand abstract relationships and may mediate between verbal explanations of the problem and the problem-solving procedures (Greeno, 1980). Unfortunately, the spatial representational systems that have been used previously have had limited generalizability. That is, they typically apply to only a narrow range of problem types. A more flexible, general system for representing and defining problems would be a useful addition to a problem solver's repertoire.

By creating a network map of the problem area, one can generate a coherent spatial representation of the issues which influence the problem. For example, a network map of personal problems (e.g., depression, anxiety) would consist of nodes made up of the major thoughts and behaviors that the individual perceives as relevant to the problem (a prototypical example). The starting node would be the major problem (e.g., anxiety). The links between the nodes would be the same type of labeled links used in prose processing, such as "characteristic" and "leads to." The map could be generated by the use of appropriate questions, such as "what are the characteristics of the starting node?," "what do these characteristics lead to?," or "what leads to the problem represented by the starting node?" Once the map has been constructed, the individual can get a complete picture of the entire problem. Additionally, potential effects of various solutions can be detected by observing results in the map if nodes are changed. An example of such a network is presented in Figure 6.

Not only can a problem area map be constructed, but a positive map can be generated to analyze the thoughts and behaviors which occur when the problem is not present. Comparison of the two maps may instill awareness of both the problem (e.g., test anxiety) and increase awareness of the problem-related cues. To investigate this possibility, a study was designed to examine treatment-based changes in self-reported behaviors and attitudes related to

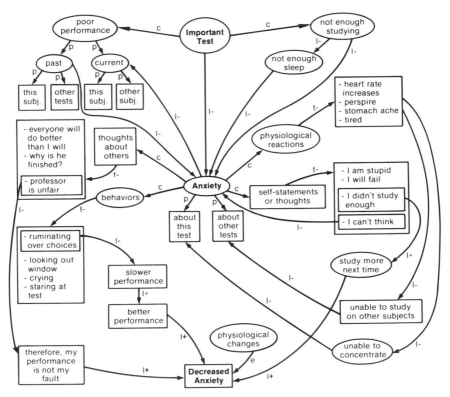

FIGURE 6. Network of a personal problem—test anxiety.

test anxiety, as well as changes in students' awareness of cues and consequences of anxiety.

Fifty members of the Techniques of College Learning class at T.C.U. were randomly divided into experimental and control groups. The experimental group used the networking strategy to map test anxiety. The control group was taught to use networking for writing term papers. All students were administered the test-taking questionnaire and the test anxiety scale (Sarason, 1978) before and after the experimental sessions. Additionally, a test composed of a subset of questions selected from the 1980 Scholastic Aptitude Test (SAT) was administered to examine the effects of the treatments on test performance. The students were allowed 10 minutes for the verbal section (40 questions) and 10 minutes for the math section (22 questions). The results suggested that networking the problem area of test anxiety does increase awareness of the problem, especially for the test-anxious students. The results also indicated that the students who networked learned some ways to control their test-taking activities, so that performance was not as severely inhibited even though high anxiety was still reported by some of the students. Further research is being initiated to replicate this study and to extend the use of networking to other problem areas.

HEARING-IMPAIRED STUDENTS

Long and his colleagues (see Chapter 5 of this volume) have employed a variant of the networking procedure presented in this chapter with hearing-impaired students at the National Technical Institute for the Deaf. Their version of networking employs the six relationships of characteristic, example, definition, sequence, compare–contrast, and reason–results.

Based on experiential and empirical results, the networking approach aids such students in shifting from a principally "bottom-up" processing approach to a moderated "top-down" processing approach. This shift seems particularly beneficial for hearing-impaired students, since they typically have difficulty with syntax, vocabulary, and the indentification of key ideas. This research-and-development aspect of networking is still in its formative stages, but the initial results appear to be quite promising.

NODE ACQUISITION AND INTEGRATION TECHNIQUE

Diekhoff has developed a spatial learning strategy, the Node Acquisition and Integration Technique (NAIT), which is also primarily based on network models of long-term memory structure (Diekhoff, Brown, & Dansereau, 1982.). NAIT involves students in constructing organized cognitive networks via four enabling steps. Each of these steps or stages is subsequently described.

Stage 1: Identification of Key Concepts

The first step in constructing the network is to identify the key concepts in the to-be-learned material. These key concepts form the initial nodes of the network. Key concepts can be explicitly identified by the instructor by providing them to students or they can be identified by students through the application of selection heuristics (e.g., italized terms, headings, terms defined by the author, glossary terms).

Stage 2: Relationship-Guided Definition

In this step, the student begins to build a semantic network around the key concepts by identifying relational information in the to-be-learned material that can be linked to each of the key concepts. Six types of relationships are employed in the process: (1) characteristics or descriptors, (2) anteced-ents, (3) consequences, (4) evidence, (5) subsets, and (6) supersets.

This step is accomplished by the student's completing definition work-sheets. When these worksheets are completed for each key concept, the stu-dent's semantic network may be envisioned as a series of unconnected pin-wheels, each with a key concept at its hub, with radiating spokes consisting of relationship links that connect the hub to defining information.

Stage 3: Elaboration

After all of the definition worksheets are completed, the student engages in elaboration activities which are designed to (1) prevent the foregoing activities from being merely an exercise in transcription and (2) capitalize on the theoretical advantages associated with depth of processing (e.g., Cermak & Craik, 1979). These elaborative activities, such as thinking of examples or applications of the information, serve to integrate the newly formed semantic networks into the student's existing memory structures (cf. Greeno, 1974).

Stage 4: Relationship-Guided Comparisons

In this stage, the students complete comparison worksheets, which are designed to guide them through a relationship-by-relationship comparison of the definitions of selected pairs of key concepts. The student's goal is to discover similarities, meaningful differences, and other such relationships between the two concepts being compared. Concepts to be compared in this manner may be selected by the instructor or by the student.

NAIT has been a major component of a learning strategy training pro-gram at Midwestern State University for several semesters. It is well received by students and appears to modify the cognitive processes employed by students during prose learning. Additionally, experimental evidence suggests that NAIT-trained students have better long-term retention and retrieval of prose than untrained controls. (See Diekhoff *et al.* [1982] for a complete description of the strategy and the empirical evidence.)

CONCEPT STRUCTURING

The Concept Structuring or ConStruct procedure was developed by Vaughan (see Chapter 6, present volume) and is similar to the networking approach. This technique involves the construction of a graphic overview that depicts the perceived relationships in expository text. Specifically, a student reads the text three times, each from a different reading objective. After or during each reading, the student depicts his or her understanding of the concepts in a diagram (graphic overview).

The principal differences in the three readings occur in the level of specificity that is depicted in the concepts and relationships. On the first reading, the student identifies the hierarchial relationships in the text, e.g., topics and subtopics. This is more of a survey of the material than a true reading, and the student's objective is to create a graphic framework or sketch of the material.

On the second reading, the student engages in "study-type" or analytical reading. The student's objective in this phase is to comprehend the information and to add to the graphic overview sufficient concepts and relationships to represent this understanding. No effort is directed toward memorizing or remembering the information.

The third reading involves skimming the entire passage and adding to the graphic overview any concepts and relationships that may have been omitted in the second reading. Following this, the student studies the graphic overview to reinforce understanding and to facilitate recall of the concepts and their relationships.

Evidence for the efficacy of the ConStruct procedure has been provided in several studies using different subjects and materials. Details of the procedure and the empirical evidence are provided in Chapter 6, present volume.

SUMMARY

In this chapter the networking technique developed at Texas Christian University was reviewed. This review included (1) node–arc representations of human memory as a theoretical basis for the strategy, (2) the major empirical studies conducted with the strategy, (3) related applications of the technique, and (4) other techniques which originated from, or are highly similar to, the networking method.

The networking approach has a solid theoretical foundation, and sufficient empirical evidence exists to argue that the technique facilitates text processing by students. Even though the results obtained to date are generally positive, there are a large number of important issues that require resolution. First, we have focused almost exclusively on relatively short-term assessment of the effects of training. The only long-term follow-ups that have been done were by questionnaires administered 3 months after the completion of training. Although these questionnaire assessments indicate that the students continue to be positively influenced by the strategies, we do not have evidence as to whether the objective text processing results would still pertain after a long-term delay. We plan to address this issue in future studies.

In addition to our lack of knowledge about the long-term benefits of training, we also know very little about the relationships between Individual difference variables and training effectiveness. In some of the studies, we have attempted to relate variables such as verbal ability, field independence, and internal–external locus of control to changes from pretraining to posttraining, but we have been unable to observe reliable interrelationships (although there seems to be a tendency for students in the midrange of verbal ability to benefit most from strategy training). If we could establish such reliable interrelationships, training could be tailored to the needs and skills of the individuals involved.

Additionally, very little empirical work has been conducted on the related applications of networking (e.g., general problem solving, instructional aid). All of the potential applications represent a fertile area for future research.

REFERENCES

Baddeley, A. D. (1976). *The psychology of memory*. New York: Basic Books.

Battig, W. F. (1979). The flexibility of human memory. In L. S. Cermak & F. I. M. Craik (Eds.), *Levels of processing in human memory*. Hillsdale, NJ: Erlbaum.

Brooks, L. W., Dansereau, D. F., Holley, C. D., & Spurlin, J. (1983). Generation of descriptive text headings. *Contemporary Educational Psychology 8,* 103–108.

Brooks, L. W., Dansereau, D. F., Spurlin, J., & Holley C. D. (1983). Effects of headings on text processing. *Journal of Educational Psychology 75,* 292–302.

Campbell, D. T., & Stanley, J. C. (1966). *Experimental and quasi-experimental designs for research*. Chicago: McNally.

Cermak, L. S., & Craik, F. I. M. (Eds.). (1979). *Levels of processing in human memory*. Hillsdale, NJ: Erlbaum.

Collins, A. M., & Quillian, M. R. (1969). Retrieval time from semantic memory. *Journal of Verbal Learning and Verbal Behavior 8,* 240–247.

Collins, K. W., Dansereau, D. F., Holley, C. D., Garland, J. C., & McDonald, B. A. (1981). Control of concentration during academic tasks. *Journal of Educational Psychology 73,* 122–128.

Conrad, C. (1972). Cognitive economy in semantic memory. *Journal of Experimental Psychology 92,* 149–154.

Dansereau, D. F. (1978). The development of a learning strategies curriculum. In H. F. O'Neil, Jr., (Ed.), *Learning strategies*. New York: Academic Press.

Dansereau, D. F., Brooks, L. W., Holley, C. D., & Collins, K. W. (1983). Learning strategies training: Effects of sequencing. *Journal of Experimental Education 51,* 102–108.

Dansereau, D. F., Collins, K. W., McDonald, B. A., Holley, C. D., Garland, J. C., Diekhoff, G. M., & Evans, S. H. (1979a). Development and evaluation of a learning strategy training program. *Journal of Educational Psychology 71,* 64–73.

Dansereau, D. F., McDonald, B. A., Collins, K. W., Garland, J. C., Holley, C. D., Diekhoff, G. M., & Evans, S. H. (1979b). Evaluation of a learning strategy system. In H. F. O'Neil, Jr., & C. D. Spielberger (Eds.), *Cognitive and affective learning strategies*. New York: Academic Press.

Diekhoff, G. M., Brown. P. J., & Dansereau, D. F. (1982). A prose learning strategy training program based on network and depth-of-processing models. *Journal of Experimental Education 50,* 180–184.

Ellis, A. (1963). *Reason and emotion in psychotherapy.* New York: Stuart.

Frijda, N. H. Simulation of human long-term memory. (1972). *Psychological Bulletin 77,* 1–31.

Gagne, R. M. (1977). *The conditions of learning* (3rd ed.), New York: Holt.

Greeno, J. G. (1974). Processes of learning and comprehension. In L. W. Gregg (Ed.), *Knowledge and cognition.* New York: Wiley.

Greeno, J. G. (1980). Trends in the theory of knowledge for problem solving. In D. T. Tuma & F. Reif (Eds.). (1980). *Problem solving and education: Issues in teaching and research.* Hillsdale, NJ: Erlbaum.

Holley, C. D. (1979). An evaluation of intact and embedded headings as schema cuing devices with non-narrative text (Doctoral dissertation, Texas Christian University, 1979). *Dissertation Abstracts International 40,* 4491A. (University Microfilms No. 80–02, 220)

Holley, C. D., & Dansereau, D. F. (1981). Controlling for transient motivation in cognitive manipulation studies. *Journal of Experimental Education 49,* 84–91.

Holley, C. D., Dansereau, D. F., Evans, S. H., Collins, K., W., Brooks, L. W., & Larson, D. (1981). Utilizing intact and embedded headings as processing aids with nonnarrative text. *Contemporary Educational Psychology 6,* 227–236.

Holley, C. D., Dansereau, D. F., McDonald, B. A., Garland, J. C., & Collins, K. W. (1978). *Networking as an information processing approach to classroom performance.* Paper presented at the Annual Meeting of the Southwestern Educational Research Association, Austin, TX.

Holley, C. D., Dansereau, D. F., McDonald, B. A., Garland, J. C. & Collins, K. W. (1979). Evaluation of a hierarchical mapping technique as an aid to prose processing. *Contemporary Educational Psychology 4,* 227–237.

Jacobsen, E. (1938). *Progressive relaxation.* Chicago: University of Chicago Press.

Kintsch, W. (1974). *The representation of meaning in memory.* Hillsdale, NJ: Erlbaum.

Larkin, J. H. (1980). Teaching problem solving in physics: The psychological laboratory and the practical classroom. In D. T. Tuma & F. Reif (Eds.), *Problem solving and education: Issues in teaching and research.* Hillsdale, NJ: Erlbaum.

Lindsay, P. H., & Norman, D. A. (1977). *Human information processing: An introduction to psychology* (2nd Ed.). New York: Academic Press.

Long, G. L. (1976). The development and assessment of a cognitive process based learning strategy training program for enhancing prose comprehension and retention (Doctoral dissertation, Texas Christian University, 1976). *Dissertation Abstracts International 38,* 2B. (University Microfilms No. 77–44, 286)

McDonald, B. A., Dansereau, D. F., Garland, J. C., Holley, C. D., & Collins, K. W. (1979). Pair learning and the Transfer of text processing skills. Paper presented at the annual meeting of the American Educational Research Association, San Francisco, CA.

Maultsby, M. (1971). *Handbook of rational self-counseling.* Madison, WI: Association for Rational Thinking.

Meichenbaum, D. H., & Goodman, J. (1971). Training impulsive children to talk to themselves: A means of self-control. *Journal of Abnormal Psychology 77,* 115–126.

Meichenbaum, D. H., & Turk, D. (1975). *The cognitive-behavioral management of anxiety, anger, and pain.* Paper presented at the Seventh Baniff International Conference on Behavioral Modification, Baniff, Canada.

Newell, A., & Simon, H. A. (1972). *Human problem solving.* Englewood Cliffs, NJ: Prentice-Hall.

Norman, D. A., Rumelhart, D. E., & the Lindsay, Norman, & Rumelhart (LNR) Research Group. (1975). *Explorations in cognition:* San Francisco, CA: Freeman.

Polya, G. (1957). *How to solve it.* Garden City, NY: Doubleday.

Quillian, M. R. (1968). Semantic meaning. In M. Minsky (Ed.), *Semantic information processing.* Cambridge, MA: MIT Press.

Quillian, M. R. (1969). The teachable language comprehender. *Communications of the Association for Computing Machinery 12,* 459–475.

Rosch, E. H. (1973). On the internal structure of perceptual and semantic categories. In T. Moore (Ed.), *Cognitive development and the acquisition of language.* New York: Academic Press.

Rumelhart, D. E., Lindsay, P. H., & Norman, D. A. (1972). A process model for long-term memory. In E. Tulving & W. Donaldson (Eds.), *Organization of memory.* New York: Academic Press.

Sarason, I. G. (1956). Effect of anxiety, motivational instructions and failure on serial learning. *Journal of Experimental Psychology 51,* 253–260.

Sarason, I. G. (1978). The test anxiety scale: Concept and research. In C. D. Spielberger & I. G. Sarason (Eds.). (1978). *Stress and anxiety* (Vol. 5). Washington, D.C.: Hemisphere.

Smith, E. E., Shoben, E. J., & Rips, L. J. (1974). Structure and process in semantic memory: A featural model for semantic decisions. *Psychological Review 81,* 214–141.

Wolpe, J. (1969). *The practice of behavior therapy.* New York: Pergamon.

CHAPTER 5

Networking: Application
with Hearing-Impaired Students

GARY LONG   *STEPHEN ALDERSLEY*

INTRODUCTION

In this chapter we present our conceptual framework for developing learning strategy and reading comprehension materials for hearing-impaired students; we also describe the materials and the instructional process, and present some initial observations and evaluation of results. The chapter describes our efforts to train students to use a text classification scheme, combined with a technique for analyzing concept relationships. Our goal is to help students with English language deficiencies to identify important concepts when reading and summarizing the gist of passages.

In a review of text analysis procedures, Tierney and Mosenthal (1980) advise a measure of caution in applying such procedures to classroom reading instruction. Although their remarks are well-taken, there is some evidence that making the inherent structure of text explicit to students may indeed have beneficial effects on reading comprehension (Brown, Campione, & Day, 1981).

Since 1981, we have been engaged in a project to examine the effects of

SPATIAL LEARNING STRATEGIES
Techniques, Applications, and Related Issues

instruction in one particular text analysis procedure, networking, on the reading comprehension of students at the National Technical Institute for the Deaf (NTID). NTID is a post-secondary college for deaf students at the Rochester Institute of Technology (RIT), and is mandated by the federal government to conduct research for application in the education of deaf students at RIT and elsewhere.

What follows are our reflections on the development and use of the text analysis paradigm applied to instruction of a handicapped college population. As a result of their hearing impairment, the English language abilities of NTID students are different from those of a hearing student population. This fact has led us to investigate text analysis as an instructional approach to developing reading *comprehension*, rather than as a technique for enhancing reading *recall*.

NETWORKING: RATIONALE

As a text analysis procedure, networking involves the breaking down of text into individual constituent ideas, which are then linked together by one of six different conceptual relationships (i.e., example, definition, sequence, characteristic, compare–contrast, reason–result). The resultant network of linked ideas becomes an alternative visual representation of the material in the original text.

The technique was devised as a learning strategy, an information-processing operation that would facilitate knowledge acquisition, storage, and retrieval. Initially, emphasis was placed on the use of the procedure as an aid to remembering what has been read (Long, Hein, Coggiola, & Pizzente, 1978). Empirical support for such emphasis comes from numerous studies which have shown that reorganization of material to be learned leads to better recall (Divesta, Schultz, & Dangel, 1973; Mandler, 1968; Myers, Pesdek, & Carlson, 1973; Shimmerlik, 1978). Among other things, networking is a reorganization strategy applied to text.

Specific use of the networking procedure as a learning strategy with beneficial effects for recall has been demonstrated by Holley, Dansereau, McDonald, Garland, & Collins (1979). Their study produced two results of interest to us here. First, students with lower GPAs appeared to derive the greatest benefit from the networking training; and second, the effect of networking was most pronounced in the area of recall of main ideas. This area—deriving main ideas from text—will be one of the principal topics of discussion in this chapter.

LEARNING VERSUS COMPREHENDING

The emphasis in all of the work cited so far has been on the role of the learning strategy in enhancing recall. Implicit in this emphasis is the assumption that students understand what they read in the first place. Initial comprehension is taken for granted, although this cannot always be assumed. Bransford and Johnson (1972) make the unremarkable but necessary point that "although considerable research is needed to assess the relative contributions of comprehension versus retrieval processes to remembering, it seems clear that there is little reason to expect retrieval cues to augment recall for prose appreciably if students have not understood the meaning of the passage" (p. 721).

To highlight the saliency, for us, of the distinction between learning and comprehending, it is important to review briefly the current understanding of what is referred to as "the meaning of a passage." The constructive or interactive orientation to reading comprehension argues that comprehension is an interactive process involving text and reader variables (Spiro, 1981). Text variables are linguistic in nature and comprise syntax, both at the sentence and discourse level, and lexicon. Reader variables include what have been called *textual* and *content schemata* (Anderson, Pickert, & Shirley, 1979; Anderson, Spiro, & Anderson, 1978). Textual schemata relate to the reader's knowledge of how texts are constructed, whereas content schemata comprise the cognitive organization of the reader's knowledge about the world in general. In the constructive theory of reading comprehension, specific schemata—both textual and content—having been triggered by a given text, give rise to expectations about the meaning of the text and powerfully influence its interpretation.

Given the elegance of the interactive model of reading comprehension, it is important not to simply infer that the sole responsibility of the reader is to have developed the necessary content and textual schemata relevant to a specific text. Naturally, the reader must also have developed *linguistic schemata* to enable him or her to use the text-base to get at what Spiro (1981) calls the skeleton or blueprint for the creation of meaning. We have used the schematic in Figure 1 to illustrate this point to our students.

The product of the reader's bringing to bear his or her linguistic, textual and content schemata on the text is that elusive notion, reading comprehension. Measurement of this product has given rise to another whole area in the field of reading research (e.g., Anderson, 1972; Surber & Smith, 1981). One formal measure that has received much attention is the ability to disembed main ideas. Brown and Smiley (1978) regard this as a "naturally occur-

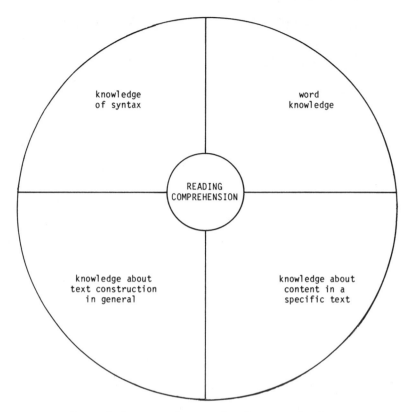

Figure 1. Important elements of reading comprehension.

ring ability" in children and adults. Based on her research, Brown (1981) argues that good readers spontaneously abstract the main ideas of an oral or written communication even when no deliberate attempt to do so is instigated. This ability to abstract main ideas in text was established as a goal in our training of hearing-impaired learners.

NETWORKING AND READING COMPREHENSION

The preceding review provides a background of considerations and theoretical principles derived from research on normally hearing students. About 2 years ago, we explored the possibility of using the networking procedure as a component in the reading instruction curriculum at NTID. We were aware of the considerable difficulties faced by deaf students in the reading process and we felt, at that time, that the conceptual–organizational features of the networking system might enable deaf students to better identify main ideas in text.

Studies of hearing-impaired students throughout the United States indicate that the average reading skills of deaf 18-year-olds and adults are at the fourth grade level (Cooper & Rosenstein, 1966; Trybus & Karchmer, 1977). As for the select group of deaf students registered at NTID, the average reading comprehension grade equivalent at time of entry (California Reading Test, Junior High Level) is 8.46 (Crandall, 1980a). However, several researchers have cast doubt upon the validity of even these low scores, notably Moores (1971) and LaSasso (Davey, LaSasso, & Macready, 1982) who argued that standardized tests may seriously overestimate the true comprehension skills of deaf students. The extent of this overestimation is not known.

Much work has been done in an effort to determine the nature of deaf students' reading problems. Studies carried out at NTID and elsewhere have shown distinct differences between deaf and hearing students in the areas of syntactic knowledge (e.g., Charrow, 1974; Quigley, Wilbur, Power, Montanelli, & Stinkamp, 1976) and lexical knowledge (e.g., Conley, 1976; Walter, 1978). The deleterious effects of complex syntax combined with difficult vocabulary on the reading comprehension of deaf students have been demonstrated by Drury (1981). Comparable deficits in schematic knowledge of both the textual and content variety have been less easy to demonstrate, but the folklore of instructors of the deaf abounds with anecdotal evidence of experiential deficits which may be assumed to have direct effect on schema development.

The ability of deaf students to extract main ideas from text compares unfavorably with that of their hearing peers. Coggiola (1982) recently demonstrated this by obtaining a number of measures from hearing and hearing-impaired students, related to the identification of important text ideas. The hearing students significantly outperformed the hearing-impaired students on all measures.

Notwithstanding our knowledge of the considerable problems faced by deaf students in the reading process, we felt that Brown's (1981) suggestion—that poor readers can benefit from instruction in a strategy to deduce main ideas by looking at text structure—should be given a closer examination with NTID students. At the same time, aware of the warning of Bransford and Johnson (1972) that the reader has to understand the text before he or she can be expected to remember (reorganize) it, we felt that the population most likely to benefit from training in networking would be students who placed at or near the top of the NTID student body on English language skills. These students have the following characteristics:

1. The average pure-tone threshold in the speech range for the better ear is approximately 100 dB (range: 33–120 dB), which indicates that these students are profoundly deaf and that their level of hearing is not useful for everyday conversation.
2. The mean grade equivalent score on the California Reading Comprehension Test, Junior High Form, is approximately 10.54 (range: 9.1–12.0).
3. The mean score on the NTID writing test (Crandall, 1980b) is approximately 9.18 (range: 7.5–10.0), which indicates that most of the errors made by these students are mechanical in nature.

Strategy Training Program

After a 10-week pilot course using materials already designed as part of a learning strategy training program (Long, Hein, & Coggiola, 1979), we revised our approach and prepared a second workbook (Aldersley & Long, 1980). This new workbook was aimed at encouraging students to use networking to extract the main ideas from text and to define the relationships of subordinate ideas to them. Fifty-one students received this instruction over the course of a 10-week academic quarter.

During the first hour, a pretest was administered which was based on two passages with a variety of task requirements. The first passage was 600 words in length and dealt with the topic of death and dying. Students were asked to read the passage and then (1) summarize it in two sentences; (2) answer six multiple-choice questions on what they had read, each of which involved manipulation of one of the six networking relationships; and (3) rate, by order of importance, clause units that were taken verbatim from the text and presented in ten sets of three clauses per set. The second passage—an anecdotal, 650-word report of communication behavior in cats—was then given to the students and the only requirement was to read and summarize it. Students were allowed to use the passages while answering the questions because we were interested in the ability to comprehend main ideas rather than recall. Summaries were rated on a 10-point scale and the multiple-choice questions were each worth 2 points. The ratings of 10 NTID faculty were used to establish a scoring key for the relative importance of each clause. Student ratings of clause importance were compared to faculty ratings and 1 point was given for each correct rating, thereby providing a maximum score of 30 points.

Following the pretest, the next 2 hours were spent introducing the six relationships (example, definition, characteristic, compare–contrast, reason–result) as they occur at the sentence level. Students were given consider-

able practice in this kind of analysis, including two 1-hour homework assignments. The fourth hour was spent progressing to more complex passages of
up to 50 words; the analysis of these typically involved the identification of
two or three different relationships. During the fifth hour a quiz was given,
to ensure adequate comprehension and use of the networking procedure at
the complex sentence level. The sixth hour was devoted to an introduction to
networking at the paragraph level. At this point an effort was made to emphasize the hierarchical nature of textual information, in terms of levels of
importance. A diagram was presented (Figure 2) which served as a reference
point for the remainder of the course. Students were encouraged to apply the
levels of importance hierarchy and the associated questions to all texts, in the
process of analyzing them according to the networking procedure.

The seventh, eighth, and ninth hours of the course were spent practicing
using the networking system with passages of various kinds and lengths of up
to 500 words. These passages were not systematically chosen; the main selection criterion was the intuitive judgement, based on experience, that the
content should be somewhat difficult for the average student in the group. In

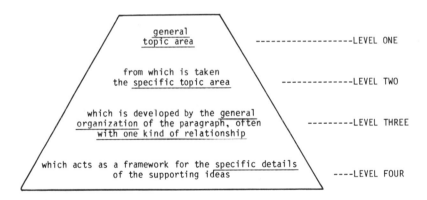

When you have a paragraph to network, start at the top of the heirarchy at LEVEL
ONE and ask yourself the following questions.

- LEVEL ONE   In a word or short phrase, what is the writer's general topic
                 area?

- LEVEL TWO   In a phrase or short sentence, what specific area within the
                 general topic area does the writer want to focus on?

- LEVEL THREE   How does the writer organize his information in general? What
                 is the main kind of relationship that the writer uses to
                 organize his information?

- LEVEL FOUR   How has the writer organized the specific details of his
                 supporting information? What relationships are involved?

FIGURE 2. Levels of importance hierarchy and instructions to students.

the tenth week a posttest was given which mirrored the pretest; however, students were required to network the "death" passage before performing the comprehension tasks.

RESULTS OF THE INITIAL PROGRAM

Analysis of the precourse–postcourse changes in scores on the death summary question indicated a significant increase ($p < .01$) in students' abilities to summarize the gist of the death passage in two sentences. Analysis of students' precourse–postcourse responses to the summary question for the cats passage also indicated a significant increase ($p < .01$) in their ability to summarize the important ideas in the passage. Thus, following the networking training, students were apparently better able to identify and summarize the gist of a passage they had networked (death passage), as well as a passage they had studied but not networked (cats passage).

Analysis of students' precourse–postcourse responses to the concept relationship questions for the death passage also indicated a significant increase ($p < .01$) in their ability to answer detailed, factual questions which utilized the six relationships emphasized in networking. Analysis of student precourse–postcourse responses on judging the relative importance of clauses also indicated a significant increase ($p < .01$) in their ability to judge the relative importance of the clauses presented in triads.

It is possible that these results were confounded by the use of the same passages and tests for precourse and postcourse assessment. Specifically, the significant effects may have been due to practice or the retention of information from pre- to post-assessment. This argument is substantially diminished in the present case because of the 10-week delay between precourse–postcourse assessment, and the use of a procedure in which students were able to refer to the passage during assessment. Although this confounding factor cannot be completely discounted, it seems likely that the networking training had a positive influence on students' ability to select the important material and summarize the gist of the passages.

The results of this evaluation of the networking procedure were gratifying. In considering possible causes for the improvement shown by the students, we return to our original rationale for teaching text analysis procedures, which was couched in terms of requiring the student to reorganize the material. Reorganization is believed to be a significant process, not necessarily because of the cognitive results of the reorganization but because of the *process* of reorganizing. In reorganizing the textual material in a specific (networking) fashion, the student must pay close attention to the text. He or she thereby becomes an "active" learner (Shimmerlik, 1978) with a better chance of remembering the material (and, for our purposes, of understanding the material in the first place).

Two less propitious results of this initial program were not revealed in the formal evaluation results, but were observed in the lessons and homework discussions. First, with several of these practice passages, students were not able to successfully identify any main or superordinate idea with which to commence their networks. Second, it became apparent that the passages we had chosen were of different genres or structures and that the networking system, as we were presenting it, did not account for such differences. For example, by not making any distinction between persuasive and informative texts, we were teaching the students to wield a rather blunt instrument.

The problem of identifying the main ideas or gist of a passage is one which has been well recorded in the literature. Jones (1980), for example, in her attempts to put text analytic procedures to work in reading instruction, reports that instructing low-achieving students to paraphase, summarize, or find the main idea is insufficient without defining each of these strategies in very concrete terms and providing some kind of instruction which helps students to learn how to apply each strategy. This sentiment is echoed by Brown *et al.* (1980) who argue that "merely instructing students to make their summaries as brief as possible and to omit unnecessary information was not an explicit enough guide for junior college students" (p. 19). Consequently, we set out to help students systematically identify the type of text that they are studying as an initial step toward selecting the most important ideas.

NETWORKING AND READING COMPREHENSION: A REVISED APPROACH

Given promising results and what appeared to be a relatively clear problem statement, we began to design a new set of materials that would mitigate the drawbacks of the set we had been using. Brewer's (1981) review of the possible usefulness of literary theory for discourse analysis provided us with a starting point. His discussion of three underlying discourse structures—description, narration, and exposition—in conjunction with four discourse "forces"—informative, entertaining, persuasive, and literary–aesthetic—seemed promising. Introducing considerations regarding the intent of the writer, together with a typology of text structures, suggested the possibility of being able to "kill two birds with one stone." If students could begin their search for the main ideas of a text with a structured set of preliminary questions about the orientation of the writer and the type of text confronting them, perhaps they would be able to form expectations about what the main ideas might be. Students would be better prepared for their search for main ideas by virtue of a strategy for identifying the writer's orientation and the text type.

With this rationale, we devised a text classification system (Table 1) which has some elements in common with the classifications suggested by Brewer. The horizontal axis in Table 1 identifies three text types: (1) description of the world—at one (particular) time, (2) description of the world—over time, and (3) ideas about the world. These types correspond broadly to the more traditional categories of description, narration, and exposition. This redefinition seemed more easily communicable to our students. The vertical axis in Table 1 serves to encourage students to consider the role of the writer; the principal set of questions refers to what we have called the writer's *mode*. The choice here is between "informative," "personal interpretation," "personal opinion" and "persuasive." Here we differ considerably from Brewer.

Our classification scheme is pragmatic and is based on the texts that were used by our students while we were engaged in developing the new set of materials. As such, it makes no claims to exhaustiveness. Indeed, any classification scheme, as long as it provides the reader with an accurate textual schema, will likely serve the purpose of getting the student to think about the text confronting him or her in a novel, structured, and motivating way. What we are discussing here fits into the model of reading comprehension outlined earlier (Figure 1), specifically in the quadrant assigned to knowledge of how texts are constructed (otherwise referred to in the literature as textual schemata).

Clearly we are defining this area rather broadly. We construe it as incorporating knowledge about writers and knowledge about different types of text. We also feel that knowledge about the structures that different text types manifest similarly falls under the rubric of text schemata, and it is at this point in our reasoning that we return to the networking procedure.

In combining the text classification system with the networking procedure, we have defined three specific text structures which can be represented by fairly distinct networks:

1. Given a text of the type "description of the world—at one time" that is written in either the "informative" or "personal interpretation" mode, the network will have the specific topic (that which is being described) as its main node, and the next most important ideas will be typically linked to the main node by the "characteristic" relationship (see Figure 3a).

2. Given a text of the type "description of the world—over time" that is written in either the "informative" or "personal interpretation" mode, the network will have a title (to be generated by the student) as its main node,

TABLE 1

Text Classification System

Writer's orientation	Text type		
Mode	Description of the world—at one time (specific topic–scene, place, person, etc.)	Description of the world—over time (series of events with beginning and end)	Ideas about the world—(writing about topics in general terms)
Informative			
Personal interpretation			
Personal opinion			
Persuasive			

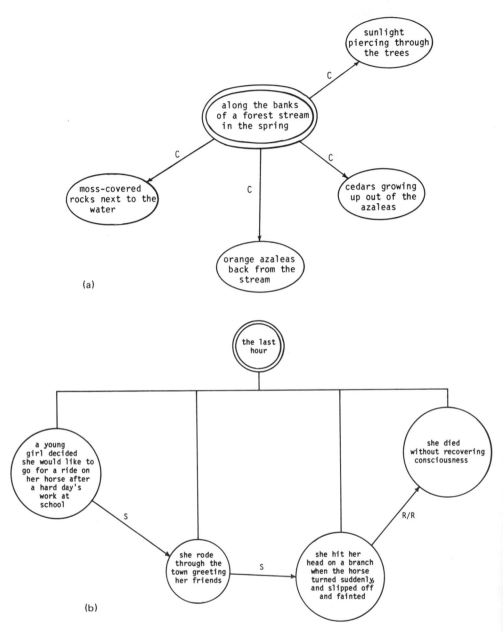

FIGURE 3. Examples of text structures that can be represented by distinct networks (C refers to characteristic; S, sequence, and R–R, result–reason): (a) text type description of the world at one particular time; (b) text type description of the world over time; (c) writer's mode; persuasive.

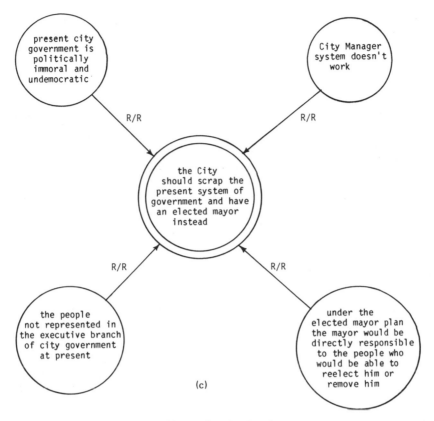

present city government is politically immoral and undemocratic

City Manager system doesn't work

R/R

R/R

the City should scrap the present system of government and have an elected mayor instead

R/R

R/R

the people not represented in the executive branch of city government at present

under the elected mayor plan the mayor would be directly responsible to the people who would be able to reelect him or remove him

(c)

FIGURE 3. (*Continued*)

and the main ideas that constitute the series of events will be linked together by either the "reason–result" or the "sequence" relationship. This type of network is unique in the system, since no named relationship links the individual ideas to the title (see Figure 3b).

3. Given a text of any of the three types that is written in the "personal opinion" or the "persuasive" mode, the network will have the writer's opinion as the main node, and the next most important ideas will all be the reasons from which this opinion results. Thus, the linking relationships will be "reason–result" (see Figure 3c).

The remaining category, texts of the type "ideas about the world" that are written in either the "informative" or "personal interpretation" mode, has proven too diverse to allow for representation in one standard type of network. When confronted with such a text, students are instructed to seek out the idea that the writer is discussing and use this as the main node, developing the network with appropriate relatonships, depending upon the information in the text. This is a somewhat unsatisfactory state of affairs, but it may well be that such texts will lend themselves to an equally structured treatment as greater attention is directed to them in the future.

In the revised curriculum, used for the first time in the spring 1982 academic quarter, the sequence of instruction was as follows. The first hour was given to some general considerations of the reading process, including a discussion of constituent reading processes incorporated in Figure 1. The second, third, and fourth hours were devoted to learning the six relationships that form the basis of the networking system. Students discussed and practiced these six relationships and their linguistic expressions in depth and by means of a variety of practice applications at the sentence and paragraph levels. After a relationship test in the fifth hour, students were introduced to the text classification system. The two axes of this system were carefully defined and students began practicing its application on texts of up to 500 words. In the seventh hour, the process of merging the text classification and the networking systems was initiated. For the remaining three hours students practiced using the two systems; by the end of the course, they had worked on 20 texts of various types and writer orientations. In every case, the end goal for the student was to produce a summary of the main ideas of the passage.

At present, the formal evaluation data are being analyzed and are not available. Informal student response, however, was enthusiastic, which is highly encouraging given the motivational problems traditionally associated with text analysis approaches (e.g., Armbruster & Anderson, 1980). This may possibly be due to the increased amount of guided "detective work" demanded by the revised curriculum.

SUMMARY

Many of the hearing-impaired students at NTID tend to be fairly passive learners who process text in a "bottom-up" fashion. This type of processing focuses on understanding word meanings and constructing the gist from the perspective of the author without active analysis. Their approach to text comprehension is understandable given the hearing-impaired learner's difficulty with vocabulary and syntax (Drury, 1981), as well as with the identification of important ideas (Coggiola, 1982). Consequently, the hearing-impaired reader typically is passive in response to the author's text schema. Our research and development activities have incorporated principles from schema theory and cognitive psychology into strategies developed for hearing-impaired students.

Our goal was to help hearing-impaired learners become active processors through the utilization of a text classification scheme and a technique (networking) for analyzing concept relationships. Students were taught to identify the type of text they are reading, to make predictions about how ideas are related and organized in the passage, and then to generate a diagram displaying the important ideas and relationships. Initial evaluations and observations of students indicated that these techniques help students select the main ideas of the passage and summarize its gist.

The students discussed in this chapter have English language deficiencies with regard to knowledge of syntax and vocabulary, as well as problems with schema generation and the identification of important ideas during reading. It was encouraging to find that these students could learn and benefit from text classification and analysis strategies. We believe that other student populations with English language deficiencies can benefit from training in spatial learning strategies.

REFERENCES

Aldersley, S., & Long, G. (1980). *Networking: A technique for organizing what you read* (Tech. Rep.). Rochester, NY: National Technical Institute for the Deaf, Rochester Institute of Technology.

Anderson, R. (1972). How to construct achievement tests to assess comprehension. *Review of Educational Research, 42,* 145–170.

Anderson, R., Pickert, J., & Shirley, L. (1979). *Effects of the reader's schema at different points in time* (Tech. Rep. No. 119). Urban, IL: Center for the Study of Reading, University of Illinois.

Anderson, R., Spiro, R., & Anderson, M. (1978). Schemata as scaffolding for the representation of information in connected discourse. *American Educational Research Journal, 15,* 433–440.

Armbruster, B., & Anderson, T. (1980). *The effect of mapping on the free recall of expository text* (Tech. Rep. No. 160). Urbana, IL: Center for the Study of Reading, University of Illinois.

Bransford, J., & Johnson, M. (1972). Contextual prerequisites for understanding: Some investigations of comprehension and recall. *Journal of Verbal Learning and Verbal Behavior, 11,* 717–716.

Brewer, W. (1981). Literary theory, rhetoric, and stylistics: Implications for psychology. In R. J. Spiro, B. C. Bruce, & W. F. Brewer (Eds.), *Theoretical issues in reading comprehension.* Hillsdale, NJ: Erlbaum.

Brown, A. (1981). Metacognitive development and reading. In R. J. Spiro, B. C. Bruce, & W. F. Brewer (Eds.), *Theoretical issues in reading comprehension.* Hillsdale, NJ: Erlbaum.

Brown, A., Campione, J., & Day, J. (1981). Learning to learn: On training students to learn from texts. *Educational Researcher, February,* 14–21.

Brown, A., & Smiley, S. (1978). The development of strategies for studying texts. *Child Development, 49,* 1076–1088.

Charrow, V. (1974). *Deaf english* (Tech. Rep.). Stanford: Instruction for Studies in the Social Sciences, Stanford University.

Coggiola, D. (1982). *The identification and use of levels of importance in text comprehension by hearing-impaired college students.* Unpublished doctoral dissertation, University of Rochester.

Conley, J. E. (1976). The role of idiomatic expressions in the reading of deaf children. *American Annals of the Deaf, 121,* 381–385.

Cooper, R. L., & Rosenstein, J. (1966). Language acquisition of deaf children. *Volta Review, 68,* 45–56.

Crandall, K. E. (1980a). English proficiency and progress made by NTID students. *American Annals of the Deaf, 125,* 417–426.

Crandall, K. E. (1980b). *Written language scoring procedures* (Working Paper). Rochester, NY: National Technical Institute for the Deaf, Rochester Institute of Technology.

Davey, B., LaSasso, C., & Macready, G. (1982). *Comparability of deaf and learning subjects' performance on selected reading comprehension tasks.* Paper presented at the Annual Meeting of the American Educational Research Association, New York.

Divesta, F., Schultz, C., & Dangel, T. (1973). Passage organization and imposed learning strategies in comprehension and recall of connected discourse. *Memory and Cognition, 1,* 471–476.

Drury, A. (1981). *Syntax, vocabulary and readability for deaf college students.* Paper presented at the Annual Meeting of the American Educational Research Association, Los Angeles.

Holley, C., Dansereau, D., McDonald, B., Garland, J., & Collins, K. (1979). Evaluation of a hierarchical mapping technique as an aid to prose processing. *Contemporary Educational Psychology, 4,* 227–237.

Jones, B. (1980). *Embedding structural information and strategy instruction within mastery learning units.* Paper presented at the Annual Meeting of the International Reading Association, St. Louis.

Long, G., Hein, R., Coggiola, D., (1979). *Networking: A technique for understanding and remembering instructional material* (Tech. Rep.). Rochester, NY: Department of Educational Research and Development, National Technical Institute for the Deaf, Rochester Institute of Technology.

Long, G., Hein, R., Coggiola, D., & Pizzente, M. (1978). *Networking: A technique for understanding and remembering instructional material* (Student Manual). Rochester, NY: Department of Educational Research and Development, National Technical Institute for the Deaf, Rochester Institute of Technology.

Mandler, G. (1968). Organized recall: Individual functions. *Psychonomic Science, 13,* 235–236.

Meyer, B. (1973). *Identifying variables in prose.* Paper presented at the Annual Meeting of the Eastern Psychological Association, Washington, D.C.

Meyer, B., Brandt, D., & Bluth, G. (1980). Use of top-level structure in text: Key for reading comprehension of ninth grade students. *Reading Research Quarterly, 16,* 72–103.

Moores, D. F. (1971). *An investigation of the psycholinguistic functioning of deaf adolescents* (Research Rep.). Research and Development Center in Education of Handicapped Children, University of Minnesota.

Myers, J., Pesdek, K., & Carlson, D. (1973). Effect of prose organization upon free recall. *Journal of Educational Psychology, 65,* 313–320.

Quigley, S. P., Wilbur, R. B., Power, D. J., Montanelli, D. S., & Stinkamp, M. W. (1976). *Syntactic structures in the language of deaf children* (Tech. Rep.). Urbana, IL: Institute for Child Behavior & Development, University of Illinois.

Shimmerlik, S. (1978). Organization theory and memory for prose: A review of the literature. *Review of Education Research, 48,* 103–120.

Spiro, R. (1981). Constructive processes in prose comprehension and recall. In R. J. Spiro, B. C. Bruce, & W. F. Brewer (Eds.), *Theoretical issues in reading comprehension.* Hillsdale, NJ: Erlbaum.

Surber, J., & Smith, P. (1981). Testing for misunderstanding. *Educational Psychologist, 16,* 165–173.

Tierney, R. J., & Mosenthal, J. (1980). *Discourse comprehension and production: Analyzing text structure and cohesion* (Technical Report No. 152). Cambridge, MA: Bolt, Beranek and Newman.

Trybus, R. J., & Karchmer, M. A. (1977). School achievement scores of hearing-impaired children: National data on achievement status and growth patterns. *American Annals of the Deaf, 122,* 62–69.

Walter, G. G. (1978). Lexical abilities of hearing and hearing-impaired children. *American Annals of the Deaf, 123,* 976–982.

CHAPTER 6

Concept Structuring: The Technique and Empirical Evidence

JOSEPH L. VAUGHAN

INTRODUCTION

Research and pedagogical literature on reading is replete with a concern about the nature of reading, and particularly the role of the reader. There seems to be a growing consensus that reading is thinking stimulated by print, whereby the reader attempts to make sense of ideas by clarifying relationships among concepts, and that such thinking is dominated by a cognitive manipulation of the concepts.

The extent to which a reader can manipulate and arrange concepts into a sensible proximity to one another may be a primary determiner of whether he or she will perceive these efforts as successful. In many reading situations the manipulation of concepts usually occurs effortlessly and apart from any conscious awareness (because of the familiarity of the ideas encountered during reading and the corresponding knowledge structure the reader possesses for those ideas). However, reading can sometimes be difficult even for accomplished readers, particularly if they lack the strategic knowledge required to control the cognitive manipulation of concepts encountered while reading.

127

SPATIAL LEARNING STRATEGIES
Techniques, Applications, and Related Issues

From my perspective, the present volume is based on the premise that learning is a facile activity if the learner has skills or strategies to metacognitively control and manipulate the circumstances that affect learning. This premise carries particular importance in contemporary society, where the need seems greater than ever to prepare learners for a world in which success may well depend on the ability to select and manipulate information pertinent to specific needs and purposes. To achieve that objective, a general learning strategies curriculum would seem reasonable, if not imperative.

As for a reading curriculum, the emerging focus of instruction favors the development of active, critical readers (e.g., Durkin, 1980; Estes & Vaughan, in press; Harste, 1982; Pearson & Johnson, 1978; Tierney & Cunningham, 1980). The prevailing theme seems to be that maintaining control over the most difficult reading situations is possible for a reader who possesses, in his or her repertoire of learning strategies, a systematic and effective approach to the cognitive manipulation of concepts. The goal of reading education, therefore, is twofold: (1) to make readers familiar with those factors affecting their attempts to make sense of ideas while reading, and (2) to provide them with opportunities to become adept at controlling even the most difficult reading activities. The purpose of this chapter is to describe a procedure that readers can use to successfully process information from the most difficult reading situation they are likely to encounter: an expository, academic textbook.

ANATOMY OF THE PROBLEM

This reading strategy was developed in response to a problem encountered by students in a variety of settings: medical school, college, and junior and senior high schools. Inherently, the problem is that many students, including so called "good readers," have difficulty comprehending the information in many, if not most, of their textbooks. Through an analysis of textbooks and interviews with teachers and students, three factors emerged as the primary contributors to this problem: (1) certain nonfacilitative characteristics of expository textbooks, (2) the novelty of the concepts to the readers, and (3) the readers' limited repertoire of learning strategies (Vaughan, Stillman, & Sabers, 1978). Each of these factors is subsequently discussed.

Although the difficulties inherent in typical expository textbooks are not, as yet, clearly specifiable, research efforts related to this are in progress (e.g., Anderson & Armbruster, 1981; Deese, Estes, Shebilske, & Rotondo, 1980; Tierney, Schallert, & Ulerick, 1981; also see Schallert, Ulerick, & Tierney, Chapter 12, present volume). An extensive review of existing research findings is not feasible here; however, expository textbooks have frequently been found to contain linguistic flaws, including a lack of unity, cohesion, and semantic elaboration. A primary characteristic of these texts is the listing of detailed facts with few cohesive ties either among the details or between the facts and the main points they potentially clarify. Armbruster and Anderson (Chapter 9, present volume) maintain that expository textbooks can be notoriously inconsiderate of the reader. Rather than facilitate the communication intended and desired by the author, many expository textbooks tend to confound and distract the reader's search for understanding.

The extent to which a reader is likely to comprehend concepts expressed in a textbook is largely determined by his or her familiarity with those concepts. Because the function of most reading assignments is to expose students to new learning, readers of academic textbooks typically encounter concepts with which they have only a cursory familiarity. The difficulty caused by lack of prior knowledge is predictably high for the reading of expository material, and it can become much higher when authors use unfamiliar, precise, technical vocabulary to present and discuss unfamiliar, complex concepts. Many students are thereby left to struggle with new ideas as best they can, at least until some postreading discussion.

The third factor that influences the reading of expository text is the reader's repertoire of strategies for processing the information. Unfortunately, many readers are not aware of alternative learning strategies (e.g., Brown, 1981; Dansereau, 1978; Tierney & Cunningham, 1980; Vaughan, 1982b). Further, alternative strategies that are often presented to students are frequently too vague to be of much value and often have little empirical verification in spite of their popularity (e.g., SQ3R). Even when empirically verified strategies are shared with students, especially senior high school and college students, the students often seem to reject the new strategies and rely on more familiar ones, even if they recognize the merits of such strategies (Brown, 1981).

Although the difficulties in comprehending expository text can be traced largely to the three factors just discussed, two other factors emerged during our investigations, and these may be of equal importance for resolving difficulties. First, readers typically perceived themselves as the problem. Few students realized the importance of a considerate text or the relationship between new learning and prior understandings. Nor do they realize that they *can* manipulate and structure conceptual relationships, much less how to actually do so. Part of our solution has been to help these readers accept the stance that they are not necessarily poor readers when they have difficulty understanding expository text. The second additional factor is the reader's purpose for reading. Frequently, the purpose is externally imposed by a teacher, rather than established by the reader. In fact, the purpose is usually determined not even by the teacher, but by the teacher's test.

While the foregoing linguistic and cognitive features are critical to the problem of comprehending expository text, these factors are amplified by issues related to affect and volition, In our work, resolution of these issues presented a greater obstacle than the development of a strategy that students could use to structure concepts (Dansereau [1978] and Dansereau, Collins, McDonald, Holley, Garland, Diekhoff, & Evans [1979] use what they distinguish as *support* and *primary* strategies, respectively, for resolving these problems).

CONSTRUCT PROCEDURE

This learning strategy derives its name from the notion of *con*cept *struct*-uring, an expression that is intended to suggest a cognitive manipulation of concepts. In this regard, it is similar to other spatial learning strategies described in this volume (e.g., mapping, networking, graphic postorganizers), yet the ConStruct procedure is distinct in two ways. First, it assumes that the reader's knowledge of the concepts under scrutiny is limited, perhaps even nonexistent. Thus, before a reader can begin to manipulate conceptual relationships, he or she must develop a personal acquaintance with the concepts, at least to the point of having a sense of their gist. Second, this strategy does not require the user to identify explicitly the relationships that exist among concepts, a feature that is integral to many of the other spatial techniques. The reader relates concepts as he or she tacitly perceives them. Labeling the relationships may provide a potential improvement to this procedure, but it seems quite effective without such labeling and any benefits would have to be weighed against the increased complexity (as perceived by students). The ConStruct procedure involves the integration of varied readings of an expository text with the construction of a diagram that depicts the conceptual relationships as a reader perceives them. After or during each of three readings, the reader depicts his or her understanding of the concepts. I chose the term *graphic overview* for the resulting diagram because the reader is trying to display on paper an overview of the concepts, including various hierarchical conceptual levels, so that when it is completed the overview graphically represents the reader's understanding of the concepts and their relationships to one another. Figure 1 illustrates application of the procedure as it might be used by a student who is studying a tenth-grade biology selection on how the digestive system works.

Initially, the reader *surveys* the selection to try to identify the topic and the major subparts of the topic. During this initial search for understanding, the reader should use as much information as is available (e.g., titles, subheadings, introductory paragraphs, first sentences, summaries, pictures, dia-

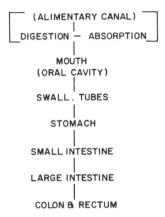

FIGURE 1. Superordinate level (first-stage) graphic overview.

grams). If the reader is fortunate enough to be using a considerate text, the structure of the concepts is likely to become clear rather quickly, as well as their gist. If the text is inconsiderate, this initial survey is more difficult; even so, the reader must strive to identify the major topic and its most important supporting concepts. (With inconsiderate texts, a reader may find it necessary to perform a thorough reading on the "first pass." In such cases he or she must avoid being distracted from the survey task of determining the gist of the passage.) Once the reader identifies the superordinate concepts for the selection, those concepts should then be diagrammatically depicted in the first stage of the graphic overview (see Figure 1).

The second phase of the ConStruct procedure consists of a careful "study-type" reading, what some call analytical reading (e.g., Adler and van Doren, 1972). During this second reading, the reader is directed to seek understanding but to make no special effort to remember. Despite the emphasis on understanding, readers are advised "to note but do not worry about" those sections they may not completely understand (because they will return to those ideas later) and to pay attention to details primarily for the purpose of comprehension (instead of memorizing them). Either during this second reading or immediately after it, the reader elaborates on the first stage of the graphic overview. It is important that students realize that the concepts added to the graphic overview during this second reading are those that are essential for clarifying the major topics or subtopics; "nonessential" details are added later. What constitutes an important supporting concept as compared with a nonessential detail is often debatable, so this too is usually best left to the discretion of the individual reader. During the initial learning of

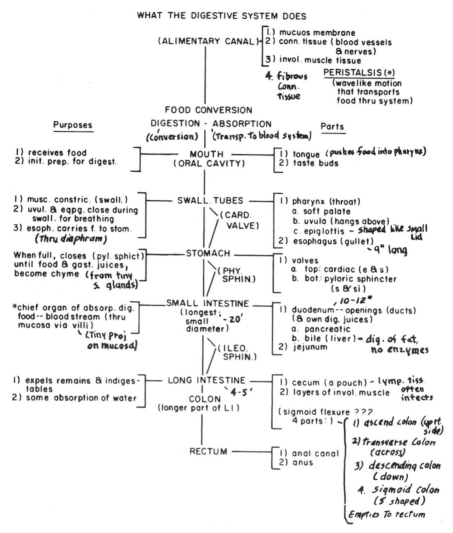

FIGURE 2. Second-stage graphic overview.

this strategy, however, students are encouraged to justify why they included or excluded some of the debatable concepts. Figure 2 illustrates a second-phase elaboration.

After the second phase of the ConStruct procedure, and before beginning the final reading, the reader should reexamine any portion of the selection that was previously not understood. Sometimes readers will discover that, based on the elaborations occurring in phase two, some concepts which

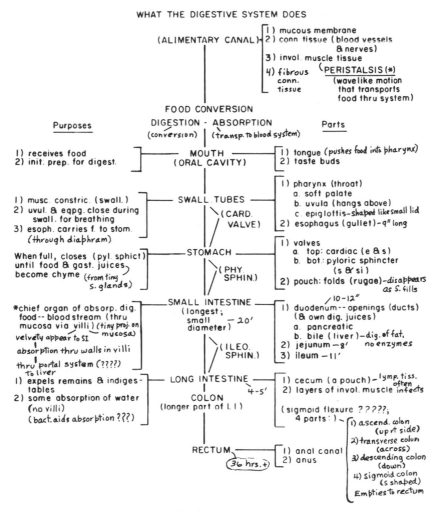

FIGURE 3. Completed (third-stage) graphic overview.

were previously unclear will now make sense. If this occurs, the reader should insert the clarified concepts into the graphic overview.

The third reading involves scanning the selection to identify nonessential detailed information and to insert it into the graphic overview. Figure 3 presents a finalized graphic overview which was created by a student during one of our validation studies. In this figure, the student indicated with several question marks her confusion about the sigmoid flexure. (Because the question marks were not removed from the finalized overview, apparently the reader still did not understand that portion of the text.)

In the final step of the ConStruct procedure, an extension of the third phase, the reader skims the entire selection to verify that he or she has satisfactorily included all the important information in the graphic overview. Then the reader studies the graphic overview to reinforce understandings and to facilitate recall of the concepts and their relationships. Any concepts that remain confusing are noted so that they can be clarified with the instructor (or other resources).

EMPIRICAL EVIDENCE

Evidence for the effectivness of the ConStruct procedure has been collected in three separate studies. The purpose of these investigations was to determine whether readers' use of this strategy enhanced their comprehension of complex, unfamiliar concepts presented in their expository textbooks. The studies differed in terms of grade level, subject area, and specific issues addressed; consequently, I discuss the context for each study separately and, in the case of the initial study, something of the evolution of the strategy. The findings of these studies are discussed following their descriptions.

Background to the Initial Study

The ConStruct procedure was originally conceived in response to a need expressed by medical students in a first-year class at the University of Arizona College of Medicine. Approximately 50% of students in the class were having difficulty passing tests on text chapters in two courses, physiology and neuroanatomy. Because some students were beginning to develop a low self-concept, associated with being "poor readers" destined to fail medical school, I was requested to provide assistance to the students.

Being uncertain as to the exact nature of the problem, I began to explore some medical education literature and concluded that the problem was hardly unique to students at the University of Arizona. For example, Barnes, Albanese, Schroeder, Weshselblatt, and Muehl (1977) had noted, "the ability to read effectively is not necessarily a part of the armamentarium of medical students" (p. 126) Based on an analysis of the students' primary textbooks, the expectations demanded by the faculty, and a needs assessment inventory, several conclusions were drawn. First, students were identified as relatively fluent, accomplished readers. If the problem had existed with only a small proportion of these students, other factors may have been considered (e.g., inappropriate admissions procedures); however, these students had previously excelled in their academic careers and perceived themselves to be above-average readers. Second, based on an analysis of faculty-constructed tests, students were expected to recall specific, detailed information about complex issues. Third, the information presented in the text, though logically organized, was also of a detailed nature and was predominantly unfamiliar to the students. In effect, then, these students were required to learn and retain detailed information for which they had limited previously developed schemata.

The proposed solution to the problem was to help the students progress through a gradual familiarization with the concepts as they attempted to construct meaning from their texts. The instructional program that was designed focused on the use of reader-constructed graphic overviews, what Barron calls "graphic postorganizers" (see Barron & Schwartz, Chapter 13, this volume). These overviews represent a graphic depiction of the "hierarchical and parallel relationships among the concepts in the learning passage represented in schematic form" (Barron & Stone, 1974). This device was first developed by Barron (1969), and research related to its use has suggested that it is most useful when students create an overview after reading a selection. Given Barron's research supporting reader-constructed overviews *after* reading, it was hypothesized that readers could create such a graphic depiction *as they read*. It was surmised that this would allow the reader to gradually develop an understanding of the new information conveyed in the text, and thereby to identify hierarchical and parallel relationships among the concepts (as with networking or semantic mapping) and consequently to generate a sufficiently developed schema for assimilating additional information.

Unfortunately, the information in the texts was organized in a manner that presented a major obstacle to this approach. Specifically, each chapter could be broken down into three predominant hierarchical levels of information. On the highest level were general concepts extending throughout the passage, usually one to three overriding ideas. Relating to these general ideas were several major subordinate concepts that provided explication and elaboration of the general ideas. These were considered second-order concepts and were labeled as such for instructional purposes. The third level contained numerous detailed pieces of information that provided the in-depth understanding emphasized by the faculty. The texts were typically presented in such a way that the general, overriding concepts were introduced in a prefatory section at the beginning of the chapter. The author then proceeded to cover each of the major subordinate concepts individually and in depth.

As students sought to understand the material, they were likely to focus on one subordinate idea at a time, along with the numerous detailed ideas presented in direct relation to the subordinate idea. Such an approach somewhat impedes comprehension because the parallel relationships are usually processed tangentially as students proceed to subsequent subordinate ideas.

In addition, many of the detailed pieces of information are not clarified until the parallel relationships among subordinate ideas are identified. In other words, if students tried to progress through the text as it was presented, they would be limited in their efforts to construct an overview of each subordinate idea, including the related details, unless and/or until they first identified parallel relationships among the major subordinate concepts.

This problem was resolved by modifying the original plan. In the needs assessment inventory, students had indicated that they read each chapter at least twice and, in most instances, three times. They further indicated that each time they read the material in the same way and with the same purpose—"to learn it all as well and as thoroughly as possible." This approach to reading is contraindicated by Smith's (1975) suggestion that "If you cannot comprehend . . . , let alone remember, you should try to read through faster, before worrying about the detail, in order to get the feeling of what entire passages are about" (p. 251).

The instructional program was modified to have students read each chapter three times, but each would be a different type of reading. On the first reading they were to read inspectionally to identify the overall ideas presented in the selection. Such a reading included the prefatory section; the diagrams, charts, and other visual aids; the first paragraph of each new subheading; and the summary. The second reading was intended to identify the gist of each subsection without concern for the detailed information. The objective was to identify the major subordinate ideas within the selection and the parallel relationships among the subordinate concepts. Further, the hierarchical relationships between the general concepts and the major subordinate ideas were to be identified. During the final reading, students were to identify the detailed information, and the hierarchical and parallel relationships among the detailed information and the higher-order concepts. During each of the three readings, students were directed to construct a graphic overview as they read. With each subsequent reading, they added to, modified, and/or deleted information from their graphic overviews. Thus, the ConStruct Procedure was created.

STUDY 1: MEDICAL STUDENTS

In the initial study, 36 first-year medical students volunteered for the program and were randomly assigned to two groups. Group A received a 4-week training program consisting of a pretest, strategy instruction, and a posttest. Instruction included an explanation of the strategy and four 2-hour practice sessions using material from their physiology or neuroanatomy classes.

All tests were composed of open-ended, cued-response questions based on selections taken from current assignments in the students' textbooks. No time limits were imposed on either their reading or the tests. The questions were designed to assess comprehension at three conceptual levels: superordinate, subordinate, and specific (Vaughan, 1981). For questions to be classified as superordinate, expected responses had to span the entire selection and, in effect, represent the gist of the passage. Subordinate questions were those that solicited information regarding major subtopics, including detailed information considered *essential* to the understanding of the subtopics. Specific questions were those that solicited nonessential details (i.e., they were not essential to comprehending either the gist of the selection or the gist of the subtopics). Analysis of the students' typical classroom tests indicated that the questions usually fit our definition of specific questions. (The instructors rationalized that tendency by arguing that if students remembered the nonessential details their understanding of the higher-level concepts could be assumed, an obviously faulty premise).

Findings from this study were based on a comparison of the pretest-to-posttest scores on comprehension and reading rates for students in Group A. Because the passages for the pretests and posttests were different, students in Group B served as a control group. This was accomplished by providing no instruction for students in Group B (see Holley and Dansereau [1981] for a discussion of no-treatment controls in this context). At the same time that the posttest was administered to students in Group A, it was also given to the control group (Group B), and served as their pretest. The passage for that test was a 3684-word passage on the mesencephalon. The findings are discussed concomitantly with those of the two other studies.

STUDY 2: TENTH-GRADE STUDENTS

A second study was conducted with students in four tenth-grade biology classes to determine whether this strategy could be put to effective use by high-school students. Students had reportedly been randomly assigned to these four classes at the beginning of the year and a comparison of standardized test scores of reading comprehension indicated no significant differences among the groups. Two of the classes were assigned to the experimental condition and the other two classes served as controls.

Students in the experimental classes received 12 weeks of instruction in the use of the ConStruct Procedure following the basic plan delineated at the end of this chapter. Emphasis was placed on their using the strategy in class on text assigned by their teacher. After each phase of the strategy, students discussed any successes and problems they were experiencing. Twenty-one instructional sessions (50 minutes apiece) were devoted to students' learning the strategy. The posttest-only design consisted of an 18-question, cued-response exam with six questions at each of the three conceptual levels discussed earlier.

Students in the control classes read and discussed their assignments in class during the 12-week period that corresponded with the instructional period for the experimental group. Thus, they became accustomed to reading their assignments in class; discussion focused on what they understood and/or did not understand. The control group read the same selection on the same day as the experimental group and took the same test. The testing passage was an 847-word passage on the circulatory system. No time limits were placed on either reading the text or responding to the test questions. The results are presented after a description of the third study.

STUDY 3: EIGHTH-GRADE STUDENTS

A third study was conducted with students in five classes of an eighth-grade history course (Vaughan, Taylor, & Meredith, 1980). Two classes, one in the morning and one in the afternoon, comprised the control group. Each of the other classes were randomly assigned to one of three experimental conditions. Class A learned to apply the ConStruct Procedure. Class B learned to develop a graphic postorganizer after reading their text assignments once. Class C learned to read the assignments three times using the varied reading incorporated into the ConStruct Procedure, but without making the graphic overviews.

No evidence existed to indicate that the students had been randomly assigned to these classes, and their teacher believed that differences did exist in reading ability among the classes. A pretest based on the format used in the second study confirmed that the classes did not contain students with comparable reading ability. Consequently, an analysis of covariance was used to examine the various effects, using the pretest as the covariate.

The posttest was designed so each of the 12 open-ended, cued-response questions could be classified in two ways. First, the questions could be analyzed according to the previously discussed conceptual hierarchy (superordinate, subordinate, or nonessential specific). Second, the questions could be analyzed according to whether the elicited information was textually explicit or inferential. The posttest passage was an 879-word passage on how the United States became involved in World War I.

The experimental groups received 19 instructional sessions following a plan similar to that described at the end of this chapter, with portions deleted for those groups that only received training with part of the strategy. During this same period, students in the control groups read and discussed their assignments in class. Following the instructional period, students read the posttest selection (the next assignment in their textbook) and took the test. Three days later, students retook the same test without rereading the selection.

RESULTS OF THE THREE STUDIES

The findings in each of the studies provided support for the ConStruct Procedure. In the study with medical students, a t-test of mean percentage scores revealed significant differences in favor of the experimental group ($p < .01$). Comparisons among scores on each of the three conceptual levels found significant differences only at the specific level. Additionally, the pretest–posttest comparisons indicated significant differences for each group ($p < .01$). No significant differences were found in the reading rates (words-per-minute).

Similar positive findings were obtained in the second study. Students who used the ConStruct Procedure significantly outperformed ($p < .01$) students in the control groups. In this study, however, significant differences were not found at the specific conceptual level, but were found at both the superordinate and subordinate levels. Another difference was that the control group read the passage at a significantly faster rate ($p < .05$).

The first two studies provided empirical validation that the ConStruct Procedure is an effective learning strategy, but did not provide much evidence on the questions of *why* or *how* it works. The third study verified the findings from the previous investigations. The analysis of covariance for main effects indicated significant differences among the groups on the posttest ($p < .05$) and the delayed posttest ($p < .01$). Pairwise comparisons of the group means using Tukey posthoc tests indicated that those students who used the ConStruct Procedure performed significantly better ($p < .01$) on the posttest and the delayed posttest than did either of the control groups. Only one other significant difference was found for the pairwise comparisons: students who designed graphic postorganizers in conjunction with one reading performed significantly better than one of the control groups on the delayed posttest.

At the superordinate conceptual level, no differences were found at the time of the posttest. On the delayed posttest, however, students who used the ConStruct Procedure scored significantly better ($p < .01$) than either control group. The mean scores indicated that this difference was due to recall deterioration by the control groups; these groups barely maintained 50% of their posttest performance, whereas the ConStruct Procedure students maintained 85% of their earlier performance.

Analysis of the scores for subordinate concepts revealed that the users of the ConStruct Procedure recalled significantly more ($p < .05$) of these major subtopics and their essential supporting details than did either control group on both the posttest and the delayed posttest. No other significant differences were observed for subordinate concepts.

At the specific conceptual level, no significant differences were found among the groups. Although this contradicts the findings with the medical school students, it does confirm the results from the second study. Although a cursory glance would suggest an inconsistency in these results, discussions with medical students indicated that they typically read their assignments to understand, not to memorize. They recognized the futility of trying to memorize details when their purpose was to understand all they could about their chosen profession. On the other hand, adolescents tend to read to pass teachers' tests and, as they often reveal, they usually read to memorize definitions and details because, as several students told us, "that's what teachers test." The mean scores for the two groups in the third study were highest on the specific conceptual level: that is, the control groups scored highest on those questions they perceived as being most important. Hence, no real inconsistency exists here; readers do read for different purposes. Further, they should score best on those items to which they assign the greatest importance.

When the mean scores across the three conceptual levels were examined for the several groups in this study, considerable variability existed for all groups except the students who used the ConStruct Procedure. It seems reasonable to conclude that this strategy does help students gradually develop their understanding of concepts at various hierarchical levels, and provides them with a strategic approach to recognizing relationships among concepts.

On the scores for textually explicit information, students who used the ConStruct Procedure and those who constructed a graphic postorganizer after one reading performed significantly better ($p < .01$) than either control group on both the posttest and the delayed posttest. No other significant differences were found. These findings suggest that the conscious manipulation of concepts into a visual array improves recall performance of information explicitly stated in expository texts, compared to less active strategies such as just reading. Presumably, this occurs because the graphic display improves comprehension and thereby aids memory. Whether this is due to constructive nature of this task, the personalized visual mnemonic, or an interaction of the two is not clear from these studies. Research with similar activities (e.g., networking, semantic mapping) would suggest that the active involvement is an important factor, given the consistently positive findings with those similar strategies and the inconsistent findings with studies using teacher-constructed overviews in which students are presented with a completed graphic display (e.g., Moore & Readence, 1980). Regardless of how one interprets these findings, the construction of graphic displays by students does enhance recall of textually explicit information.

With respect to the inferential questions, those students who read the material three times and those who used the ConStruct procedure performed significantly better ($p < .05$) than all other groups on the posttest. This finding suggests that students who used varied approaches to reading expository material tend to develop a broader sense of the concepts than those who read the material only once. On the delayed posttest for these questions, only the students who used the ConStruct procedure retained their inferential performance. The varied readings component of the ConStruct procedure seems to contribute heavily to inferential performance, and the graphic overview component appears to aid in long-term retrieval.

SUMMARY OF THE EMPIRICAL EVIDENCE

The empirical evidence for the ConStruct procedure supports its value as a strategy that enhances readers' recall of expository text. Students who used this strategy consistently outperformed other students on all types of concepts examined. The two major elements of the strategy, three varied readings and construction of a graphic overview, were found to contribute differentially to its overall effectiveness. The time required to use this strategy is not significantly greater than the time typically required for conscientious study of the material, as indicated in the study with medical students.

While the ConStruct procedure has consistently been shown to have empirical validity, several cautions should be noted. This strategy was designed and is intended for use with unfamiliar, complex expository text. It may be effective with text that is less complex and/or presents concepts familiar to a reader, but those conditions have not been investigated empirically. In other reading situations, other strategies that require less time may be equally or even more effective. No claim is made for this strategy other than its intended purposes and its empirically validated uses. Further, it is a reader strategy, not a teacher strategy, and it requires approximately 20 sessions for adolescents to become proficient in its use. Older students may be able to learn and apply it in less time, as was the case with medical students. Another uninvestigated aspect of the strategy is the issue of labeling conceptual relationships, as is done with networking and semantic mapping. Would such explicit labeling increase the effectiveness of this strategy? Would adding three differential readings to networking and semantic mapping increase their effectiveness? Further, can the ConStruct procedure facilitate the development of students' metacognitive awareness of strategic approaches to reading? Finally, can students who learn to use this strategy eventually discard the pencil–paper construction of a visual graphic display and maintain similar effectiveness in their comprehension by constructing a mental image of the conceptual relationships? These and other questions remain to be explored.

INSTRUCTIONAL SUGGESTIONS

A primary feature of the research on the ConStruct procedure has been its context. All of these studies have been pursued to determine whether the strategy can be learned and used in typical classroom situations. The following suggestions for teaching the strategy have evolved from classroom observations (Vaughan, 1982a).

1. *Teach ConStruct in context.* ConStruct is intended for, and has been validated with, readers who have difficulty comprehending complex, expository text. Students should learn to use ConStruct by applying it to their regular textbooks in the regular classes. Although this initally requires the use of class time for students to read what would usually be homework assignments, teachers who have been willing to do so have reacted favorably. After learning the strategy, many students substantially increased their understanding of the text when they returned to reading their assignments outside of class. Further, even while learning to use ConStruct, students are more attentive to, and involved in, discussion of content because they understand what they are studying. Hence, teachers often report that time is actually saved, even during the instructional period for the strategy, because information does not have to be repeated.

2. *Explain what you are doing.* In those instances in which we have told students that we realize they are having trouble understanding and remembering what they read in their textbooks, they are relieved to hear that someone knows and cares. When we were less than honest about what was going on, we encountered resistance from many students, especially successful ones, because they were reluctant to abandon strategies that were comfortable and familiar.

3. *Be patient.* The optimum period for adolescent students to learn and to become adept at using the Construct procedure appears to be 10 weeks, with two sessions per week. Some students learn more quickly than others, so patience is important.

4. *Model the graphic overview.* Graphic overviews are a crucial dimension of the ConStruct procedure, but few students have been exposed to

them. Before actually introducing students to ConStruct, it is benefical to design some graphic overviews on the board as part of class discussions. The value of such modeling cannot be overemphasized. Because students see the product of their thinking as it grows, they understand the construction process better. This facilitates their learning the ConStruct procedure when it is later introduced.

5. *Involve students during modeling.* As an extension of item four, students' ideas and input, relative to the content and the location of the content, should be used in constructing and modeling the graphic overviews. Using graphic overviews without student participation is likely to have little value.

6. *Introduce ConStruct as an integrated strategy.* Students must understand the whole of ConStruct before they begin to learn its parts. Because it is complex, students will need to learn the strategy gradually; but to avoid students' perceiving the parts separated from the whole, we have found it essential to describe the entire strategy from the outset. Then, we relate the parts to the whole as each part is introduced. This continuous reference to the whole helps students integrate, adopt. and sometimes even modify ConStruct into their own study tactics. Thus, the intial step when introducing students to the ConStruct procedure is to outline it for them in much the same way as it is presented earlier in this chapter.

7. *Learning ConStruct is like using building blocks, only starting at the top.* Several variations of teaching ConStruct have been tried, but one particular sequence seems to work best. In general, the greatest success results from a straightforward presentation of the parts in the order they are actually used when the integrated whole is applied. The specific sequences are as follows:

    a. *As an introduction, teach students why and how to survey a selection.* Few students understand the value of a survey reading; even fewer know how to do it correctly. Of course, surveying strategies vary depending on what "overview cues" a text provides. We have had most success with a discovery approach rather than with giving explicit directions for a particular passage. Following a survey of each selection, we discuss students' responses to the question, "what will the selection be about?" Then we discuss what they did when they surveyed, and why. By sharing their successes, students learn new ways to survey from each other.

    b. *Begin overview construction with top-level content only.* After students have been exposed to graphic overviews and surveying, we ask each student to design a top-level graphic overview for a selection they have just surveyed. To help students overcome any initial consternation, we encourage them to return to the text. We also walk around the class providing encouragement and reinforcement. After students have designed their own top-level graphic overviews, we ask a student to put his or her overview on the board. We discuss it and emphasize that it represents one way, certainly not the only way, to depict the general concepts. After discussions, we ask the students to read the selection carefully. As they do, we examine the other students' top-level overviews. When we discover one with a different perspective from the overview on the board, we ask the student to share it with the class, after all students have concluded their careful reading. During such a sharing session, the class discusses the different examples of top-level overviews and may well conclude that some are more appropriate for the selection than the one originally discussed. This activity encourages students to revise their own top-level overviews, if and when they discover a more appropriate general structure. Later, when students are using ConStruct on their own, they feel free to make such modifications.

c. *Encourage reading to understand, not to memorize.* Students, especially adolescents, should be encouraged to focus their attention during reading on understanding, rather than trying to memorize details for teachers' tests. This can be done during the general introduction of the procedure, or as a general strategy that is not necessarily related to ConStruct. The latest that such a tactic should be introduced is when students read analytically during the second phase of the strategy. At the same time, students should be encouraged to identify those sections of the text they do not understand.

d. *Following analytical reading, second-stage graphic overviews should be developed as an extension of the superordinate overview.* While teaching students to learn the ConStruct Procedure, we have never ignored or de-emphasized the course content. Even in the initial stages of instruction, students discuss the content of each selection after their analytical readings. Because the students have been introduced to graphic overviews prior to the instructional sessions on ConStruct, we can elaborate on the superordinate graphic overview after they read the selection carefully. We do, however, avoid adding the specific level (nonessential) concepts to the overview at this time. Helping students make the distinction between key supporting details and nonessential details is an important part of this phase of the instructional program. Students often try to include nonessential details in the overview following the second reading, before they actually perceive how those specific concepts are related to the higher-level subordinate concepts. Teacher-guided discussion at this point is essential; just telling students to shift their focus from details to important subconcepts is not enough. Making such a shift is not easy to do; besides, the person who might be telling them to do so is the same person (their teacher) who is likely to have been testing nonessential details.

Students should begin to develop their own graphic overviews gradually, following the second reading. We suggest two steps. First, before students try this on their own, the teacher should elaborate on the top-level overview that has been placed on the board. Again, be sure to involve students in the discussion of where concepts fit into the overview and why. Encourage students to refer back to the text to clarify suggestions. Encourage them to justify inclusion of details at this point, so they can begin to sense the distinction between important supporting details and nonessential details. Where disagreements arise, however, a particular perspective should not be imposed on the students; their view of importance may well differ from that of a teacher (or other students) and their understanding is what we are trying to develop. After several sessions of group construction of second-stage graphic overviews, students are usually prepared to try them on their own. They will need to discuss their own efforts with others and will need encouragement in their efforts.

e. *Help students learn to scan.* Students who do not learn to differentiate in their three readings will quickly come to perceive this strategy as a cumbersome activity. Three analytical readings of the text is not part of this strategy. Students should be reminded that they have already read the material carefully and do not need to do so again. Instead, they need to review the text to locate those sections that were previously identified as "nonsense" to see if they now make sense. They also need to scan to locate those details that are nonessential, but are to be added to their overview.

f. *Students insert nonessential details into the graphic overview.* Details are much better understood and remembered when perceived in relation to other details and to more general concepts. Students have little difficulty accomplishing this final step if all has gone before as it should.

8. *Encourage practice, sharing, and discussion.* Once students have begun to get a sense of how to use this strategy, practice is essential to develop proficiency. If their proficiency is important to the teacher, nothing will demonstrate this to students more quickly than con-

tinued use of class time for practice. As students use ConStruct more frequently, they will make personal adjustments and fine-tunings that will work best for them. We have found it helpful to allow class time for discussions in small groups for students to share their successes and problems, especially when problems continue to arise due to inconsiderate texts.

CONCLUSION

Several key points related to the ConStruct procedure deserve reiteration. This strategy is intended for use with expository text, particularly those texts that are used in academic classrooms. It has never been examined as a way to approach other types of text, although it could be tried with some types of poetry (e.g., *Paradise Lost*) where the meaning is at times difficult to discern. Further, this strategy has only been empirically verified in cases where the concepts being learned are largely unfamiliar and the reader needs several exposures to the ideas before they begin to coalesce with some degree of familiarity. When a reader is already somewhat familiar with the concepts, he or she would probably find that other strategies (e.g., graphic postorganizers) would be a more appropriate choice. Students who use the spatial learning strategies discussed in this volume will learn to modify and apply them selectively according to their own needs. When this occurs, improved performance and understanding of textual material can be anticipated.

REFERENCES

Adler, M. J., & van Doren, C. (1972). *How to read a book.* New York: Simon & Schuster.
Anderson, T. H., & Armbruster, B. B. (1981). *Characteristics of school texts.* Paper presented at the Annual Meeting of the National Reading Conference, Dallas.
Barnes, H. V., Albanese, M., Schroeder, J., Weshselblatt, S., & Muehl, L. (1977). A reading course for medical students. In P. L. Stillman (Ed.), *Update: Introduction to clinical medicine.* Washington, DC: Association of American Medical Colleges.
Barron, R. F. (1969). The use of vocabulary as an advance organizer. In H. L. Herber & P. L. Sanders (Eds.), *Research in reading in the content areas: First year report.* Syracuse, NY: Reading and Language Arts Center, Syracuse University.
Barron, R. F., & Stone, V. F. (1974). The effect of student-constructed graphic post organizers upon learning vocabulary relationships. In P. L. Nacke (Ed.), *Interaction: Research and practice for college-adult reading* (NRC Yearbook 23). Clemson, SC: National Reading Conference.
Brown, A. L. (1981). Metacognition: The development of selective attention strategies for

learning from texts. In M. L. Kamil (Ed.), *Directions in reading: Research and instruction* (NRC Yearbook 30). Washington, DC: National Reading Conference.

Dansereau, D. F. (1978). The development of a learning strategies curriculum. In H. F. O'Neil, Jr. (Ed.), *Learning strategies.* New York: Academic Press.

Dansereau, D.F., Collins, K. W., McDonald, B. A., Holley, C. D., Garland, J. C., Diekhoff, G., & Evans, S. H. (1979). Development and evaluation of a learning strategy training program. *Journal of Educational Psychology, 71,* 64–73.

Deese, J., Estes, T., Schebilske, W., & Rotondo, J. (1980). *Learning from science textbooks: Text structure, reading strategies, and comprehension.* Symposium presented at the National Reading Conference, San Diego.

Durkin, D. (1980). Reading comprehension instruction in five basal reader series. *Reading Research Quarterly, 16,* 515–544.

Estes, T. H., & Vaughan, J. L. (in press). *Reading and learning in the content classroom* (2nd ed.). Boston: Allyn & Bacon.

Harste, J. C. (1982). *Text and context.* Presentation at the International Reading Association, New Orleans.

Holley, C. D., & Dansereau, D. F. (1981). Controlling for transient motivation in cognitive manipulation studies. *Journal of Experimental Education, 49,* 84–91.

Moore, D. W., & Readence, J. E. (1980). A meta-analysis of the effect of graphic organizers on learning from text. In M. L. Kamil & A. J. Moe (Eds.), *Perspectives on reading research and instruction* (NRC Yearbook 29). Washington, DC: National Reading Conference.

Pearson, P. D., & Johnson, D. D. (1978). *Teaching reading comprehension.* New York: Holt.

Smith, F. (1975). *Comprehension and learning.* New York: Holt.

Tierney, R. J., & Cunningham, J. W. (1980). *Research on teaching reading comprehension* (Tech. Rep. No. 187). Urbana, IL: University of Illinois, Center for the Study of Reading.

Tierney, R. J., Schallert, D. L., & Ulerick, S. (1981). *Learning from informative text.* Symposium presented at the Annual Meeting of the National Reading Conference, Dallas.

Vaughan, J. L. (1981). Analyzing reading comprehension: An initial investigation of an approach that combines skills area and concept level questions. In P. L. Anders (Ed.), *Research on reading in secondary schools* (Monograph no. 7). Tucson: University of Arizona.

Vaughan, J. L. (1982a). Use the ConStruct Procedure to foster active reading and learning. *Journal of Reading, 25,* 412–422.

Vaughan, J. L. (1982b). *Understanding and remembering.* Paper presented at the Annual Meeting of the International Reading Association, Chicago.

Vaughan, J. L., Stillman, P. L., & Sabers, D. L. (1978). *Developing ideational scaffolds during reading.* Paper presented at the Annual Meeting of the National Reading Conference, St. Petersburg.

Vaughan, J. L., Taylor, N. C., & Meredith, K. E. (1980). *Effect of the ConStruct Procedure on comprehension and retention of concepts presented in extended expository text.* Paper presented at the Annual Meeting of the International Reading Association, St. Louis.

CHAPTER 7

Schematizing: Technique and Applications

MARCEL J. A. MIRANDE

SCHEMATIZING: BACKGROUND

It is seldom that great renewals are made in the field of study skills. The greatest discovery in this area is perhaps that of silent reading. In 1960, Borges ascribed this discovery to Ambrosius (Bishop of Milan, ca. A.D. 384), basing this on a remark of Augustine's. In The Confessions (Part VI) Augustine describes something that made a great impression on him: Ambrosius was reading a book without saying the words aloud. As Borges described it, "the man made one direct jump from the written symbol to the understanding of it, omitting the sounds in between." If we are to believe Augustine, what led to this new method of reading was something quite astounding. "What I actually think," says Augustine, "is that he read in this manner in order to save his voice."

More recently, new developments have tried to find methods of easing "the jump from the written symbol to the abstract idea." A distinction can be made between textual aids and aids that depend on the student. Examples of textual aids are advance organizers and questions in the text. Examples of aids that depend on the student (i.e., student-bound) are underlining in the text and making notes. Schematizing, considered as a spatial learning strategy, is

149

a student-bound aid in the study of selected texts. It is a technique that enables a controlled representation of information to knowledge. As used here, the term *knowledge* is considered to comprise concepts and the relationships between them. These mutually dependent concepts can be represented via a two-dimensional network or schematization.

Schematizing has various educational applications. One of these is as a learning technique when studying selected texts. In this regard, schematizing is useful in making the distinction between central and subcomponents in the texts studied. In order to do this, the student selects the most important concepts from a text and their mutual relations, and represents them in the form of a diagram.

The technique of schematizing consists of a few rules and cautionary words. We state these first. Then, we describe a course in which students who have difficulty in studying their texts are taught the technique of schematizing. Then a few applications of schematizing are described; these are part of the courses of instruction for both teachers and students at the Center for Research into Higher Education at the University of Amsterdam (COWO).

THE TECHNIQUE OF SCHEMATIZING

The technique of schematizing consists of a heuristic method for creating a graphic representation of a study text. A *text* in this sense is considered to be connected discourse regarding a group of concepts. The aim of the heuristic is to clarify how these key-concepts and their interrelations can be identified in the text, and how they can be presented in a clear manner by using a diagram or schematization.

A schematization consists of labels (words in boxes) and symbols denoting relationships (lines and arrows). Labels point out the key terms in a text and symbols indicate the relationships between these concepts. A schematization is a two-dimensional representation of the essence of the text. See Figure 1 for an example.

The schematizing process comprises three primary activities: (1) the selection of labels, (2) the establishment of relationships into an ordered schematization. Each of these activities is subsequently described.

THE LABEL AND SPECIFICATION RULES

For the selection of labels from texts, the *label rule* is introduced. This rule is based on the distinction between topic and comment in texts. A *topic* is

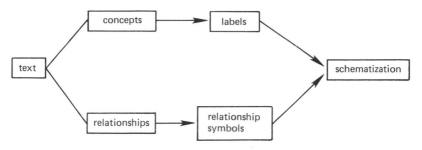

FIGURE 1. An example of a schematization.

a subject about which something is said in the text. The *comment* is what is said about the topic. The aim of the rule is to create a sharp distinction between labels and what is said about them—the *specification*. Labels are placed in the schematization; specifications are either not included or noted in a specifications list. The label rule reads as follows:

Those concepts become labels that are either: (1) introduced as new and explained in the text, or (2) already familiar but are further elaborated. Labels are represented by enclosing the identified concepts in boxes.

Put briefly, the student asks himself or herself: What concept is discussed in this sentence, this paragraph, this section? Whatever is said concerning that concept is termed its specification. In order to deal with these specifications, the *specification rule* is introduced:

A specification list consists of a list of labels. Attached to each label is a summary of the information given in the text about that label—such as characteristics or defining traits, examples, descriptions, and so on.

A specification list is thus a list containing condensed notes about one or more of the labels from the schematization. It is not always necessary to make a specifications list. If a student envisages that at a later point she or he will not be able to verbalize a schematization effectively, then making a specifications lists is well advised. I should stress here that not only descriptions or definitions of concepts are termed specifications, but also information about concepts. Further refinement on this rule is concerned with limiting, as much as possible, the number of specifications identified.

As an illustration of the two rules, consider the following:

An animal is termed omnivorous if it eats both vegetable and animal food.

The word *omnivorous* is introduced as a new concept, and that concept is defined. In this sentence, omnivorous is the label, and the specification is "animal that eats both vegetable and animal food."

The church, for generations the house of God, is now also used as a tea-room and a place in which to hold meetings.

In connection with the concept *church*, which we assume to be familiar, a new piece of information is given. This new information is the specification.

The Relation Rule

The second schematizing activity consists of identifying relations between the labels that have been selected. Here the *relation rule* is introduced. This is a pragmatic rule, concerned with the construction of schematizations.

From one label, at least one relationship should connect with another label or another relationship. It should be apparent from the text which label or which relationship is involved. Relationships are represented by lines or arrows.

The relation rule is not based on a classification of relationships between concepts, but simply identifies that a relationship exists between two labels. The precise nature of this relationship should either be remembered or inferred from the schematization. It should be sufficient simply to show lines where there is some relationship; however, we have discovered in practice that in order to read back a schematization it is useful to add some other relationship symbols.

As shown in Table 1, lines per se represent static relations such as classifications, characteristics, time–space, comparisons, and so forth. Arrows

TABLE 1

Relationship Symbols

symbol	description
⟶	dynamic relationships
——	static relationships
═══	similarity
⟵⟶	interaction
⟷⟷	denial

represent dynamic relationships such as conditional and cause-and-result. It is possible to conceive of further relationship symbols, for example, using plus and minus signs to indicate positive or negative influences. The individual using the symbol system is free to expand and personalize it.

THE ONLY ONCE RULE

The third schematizing activity consists in the construction of clearly organized schematizations. A number of practical tips are given in this connection and the last rule is introduced, the *only once rule:*

One specific label may only appear once in a schematization.

This rule implies that when a key concept appears more than once in a text, a further label should not be made. The application of this rule contributes to the coherence in the construction of schematizations and the integrated knowledge of a text. Practical tips for the construction of clear schematizations include:

1. *Directions*   The schematization should direct the reader from left to right, from top to bottom, or from a central point outwards.
2. *Crossing lines*   Avoid as much as possible lines and arrows that cross one another.
3. *Long lines*   Avoid long lines and arrows, especially if outside the schematization.
4. *Summarizing*   Define labels as succinctly as possible, but do not use alternative terminology.
5. *Trimming*   "Side shoots" can be trimmed, unless they form an essential part of the schematization.
6. *Shrinking*   Knowledge that is already familiar does not necessarily need to be included in the schematization.
7. *Composite Labels*   A composite label consists of two or more interrelated labels and is represented by enclosing the label combination in a box.

A TEACHING EXAMPLE

To better illustrate the application of the technique, a teaching example, based on a short passage of text, follows:

Memory usually implies the retention of a previous event, but a large number of processes are involved in this retention. We can define three logical catego-

FIGURE 2. A schematization of a text about memory.

ries of operations. First, there is acquisition, when the outside stimulus is perceived, and a representation (code) is made of it in a storage system. Second, there is storage, in which the representation is retained. Third, there is retrieval, in which the required information is sought and recalled from the storage system.

The specifications list is:

1. Memory: the retention of events
2. Operations: three logical categories
3. Acquisition: outside stimulus perceived, representation (code) of this input into storage
4. Storage: the representation is retained
5. Retrieval: desired information sought and produced from storage.

An example of the schematization is presented in Figure 2.

This teaching example is from our course in which students learn to apply the procedure of schematizing. The rules and recommendations are explained, after which students are able to make a schematization of this text, similar to that given in Figure 2. They are also able to employ a composite label in this schematization, as represented in Figure 3.

THE STUDY SKILLS COURSE: STUDYING VIA SCHEMATIZING

Initially, learning to schematize was a problem for students who had preexisting study difficulties. According to Daalder (1976), after half-a-day's

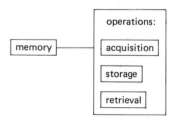

FIGURE 3. A schematization with a composite label.

instruction in schematizing, the students were not sufficiently able to apply the technique to their own field of study. Mirande and Camstra (1978) made the assumption that, although the principle of schematizing could be understood relatively quickly and easily, learning to apply the strategy required a carefully devised program, in which the components of schematizing were dealt with in a structured and sequential manner. With this premise, they developed a course that could be used either for individual-study or for group-study.

The program of the group-study course consisted of six sessions, each approximately 2 hours in length. For each session there was also some homework. Almost all of the students in the group-study program learned the system of schematizing. On the other hand, those students who took the individual-study program, although they had exactly the same exercises and the same amount of time—but without a teacher and not in a group situation—by and large did not learn the system of schematizing. These students, as well as the members of the group-study program, had enrolled in the course because they were having difficulties with their studies; an individual-study program was apparently inappropriate for this type of student.

Using the foregoing experiences, the course was restructured into its present format, which includes detailed specifications regarding the enrollment, the "intake," the exercises to be done, and the homework to be given (Mirande & van Bruggen, 1981). This standardized format is employed to carry out a longitudinal research program in which the course is presented in the same way many times. The enrollment attracts students who experience difficulties in distinguishing between major and subsidiary themes in texts. The "intake" consists of a lecture in which: (1) information is given about the content and method of the course, (2) an attempt is made to clarify the study difficulties of the student, and (3) arrangements are made regarding student participation in the course. The course, which consists of six 2-hour sessions, is presented as a rigidly organized exercise. Sections of sessions last from 10 to 20 minutes and, in these sessions, an explanation or example is given, an assignment is executed, or an executed assignment is discussed. The time required for learning schematizing includes the six 2-hour sessions plus 10 hours of homework assignments: a total of 22 hours.

Within this course, the technique of schematizing is embedded in a kind of SQ3R procedure. At the end of the course the participants should be able to apply this procedure to their own study texts. The components of the procedure are

1. Surveying books and articles
2. Skimming chapters
3. Selecting labels and relationships

4. Arranging schematizations and subschematizations
5. Evaluating the schematizations, and if necessary,
6. Specifying labels.

Surveying and skimming can be considered top-down strategies to discover the main arguments in a text. These strategies use the outer characteristics of a text. In contrast, the selection of labels and relationships can be seen as a bottom-up strategy for finding the main themes in a text, in which this theme has to be constructed piece-by-piece by the reader.

Each of the six components of the procedure is given a four-part treatment consisting of presentation, demonstration, exercise, and feedback. Specifically, textual ideas are presented, on which a schematization rule is based. The application of the rule is demonstrated. After each demonstration, students do exercises in connection with the level demonstrated. Then, the students discuss their results with a peer, providing each other with informal feedback. Finally, the teacher also provides feedback, including the solutions and comments on the students' solutions. Initially, the rules for schematizing are applied to short passages of text, then to longer passages, and finally to passages from the students' own material.

It should be emphasized that this course is oriented toward students who have existing study difficulties. Most participants have one or more of the following symptoms of unproductive study behavior: slow reading speed, difficulty in concentration, fixating on difficult passages, becoming swamped in details, making précis that are too long and complicated, memory problems, and a diffident attitude toward studying texts. These are the symptoms that are exposed to the fundamental assumptions of the course, and in particular, to the idea of schematizing. Nonetheless, by the end of the course most students are able to make a good schematization of a text consisting of about 2000 words.

While we have experienced success with schematizing in this context, the strategy does have some limitations, particularly with the type of students previously described. Specifically, these students have difficulty identifying relationships between concepts, and application of the technique is viewed as too time consuming. Future improvements in the course will be oriented toward solving these and other problems.

ADDITIONAL EDUCATIONAL
APPLICATIONS OF SCHEMATIZING

Schematizing can be used to achieve many ends (Breuker, 1980). In this section I discuss two general applications that have been investigated at the

COWO. These applications are schematizing as a study strategy (excluding the previously described application) and as an instructional strategy.

STUDY STRATEGY

As a study strategy, schematizing is introduced to various types of students, in various ways, with a sensitivity for different study goals. First, there is a "do-it-yourself" course for individual students who do not have specific study problems (Mirande, 1981). Second, there is an elective course, which is provided for various different types of study (Mirande & van Bruggen, 1981). Third, schematizing is embedded in a regular course in Modern History in which it is used as an aid to the study of texts and also as a means of provoking group discussion over texts that have been studied (van Driesum *et al.*, 1978). Fourth, it is used as a writing strategy in another elective course, "How to Solve your Thesis-Writing Problems" (Mirande and Wardenaar, 1983). Fifth, schematizing is used in a course for secondary-school pupils on how to do homework (Mirande & Broerse, 1984).

An interesting observation from these varied offerings of schematizing is that secondary students find the technique easy to learn and apply, whereas university students still experience difficulties in schematizing after a course that consists of 22 hours of training. Secondary-school pupils appear to have less difficulty in applying the strategy with their shorter and simpler texts. Specifically, they can limit themselves to passages of text that are short units; identifying and extracting macrostructures from such passages is not required. In contrast, university students have to extract the macrostructures from the texts, and for such a bottom-up process, schematizing does not work adequately.

INSTRUCTIONAL STRATEGY

As an instructional strategy, schematizing is presented in various training courses for university teachers at the University of Amsterdam. These instructional development courses are planned and developed by the COWO and generally employ a self-study approach to learning, using a course book as a starting point. Four of these course books employ schematizing as a strategy.

In the course book *Outlining Subject Matter,* schematizing is presented as a technique for formulating study goals (Breuker, 1980). Using as a starting point the fact that students have to study certain texts, the diagrams (schematizations) of these texts are used to represent the content of the study goals. In the course book *Lecturing,* schematizing is used in two ways (van Hout, Mirande, & Smulling, 1981). First, it is used for the selection and organization of material, so as to establish a certain order for dealing with the subject matter. Second, it is used to present information during lectures, usually via an overhead projector. In the course book *Organizing Practical Work,* schematizing is used as a means of reaching agreement over the content of a practicum that is to be performed by the student (Tromp, 1978). Specifically, teachers involved with a particular practicum make individual schematizations of its proposed content. Then, group discussions are held and consensus is obtained regarding the actual content of the practicum. In contrast to the formulation of study goals from study texts, the application of schematizing for practicums and lectures does not require complicated instructions and can be more quickly and flexibly applied.

THE EFFECTIVENESS OF SCHEMATIZATION: A DEMONSTRATION

In 1982, Breuker constructed a simple experiment intended to convince university teachers of the usefulness of schematizations. This miniexperiment is carried out in about 10 minutes and usually with great success. Participants are divided into an experimental group (E) and a control group (D). For the duration of 2 minutes both groups are given the subsequent text. The experimental group is then shown a schematization of the text for 1 minute (see Figure 4), while the control group uses this extra minute to continue reading the text. After this, the participants answer two multiple choice questions on the text, without references to the text or the schematization. The text is (based on a passage from Fry, 1969):

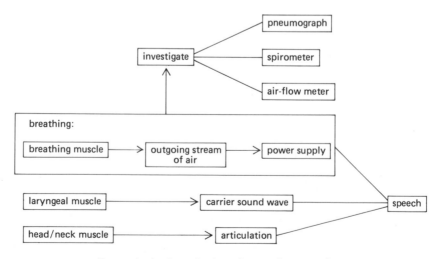

Figure 4. A schematization of a text about speech.

Three main muscle systems are employed in producing speech. The breathing muscles provide the outgoing stream of air, which is the power supply for speech. The laryngeal muscles generate the carrier sound wave of speech, and the muscles of the head and neck perform the movements of articulation. These three functions constitute variations in speech. Aspects of breathing may be investigated by using: a pneumograph to measure changes in the circumference of the thorax and the abdomen, a spirometer for showing the volume of air inspired or expired, and an air-flow meter to register variations in air-flow during a speech sequence.

The two questions are

1. What characteristics of speech can be investigated by using a combination of pneumograph, spirometer, and air-flow meter?
   a. Carrier sound wave
   b. Power supply
   c. Articulation
   d. I have to make a guess.
2. Which muscles control articulation?
   a. Head–neck
   b. Laryngeal
   c. Breathing muscles
   d. I have to make a guess.

Two predictions apply to this experiment. The first prediction is that no differences will be observed between the two groups on Question 2. This question is concerned with an explicit piece of information in the text, and the schematization does not add anything to this; it is, therefore, a control question. The second prediction is that the two groups will differ on Question 1. This question is concerned with relationships between the two main

TABLE 2

FREQUENCY OF ALTERNATIVES CHOSEN BY THE
EXPERIMENTAL (E) AND CONTROL (C) GROUPS

Group	Question 1		Question 2	
	E	C	E	C
Alternatives				
a	0	1	10	10
b	6	1	0	0
c	2	6	0	0
d	4	3	2	1

parts of the text: the description of speech (muscles used, characteristics) and the method of investigation. The link between these two main parts is the concept *breathing,* which is made explicit in the schematization.

On the last occasion when the experiment was carried out, there were 23 participants and the results were as shown in Table 2. The correct answers are respectively "b" and "a" and the results were as predicted. Specifically, the answers of the two groups to Question 1 are significantly different, whereas the answers to Question 2 are not significantly different. Perhaps Ambrosius, the first to use silent reading, would be surprised at this result. Perhaps he would even develop a preference for texts with lots of schematizations, so that he could save not only his voice, but also his memory.

DISCUSSION

In this chapter, the technique of schematizing was described. In its most typical application, as a study strategy for students with study problems, its training is embedded in a study skills course that generally employs a modified SQ3R approach. In general, the strategy has been effective in this context, although there are many research questions that have not been investigated as yet.

In a wider vein, the technique has beem employed as a study strategy and an instructional strategy in a variety of applications at the University of Amsterdam. In this regard, little empirical evidence has been collected to support its efficacy; however, experiential data suggest that it is an effective, general-purpose educational strategy.

REFERENCES

Augustine, Saint (1981). *Confessions.* Harmondsworth, England: Penguin Books.
Borges, J. L. (1960). *Otras inquisiciones.* Buenos Aires: Emece Editores.
Breuker, J. A. (1980). *In kaart brengen van leerstof.* Utrecht/Antwerpen: Het Spectrum.
Breuker, J. A. (1982). Gaan waar de woorden gaan. *Bullentin Leren van Volwassenen, 1,* 3–24.
Daalder, M. (1976). *Leren door fileren. Een cursus in het hanteren van een analysetechniek voor het begrijpen en onthouden van leerstof: Theorie en constructie.* (Doctoral dissertation). University of Amsterdam.
Driesum, R. van, *et al.* (1978). *Handboekbegeleiding met schema's. Evaluatie van een eerstejaars werkcollege nieuwe geschiedenis waarbij gebruik gemaakt werd van de schematiseermethode.* (COWO Report.) Amsterdam: University of Amsterdam.
Fry, D. G. (1969). Phonetics, experimental. In A. R. Meethan & R. A. Hudson (Eds.), *Encyclopedia of linguistics, information, and control.* London: Pergamon Press.

Hout, J. F. M. J. van, M. J. A. Mirande, & E. B. Smuling, (1981) *Geven van hoorcolleges.* Utrecht/Antwerpen: Het Spectrum.

Mirande, M. J. A. (1981). *Studeren door schematiseren.* Utrecht/Antwerpen: Het Spectrum.

Mirande, M. J. A., & Broerse, P. H. (1984) *Al doende. Een kursus in het in schema zetten van leerstof voor leerlingen van het voortgezet onderwijs* Groningen: Wolters Noordhoff.

Mirande, M. J. A., & Bruggen, J. M. van (1981) *De schematiseerkurus, draaiboek voor het geven van de kurus "Studeren door schematiseren.* (COWO Report.) Amsterdam: University of Amsterdam.

Mirande, M. J. A., & Camstra, B. (1978). *Schematiseren als leerstrategie: een exploratief onderzoek naar de kursus "Leren door schematiseren."* Paper presented at the Onderwijs Research Dag - National Congress, Utrecht.

Mirande, M. J. A. & E. Wardenaar. (1983) *Scriptieproblemen.* Utrecht/Antwerpen: Het Spectrum.

Tromp, D. (1978) *Het opzetten van practica.* (COWO Report.) Amsterdam: University of Amsterdam.

CHAPTER 8

Schematizing: The Empirical Evidence

BERT CAMSTRA   *JAN VAN BRUGGEN*

LEARNING BY SCHEMATIZING: AN OVERVIEW

Researchers who set out to investigate the functioning and effectiveness of a study skills course such as Learning by Schematizing (LbS), face a host of research problems and research questions. These pertain to both the methodology and the substantive field of research. The problems of methodology are roughly those of any "field research" paradigm. Some examples include (1) the use of volunteers, who often have biased reasons for participating as subjects, (2) frequent inability to randomly assign subjects to treatment, (3) intrusion by many experimental artifacts, (4) treatments tending to be either too time-consuming for students or too trivially short, and (5) the number of subjects typically being too small to provide sufficient statistical power.

Since Entwisle's (1960) review of research on study skills courses, researchers in this area have frequently received harsh criticism of their work. For example, Santeusanio (1974) concluded that there is insufficient evidence that college reading programs serve their intended purposes, because almost all of the favorable outcomes can be attributed to poor research meth-

163

SPATIAL LEARNING STRATEGIES
Techniques, Applications, and Related Issues

TABLE 1

CLASSIFICATION OF VARIABLES INVESTIGATED IN THE PRESENTED SERIES OF STUDIES

A. Antecedent variables	B. Treatments	C. Immediate effects	D. Intermediate effects	E. Ultimate effects
1. Study problems	1. Crash course	1. Participation	1. Amount of schematizing	1. Study results
2. Study experience	2. Closely supervised small groups	2. Drop out from course	2. Changes in schematizing behavior	2. Drop out from curriculum
3. Study behavior	3. "Active" lecturing	3. Competence in schematizing	3. Pass–fail data	—
4. Voluntary vs. obligatory	4. Part of wider study skills course	4. Evaluative opinions	4. Follow-up opinions	—
5. Intelligence: CMS	5. Integrated in study of subject matter	5. Text comprehension	5. Study behavior	—
6. Intelligence: CMU	6. Discipline—specific course	—	—	—

odology. Contrary to this conclusion, Fairbanks (1974) states that research methodology in this area has improved. Nevertheless, van Bruggen (1980) concluded that many studies still suffer from severe methodological weaknesses that sometimes explain the favorable outcomes. Research on schematizing is burdened with the same methodological problems inherent in any "field-research" project. These inherent problems are not extensively discussed in this chapter, but are pointed out where relevant.

A structuring of this field of research should preferably be done in the form of a substantive theory of studying, learning, and comprehending text. Elements of this theory are presented by Breuker in Chapter 2, present volume. Additional elements are provided by van Bruggen (1980) in a literature survey. Here, we take a modest approach, in the form of a simple classification of the variables that have figured in the experiments to be discussed. The classification conforms closely to established principles of the methodology of empirical research. The variables are classified into the following five categories: (1) antecedent variables, (2) treatments, (3) immediate effects, (4) intermediate effects, and (5) ultimate effects.

The classification itself is presented in Table 1. The categorization does not pretend to be a theory; it merely functions to organize the relations that have been investigated. Obviously, many of these so-called variables are really conglomerates of variables that could be broken down into more specific lists and structures of variables. Moreover, the series of entries under the heading of "B. Treatments" are not really variables themselves, but instances of the variable "treatments." The present format, however, is used for the sake of completeness and clarity.

In principle, all variables can be associated with all other variables. The set of relationships that could be investigated runs into the hundreds. The selection of those variables and their relationships that were actually investigated in the set of studies presented here has been guided by (1) some theory of text processing, knowledge acquisition, and study behavior, (2) some didactic and pedagogical considerations, (3) some methodological considerations, and (4) a lot of practical considerations. The overview presented in Table 1 helps the reader situate the various subsequent studies.

THE SERIES OF STUDIES

From the beginning of 1976, a series of studies have been conducted into the functioning and effects of LbS. In this section we present summary descriptions of the entire series, emphasizing the main aspects of each. This is done in chronological order, putting the research in temporal perspective. Only the most salient results are presented. In the subsequent section we present the results of the series by topic rather than by chronology. At the end of each description, references are given to more detailed reports of the studies. Each study will carry a label or title for easy reference.

THE 1976 PILOT STUDY

A preliminary version of LbS was developed by Daalder in 1975 and was tested in March, 1976, in a laboratory-type experiment. Thirty-five first-year economics students volunteered to be randomly assigned to an experimental and a control group. The experiment consisted of a training session for the E-group, and a testing session for both groups, 2 days later. The E-group studied the LbS coursebook individually, during one day, including performing the exercises in the coursebook.

In the 2-hour testing session, all students were first instructed to study a macroeconomics chapter. The controls were asked to study "as they were used to" (i.e., to use their normal study methods; cf. Holley & Dansereau, 1981). The experimentals were asked to study by schematizing and to make both an initial and a reorganized schematization of the chapter. After this, both groups were given a 30-minute reproduction task, without the texts. Specifically, the controls were instructed to produce a summary of the text and the experimentals were instructed to reproduce their final schematization. Finally, all of the students took a 60-item two-choice test on the chapter.

The results can be summarized as follows:

1. The amount of time that experimentals had to acquire the schematization method was insufficient; consequently, they did not learn how to schematize well.
2. No significant differences were found between the two groups in terms of text comprehension.

The pilot study did not demonstrate the effectiveness of either the course or the schematization procedure. It was functional in showing that better ways should be devised to teach the schematization procedure. It also indicated that (at least at that stage) more qualitative methods might be more informative as to the effects (Camstra, 1979; Daalder, 1976).

IN-DEPTH STUDY OF PROBLEM STUDENTS

A thoroughly revised version of LbS was given to students with study problems from October through December, 1977. The 23 participating students were divided into a closely supervised group (12) and a self-study group (11). This was done to determine if schematizing could be effectively learned by self-study. The closely supervised students were taught schematizing in six weekly meetings of 2 hours each, in groups containing three students per one instructor. Much attention was given to applying the procedure to texts from their own discipline, to which the homework was also directed. The self-study students were given the LbS workbook (designed for self-study, including exercises and feedback) as well as the same learning schedule that the small groups followed. They, however, had to manage their own learning progress.

The results can be summarized as follows:

1. Of the 12 closely supervised students, one dropped out during the course; the other 11 spent between 20 and 35 hours learning the technique. Of the 11 self-study students, 7 apparently dropped out (because they did not respond to follow-up attempts).

2. Only 3 of the self-study students learned the schematization procedure reasonably or sufficiently well, whereas 11 of the students in the closely supervised group mastered the technique.

3. It takes an extremely well-organized and motivated student to learn schematizing by self-study.

4. Around the third meeting, a *schematization crisis* appears, which is characterized by the students' strong doubts (e.g., schematizing longer passages still takes too much time, doubting the adequacy of their products, questioning the utility of the technique). A strong tendency to quit must be overcome here, which takes persuasion and encouragement from the instructors. When this is overcome, the crisis passes and the students become versed in schematizing. They need less time, have greater confidence, and acquire a personal style of schematizing.

5. The students generally held favorable opinions about the strategy at the end of the course, and all but one planned to use it regularly.

6. A follow-up questionnaire 3 months later showed that about half of the students had integrated schematizing into their regular study behavior. Most of the others had not done so either because they thought they had not really learned the method well enough (four students) or thought it too time-consuming (two) (Camstra, 1979; Mirande & Camstra, 1978).

A LARGE-SCALE LECTURING APPROACH

In the autumn of 1977, a large-scale implementation of LbS was conducted with 350 first-year psychology and pedagogy students in Leuven, Belgium. For various reasons, the study could not be performed as planned and should be considered a failure. However, it strongly reinforced the preceding finding about the schematization crisis and the necessity of going on with training well beyond the initial acquisition of the procedure. It also strongly suggested that schematizing is a skill that can only be acquired with thorough practice. Lecturing, even when some practice is included, clearly does not allow the amount of practice and feedback necessary for adequately applying the technique (Camstra, 1979).

Study with Students Majoring in Education

In January through March, 1978, schematizing was integrated into a broad course in study skills, which consisted of eight weekly meetings of 2 hours each, with homework. The first five meetings were dedicated to more conventional aspects of studying (e.g., improving the study environment, flexible reading, study planning, test preparation, paper writing). The last three meetings were dedicated to schematizing. The course was given in discussion group format to 29 volunteers, all of whom were majoring in education. Data pertaining to study behavior and study progress were obtained from both the experimental group and a large control group, before the course and after the course (study behavior after 5 weeks, study progress after 3 months).

The results can be summarized as follows:

1. The students that volunteered for the course were (compared with the control group of nonparticipating students) already running 1.7 *credit points* (points of credit given for each successfully completed course) behind (at the beginning of the course in December). (One point equals 40 hours of study; one year of study equals 40 credit points.) They managed to reduce this to .6 credit points during the course by making good use of "second chance" examinations. At the end of the academic year they had turned this deficit into an advantage over the controls of 2.4 credit points.

2. The experimental group differed in a few respects in the structure of their study behavior, as determined by a study behavior questionnaire developed earlier (Grosveld & van Hoof, 1976), which yields five primary factors. Initially, they reported their own study behavior as using less "study by repetition," more "study [being] test-oriented," and less "study [being] doggedly conscientious." After the course, these differences had disappeared and the experimental students reported more often that they "structure and summarize subject matter on paper."

3. It should be stressed that the preceding data pertain to the study skills course as a whole, not only to schematizing. A questionnaire oriented toward schematizing showed that the students thought they had learned to schematize "somewhat" and planned to apply it "a little bit." In general, their opinions about schematizing were favorable, but cautiously so.

4. A follow-up 5 weeks after the course showed that approximately 70% of the respondents incorporated schematizing into their regular study repertoire. These students felt that it both changed and improved their studying (Camstra, 1979; Camstra, Metten & Mirande, 1979).

INTEGRATING SCHEMATIZING WITH HISTORY STUDENTS

Roughly in the same period, January–April, 1978, schematizing was taught to 29 first-year history students, integrated within their regular discussion course on modern history. For two reasons this study did not yield any sufficiently hard data on schematizing, although it was informative as to how *not* to teach schematizing and as to students' opinions of schematizing. First, insufficient time was once again allotted to learning schematizing. It was viewed as a sideline activity, because only two meetings were specifically addressed to it. The students never even approached the "schematization crisis" and hardly learned schematizing at all. Second, the instructor developed a private variation of schematizing, in which the method turned into a method of text analysis rather than comprehension organization, which tended to degrade schematizations into boxed indices of the text instead of representing the conceptual structure (Camstra, 1979; van Driesum *et al.*, 1979).

After this series of studies, some firm decisions were made regarding the conduct of the course. In the first place it had become convincingly clear that schematizing is something to be really learned and thoroughly mastered, before any effects may be expected. This has been the impetus for the development of a very thorough "scenario" for teaching schematizing (Mirande, 1981, and Chapter 7, present volume; Mirande & van Bruggen, 1981). Though flexible enough to be implemented in a variety of ways, this scenario stresses the importance of sufficient time for learning the method and training its application. It also includes the administration of a set of tests. This latter aspect is a consequence of a systematic revision of the research strategy, applied since 1979.

In this revised strategy the main emphasis was shifted away from trying to "prove" that schematizing leads to better results, and toward trying to investigate its functioning within text comprehension processes. It was also concluded that it was necessary to develop adequate instruments for that purpose, and to collect data on a sufficient number of students. Therefore, since 1980 the course has been offered to students of the University of Amsterdam on the following basis. The course is intended for volunteers, who are allowed to enroll on the condition that they participate in the testing sessions and that they adhere to a stringent schedule. This was intended to counteract dropout during the course. To avoid demotivating these volunteers, the control group approach has been dropped. The design bears some resemblance to the "recurrent institutional cycle design" of Cook and Campbell (1979). In this design a series of treatments is administered to consecutive groups of students with varying pre- and posttests, after which aggregate pre- and posttest means can be compared. Although the design does not control for every threat to validity, it is sufficiently informative.

Another shift in emphasis has to do with the students' cognitive abilities. Breuker (Chapter 2, present volume) argues that insight and understanding of a difficult text may correlate with reasoning skills. Frijda (1977) discusses the close parallel of problem solving and text comprehension, especially the flexibility of the reader in selecting a (cognitive) schema that fits the text. A schema in this sense has close resemblance to the configuration of concepts that must be actualized in solving problems such as linear syllogisms. In Guilford's (1967) structure of intellect (SI) model this ability is called "cognition of semantic systems" (CMS). We, therefore, decided to investigate the hypothesis that CMS correlates substantially with text comprehension. If schematizing helps the reader in recognizing appropriate schemata, the course should be more beneficial for those students with a relatively low CMS ability, than for those with a high CMS score. Specifically, schematizing may provide low CMS students with a tool "to fill a void," while for high CMS students the method may be a clumsy way of externalizing what they used to do automatically and smoothly anyway.

THE LONGITUDINAL SERIES

According to the preceding procedures, LbS has been given nine times since the beginning of 1980, for a total of 206 students. The series is summarized in Table 2. The course is taught in six meetings of 2 hours each,

TABLE 2

OVERVIEW OF COURSES GIVEN AS A PART OF STUDY 6

Study 6	Course given in		Participants	Details
a	May	1980	17	Tryout of scenario
b	November	1980	23	Tryout of revised scenario
c	January	1981	14	Discipline-specific for andragogy students
d	March	1981	17	
e	May	1981	48	Two groups
f	September	1981	18	Discipline-specific for pedagogy students
g	October	1981	41	
h	January	1982	14	Discipline-specific for psychology students
i	January	1982	14	Discipline-specific for pedagogy students
			206	

preceded by an intake procedure and including a pretest and a posttest. In the first meeting the students have to study a text and take a test about that text. The texts and tests have been carefully analyzed, developed, and improved over the years. The details thereof have been reported by van Bruggen (1981a). During the course a CMS test is administered, consisting of 50 linear syllogisms (Kunst, 1978).

The data of these series of courses have been accumulated and analyzed jointly. They are presented in the next section of this chapter. These data have partly been reported in van Bruggen (1981a); some are presented for the first time.

THE LONG-TERM STUDY OF EDUCATION MAJORS

The last study to be reported pertains to a long-term following of a group of students of education, who took a course in schematizing in the beginning of 1979. Because the 1978 course in study skills turned out to be successful (please refer back to Study 4, with students of education), it was expanded and revised the next year, and many more students volunteered. Both the course and the study have been the responsibilities of our colleagues Metten and van Balen, who kindly made their data available to us.

The course was split into two parts, the first given in November, 1978, and directed toward general reading–study skills and the second given in January, 1979, and dedicated completely to schematizing. Twenty-four students participated in the basic course only, 34 in the combined basic and schematizing course, and 4 in the schematizing course only. Study progress and dropout percentages of these groups, as well as of the students that did not take any of the courses, have been collected at semiannual intervals up to September, 1981, and are presented in the following section.

FINDINGS

In this section we present the results of the preceding series of studies. We have grouped them topically rather than chronologically, and the order more or less follows the paradigm of Table 1. Where applicable, the various separate studies are mentioned.

MASTERY OF THE TECHNIQUE

Before examining the effects that schematizing may have on a variety of processing factors, it must, of course, first be ascertained whether the students have learned to schematize. In principle, this can be done in two ways, subjectively and objectively. The *subjective* method consists of having the students self-report on their own competence. This has been routinely done by means of an evaluative questionnaire. The *objective* way consists of having experts (expert schematizers and/or subject experts) judge the quality of the products (schematizations) of the subjects. This has been done informally in a number of studies. A better alternative would consist of an "automatic scoring procedure" for judging the correspondence between a subject's schematization and some "ideal" or criterion schematization. This latter approach has been attempted a few times, but has never been satisfactorily implemented (van Bruggen, 1981b; Camstra, 1979; Daalder, 1976).

The results presented here generally pertain to self-report evaluative data, sometimes checked informally against expert judgement of subjects' schematizations. We have gained the impression, by the way, that subjects are quite capable of judging the extent to which they have (or have not) mastered the schematizing technique.

In a couple of studies we clearly found that the subjects did not master the technique, or barely touched the surface. This was the case in Studies 1 (the 1976 pilot study), 3 (the large–scale lecturing approach) and 5 (integrating schematizing with history students). In all cases, the amount of training was deficient (4–6 hours in total).

In Study 2 (in-depth study of problem students), it was determined, on the basis of both self-opinion and objective judgement of the quality of student schematizations, that all 11 students in the closely supervised groups and 3 of the 4 self-study students had mastered the schematization procedure reasonably or sufficiently well. Half of those who considered themselves sufficiently good schematizers, expected to become reasonably good schematizers in the near future.

In Study 4 (study with students majoring in education), three meetings were dedicated to schematizing, directly after which the questionnaires were completed. Of the 29 students, 4 thought that they could schematize "reasonably well," 20 "somewhat," and 5 "not well at all." It is likely that this is once more related to insufficient training time. In Study 6 (the longitudinal series), of the 58 students (Studies 6b, 6d, and 6e) 33% evaluated their mastery as sufficient to good, 27% had their doubts, and 31% evaluated their mastery as insufficient.

Examining the students' schematizations of self-selected, longer text passages corroborated their self-reports of meager mastery of the technique at the end of the course. Apparently, preparing a schematization of a longer text poses some serious problems to the novice schematizer, particularly for those students that had the a priori habit of studying by creating overly detailed abstracts (i.e., they find it hard to reduce the number of labels selected).

Others have difficulties in preparing a "good-looking" schematization (see Mirande, Chapter 7, present volume, for details on the requirements of acceptable schematizations).

Our overall conclusion is that the *essentials* of schematizing can be taught in a course such as we have offered. The resulting skill, however, is at a minimum performance level. Transforming schematizing into a smoothly operating study technique takes more time and more effort. Therefore, we plan to redesign the course to give the students more opportunity to practice on longer passages of text.

IMMEDIATE EFFECTS

Immediate effects refer to those measured during and directly after the course. Under this heading, we discuss participation and dropout data, evaluative opinions of subjects and text comprehension.

Participation and Drop-out Rate

Clearly, dropout rate during the course is dependent on a great variety of factors: the duration of the course, the nature of the subjects, whether participation is voluntary or not, the quality of the teaching, and so forth.

TABLE 3

DROPOUT PERCENTAGES FOR THE SERIES OF STUDIES

Study	N: initial	N: final	% Drop out	Remarks
1	29	29	0	1-Day course
2	12	11	8	Closely supervised subjects
	11	4	64	Self-study subjects
3	320	100	—	To be ignored
4	40	29	27	8-week course
5	—	—	0	To be ignored
6a	17	14	18	
6b	23	18	22	
6c	14	14	0	
6d	17	8	53	
6e	48	34	29	
6f	18	18	0	
6g	41	24	41	
6h	14	14	0	
6i	14	8	43	
Total	269	194	28	Excluding studies 1, 3, 5

Nevertheless, we present complete dropout data, and try to draw informative conclusions from them.

Dropout rates have little meaning at this point for Studies 1 (the 1976 pilot study), because that was a one-day course; 3 (the large-scale lecturing approach), because the dropout rate occurred in a course that was a failure in many respects; and 5 (integrating schematizing with history students), because the dropout rate reflected an attitude toward the discussion class as a whole rather than toward schematizing.

The dropout rates from the other studies are presented in Table 3. In general, we may conclude that approximately 28% of the students that begin the LbS course do not complete it, for whatever reason. These results parallel those of comparable Dutch courses offered on a volunteer basis. The dropout is partially distributed at random over the course (illness, etc.) but occurs most often after the fourth session. Informal contacts with dropouts suggest that the slow pace of the course encourages some students to go at their own pace, thus leaving the course itself behind. Problems encountered with schematizing longer passages also appears to be a reason for dropping out. In summary, a 28% dropout rate, while certainly leaving room for improvement is neither uncommon nor dramatic for this kind of extracurricular course.

Evaluative Opinion of Students

As said earlier, a questionnaire soliciting the students' opinions on a variety of aspects regarding schematizing was routinely administered at the end of the course. We restrict our comments to those studies in which it was determined that the subjects had actually learned to schematize.

Study 2 (In-depth Study of Problem Students).   Opinion data were collected from 10 students in the closely supervised groups and 4 students in the self-study group. Of these 14 students, 13 valued the method positively; most often they reported that this was because the method gives structure and orientation for the necessary study activities. The same number (13 students) reported that they were going to apply the method in their regular study behavior. Of the 12 students with study problems, 9 felt that the method contributed to the solution of their problems; the other 3 found the method too time-consuming.

Study 4 (Study with Education Students).   As previously discussed, only three sessions of this study were dedicated to schematizing and, consequently, the students did not rate their competence at the end of those three meetings very highly. This was also reflected in the evaluation questionnaires. Of 24 students, 6 planned to use the method regularly, 14 "a little bit," and 4 "not at all." Of 29 students, 9 felt that the method contributed to the solution of their study problems; for 16, it contributed "somewhat," and for 4 students, "not at all." The extent to which students felt that schematizing was an aid to solving their study problems was strongly correlated with their self-perceived competence in schematizing ($r = .69$, $N = 29$). Of the 29 students, 12 expected the method to help them get better grades, 9 did not think so, and 8 had no idea.

Study 6 (The Longitudinal Series). The questionnaire responses from Studies 6b, d, and e were coded as positive, neutral, or negative. The data are summarized in Table 4, based on percentages of the 58 subjects. Generally, the students' opinions about the schematizing method and the course were fairly positive. Subjects tended to report that schematizing represented a solution to their problems, even though complete mastery of the technique was to be achieved via additional practice after the course. The students were pleased with both the *content* of the course and its rather rigid organization.

Text Comprehension

The effects of schematizing on text comprehension and the hypothesized correlations with the ability CMS have been investigated since the Novem-

TABLE 4

EVALUATIVE OPINIONS OF STUDENTS IN PERCENTAGES[a]

Question number	Question	Positive	Neutral	Negative	No reply
1	Did the course focus on your specific problem?	53	31	10	5
2	Did the course help in discriminating between main and peripheral topics?	69	12	9	10
3	Did the course correspond to your expectations?	67	17	9	2
4	Do you now feel more confident toward texts?	65	21	7	7
5	Are you competent in schematizing?	33	27	31	9
7	Have you already tried to apply schematizing?	60	N/A	40	0
9	Did you like the stringent course organization?	72	9	17	2
10	Did you appreciate the intake talk?	62	15	9	10

[a] $N = 58$; Questions 6 and 8 are qualitative.

ber, 1980, study (Study 6b). Two differing texts were used for this purpose. The first presented a survey of some basic immunological processes and the second presented concepts of Galperin's theory of the formation of mental actions. Both texts were about 1700 words in length. Two 25-question multiple-choice tests were used as dependent measures. These exams are subsequently referred to as Immunology and Galperin.

CMS was measured by means of the test, Conclusions IV (Kunst, 1978). This test consists of 50 linear syllogisms and is well-known for its high loading on the CMS factor. As a control variable, we added a vocabulary test developed by Elshout and Keizer (discussed in Elshout, 1976), measuring the ability known as "cognition of semantic units" (CMU) in the SI model. Knowledge of concepts and the ability to derive the meaning of a concept in its context seemed the most plausible rival SI factor.

The Immunology test had an average reliability $(K-R_{20})$ of .66. The Galperin test only had a mean reliability of about .47 (possibly, due to the lower reliabilities for two small groups). If we take these two groups to be exceptions, a reliability of about .60 may be assumed. Conclusions IV has a mean reliability of .89, whereas the vocabulary test has an average reliability of .82 (the last two being split-half reliabilities).

Excluding those students with missing test scores, we combined the groups and calculated the correlations between the text comprehension scores and the Guilford test scores (see Table 5). A moderate correlation exists between the comprehension test and the CMS scores, whereas the correlations with the CMU scores are virtually zero. This result supports the proposition that CMS is relevant in text comprehension.

There is, however, additional evidence to support the importance of CMS in this context. Specifically, it seems reasonable to expect rather low CMS scores among those who encounter problems in text comprehension and enroll in a course like this. Kunst (1978) tested first-year psychology students and found a mean score of 21.0. Elshout (1976) used a parallel test and obtained mean scores ranging from 15 to 22. As expected, our students

TABLE 5

INTERCORRELATIONS OF THE TEST SCORES, POOLED
GROUPS ($N = 106$)

Correlates	Galperin	CMU	CMS
Immunology test score	.44	−.04	.45
Galperin test score	—	.06	.33
CMU	.06	—	−.16

TABLE 6

COMPARISON OF CMS AND CMU SCORES BETWEEN STUDENTS WHO STAY IN COURSE
AND STUDENTS WHO DO NOT FINISH COURSE

	CMS			CMU		
	$\bar{X}$	SD	N	$\bar{X}$	SD	N
Course completed	11.7	6.54	122	21.7	7.61	122
Dropouts	9.9	6.32	34	19.5	7.12	46
Total	11.3	6.56	156	21.1	7.52	168
t (diff.) completed–dropouts	1.43	(df = 154, n.s.)		1.70	(df = 168, n.s.)	

($N = 156$) clearly scored low on CMS (see Table 6). (CMU scores for dropouts and "graduates" are also presented in Table 6.)

The first step in the analysis of comprehension scores consisted of comparing the various pre- and posttest means of the Galperin test and the pre- and posttest means of the Immunology test. For this comparison, separate one-way analyses of covariance (ANCOVA) were conducted, with CMS as the covariate ($N = 106$). The results are presented in Tables 7 and 8 for Immunology and Tables 9 and 10 for Galperin. None of these analyses were statistically significant.

There is no evidence that schematizing, in the short term, results in an improvement of text understanding as measured by our tests. (However, see Holley and Dansereau, Chapter 4, present volume, for arguments related to differential effects of exam formats.) Students complained that using the technique during the final session (study-test) was too time-consuming. Their skill with the technique apparently was insufficiently developed to

TABLE 7

ANALYSIS OF COVARIANCE (ANCOVA) IMMUNOLOGY TEST USED AS PRETEST AND AS POSTTEST

Source	SS[a]	df	MS[b]	F ratio	
Covariate CMS	272.54	1	273.54	24.94	.001
Pretest vs. posttest	9.69	1	9.69	.89	.349
Residual	1125.74	103	—	—	—
	1407.96				

[a]Sum of squares.
[b]Mean square.

TABLE 8

MEANS OF IMMUNOLOGY TEST, USED AS PRETEST
AND AS POSTTEST

Test	$\bar{X}$	N
Pretest	18.28	61
Posttest	<u>17.66</u>	<u>45</u>
	18.02	106

schematize a difficult text at a normal pace (45 minutes were alloted for studying the criterion texts).

Because of the apparent importance of CMS to text processing, the students were trichotomized on these scores. The means on the two exams for these subgroups are presented in Table 11. (Obviously, the subgrouped means are consistent with the previously discussed correlations, and are presented to highlight that relationship.) Schematizing appears to be detrimental for low CMS students in the case of the Immunology text and beneficial in the case of the Galperin text, thereby suggesting a passage-by-treatment interaction. However, the strong possibility of a testing-effect cannot be ignored, particularly given some of the low reliability coefficients that were observed.

We do feel (but this is very much an a posteriori explanation) that the complexity of the Galperin text may be responsible for this effect. The "criterion" schematization for this text is a densely interwoven network, whereas the corresponding schematization for the Immunology text is much more transparent and less interconnected. Possibly, schematizing helps low-CMS students with more complex subject matter, whereas with less complex sub-

TABLE 9

ANALYSIS OF COVARIANCE, GALPERIN TEST USED AS PRETEST AND AS POSTTEST

Source	SS[a]	df	MS[b]	F ratio	
Covariate CMS	130.58	1	130.58	12.86	.001
Pretest vs. posttest	15.11	1	15.11	1.49	.225
Residual	<u>1045.67</u>	103	—	—	—
	1191.36				

[a]Sum of squares.
[b]Mean square.

TABLE 10

MEANS OF GALPERIN TEST, USED
AS PRETEST AND AS POSTTEST

Test	$\bar{X}$	N
Pretest	16.13	45
Posttest	16.95	61
	16.60	106

ject matter, it is deleterious. This could be due to the short time that was allotted for studying the criterion texts. This, of course, is speculation.

The effectiveness of schematizing in enhancing the students' text comprehension has not been demonstrated by this series of studies. There are some indications that an effect does exist, and that it is related to CMS ability. Further research should aim at improved control and procedures in the experimental designs, including a variety of longitudinal measurements of text comprehension. The findings of Metten and van Balen, described here subsequently support this conclusion.

INTERMEDIATE EFFECTS

The term *intermediate effects* refers to those effects of schematizing that are measured in a time frame ranging anywhere from a month after the course to the end of the academic year. The two entities that have been investigated in this manner are dimensions of study behavior and study results. These findings were previously described and are only highlighted in this section. With respect to the dimensions of study behavior, in Study 4 (with educa-

TABLE 11

PRE- AND POSTTEST MEANS FOR LOW, MEDIUM, AND HIGH CMS-ERS

	Galperin test				Immunology test			
	Pretest		Posttest		Pretest		Posttest	
CMS	$\bar{X}$	N	$\bar{X}$	N	$\bar{X}$	N	$\bar{X}$	N
Low	14.9	14	16.2	20	17.3	20	15.6	14
Medium	16.4	18	16.3	20	17.7	20	17.6	18
High	17.2	12	18.4	20	19.9	20	20.2	12

TABLE 12

Study Progress, 1977 Education Groups, in Credit Points

Year: 1978	Experimentals (N = 29)		Controls (N = 91)	
	$\bar{X}$	SD	$\bar{X}$	SD
January	8.9	2.9	10.6	2.7
February	12.8	3.5	13.4	3.0
July	24.2	4.8	21.8	5.1

tion students) self-reported improvement in study behaviors were observed for the experimentals vis-à-vis the controls, using the 5-factor questionnaire developed by Grosveld and van Hoof (1976). (However, these findings are replete with missing data and must be accepted with caution.)

Study result data, which consists of a comparison of overall grades (credit points), were also collected in Study 4 at pre, mid, and post (4 months after the course) intervals. All students were able to improve their credit pointstandings by taking a series of "second chance" examinations. As previously discussed, the experimentals vis-à-vis the controls, changed a pre-course disadvantage into a postcourse advantage in credit points. These findings are presented in Table 12.

LONG-TERM EFFECTS

Study 7 (the long-term study of education majors), conducted by our colleagues Metten and van Balen, is the only study that examined truly long-term effects of the study skills course. They have been following the study careers of a cohort of education students who enrolled in September, 1978. These students could voluntarily participate in any combination of a basic course in reading study skills, starting in November, 1978, as well as a follow-up course in schematizing, starting in January, 1979. Twenty-four students took only the basic course (BC), 34 took both courses (B+S); and 4 took only the schematizing course (SC). Students' progress in terms of accumulated credit points have been collected semiannually since March, 1979. Various other data pertaining to previous education, intended study behavior, and so forth, had been collected immediately after enrollment. We only present an analysis of a subset of these data. A detailed report will be given by van Balen and Metten (in press). The cumulative study results for these groups of students are presented in Table 13.

TABLE 13

STUDY RESULTS IN MEAN CREDIT POINTS, 1978 EDUCATION GROUPS

Group		Mar 79	Sep 79	Mar 80	Sep 80	Mar 81	Sep 81
No course	N	118	109	98	91	85	84
	$\bar{X}$	10.5	27.2	38.1	53.2	67.1	92.5
	SD	4.49	8.95	10.56	13.70	15.84	22.06
Basic course	N	24	20	18	17	17	17
only	$\bar{X}$	12.5	31.2	42.7	58.1	72.8	99.6
	SD	3.16	8.08	9.80	16.07	18.71	26.57
Basic course +	N	34	34	34	34	34	33
schematizing	$\bar{X}$	14.4	35.2	47.8	65.6	76.5	110.4
	SD	2.03	3.45	4.82	8.81	9.00	11.44
Schematizing	N	4	4	4	4	4	4
only	$\bar{X}$	9.9	28.5	41.9	62.6	79.1	102.3
	SD	4.13	7.33	8.22	16.38	19.29	22.39
Total	N	180	167	154	146	140	138
	$\bar{X}$	11.4	29.4	40.9	56.9	70.4	98.0
	SD	4.24	8.56	10.18	14.00	15.42	21.80

After 3 years of study, the B+S students outperformed their cohort students who had not participated in any study skills course (NC) by 18 credit points. Post hoc comparisons between means of the B+S and NC groups at any time point revealed that the B+S students had accumulated significantly more credit points than their NC colleagues. The B+S students also performed substantially better than the BC students.

Additionally, the students were examined on a number of relevant variables pertaining to potentially preexisting differences between groups. No differences were found in students' mastery of the English or German languages (relevant because many textbooks used are in English or German), or mathematics (relevant for statistics and methodology). The only small difference found was that the students in the NC group expected to study 35 hours per week, while the other students expected to study 38 hours per week (self-reported). Subsequent analyses by Metten & Van Balen revealed a significant difference between volunteers and nonvolunteers. Volunteers tend to be younger and (not surprising) more often come directly from high school (personal communication). Together with the obvious difference that the NC students did not volunteer to take any course in study skills, some limited support is provided for arguing that the treatment group were better motivated to perform well in their studies.

Student dropout rate has to be considered when interpreting the student progress data. In the first place, the means per semester are decreased by

TABLE 14

PERCENTAGES OF STUDENTS STILL ENROLLED, 1978 COHORT

Group	Mar 79	Sep 79	Mar 80	Sep 80	Mar 81	Sep 81
NC	92	83	77	72	72	71
BC	83	75	71	71	71	67
B+S	100	100	100	100	97	97
SC	100	100	100	100	100	100

students dropping out after completion of only a few courses of the semester (these students were deleted from the analyses of subsequent semesters). Differences in dropout rate between the groups coincide with differences in mean credit points. Second, in Dutch universities, it is no exception if 50% of the students who start studying (e.g., education), do not graduate within an acceptable number of years. The percentage of students in our study who were still "in the race" at the various time points are given in Table 14. About 30% of the NC and BC students dropped out during these 3 years, while virtually no one dropped out in the B+S and SC groups. These differences in dropout rate partially explain the initial differences found in mean credit points, because dropout is highest in the first semesters.

As a routine procedure, study counselors of the Department of Education identify students who "lag behind" in their study progress. These students are invited, but not required, to contact the counselors for advisory talks. The number of students invited and responding, by group, are presented in Table 15. These figures corroborate that the students in the B+S and SC conditions had far fewer study problems in terms of lagging behind, than

TABLE 15

NUMBER OF STUDENTS INVITED AND RESPONDING, BY GROUP[a]

Year	Number	NC	BC	B+S	SC
	N	109	20	34	4
1979	Ss invited	13	0	1	1
	Ss responding	7	0	1	1
	N	91	17	34	4
1980	Ss invited	30	3	2	1
	Ss responding	16	0	2	1
	N	84	17	33	4
1981	Ss invited	25	3	3	0
	Ss responding	10	1	3	0

[a]NC = no course, BC = bacis course only, B+S = basic course plus schematizing, SC = schematizing only.

the other groups. When invited however, they do show up, contrary to half of the invited students in the other groups, who tend to ignore an invitation.

DISCUSSION

WHAT DO WE NOW KNOW ABOUT SCHEMATIZING?

In the preceding studies, we have gathered a lot of information about schematizing. It is clear that the certitude of this information can be described with the whole spectrum from absolute certainty through likelihood to pure speculation. We try to assess here which of these tags belongs to which information.

Mastery of Schematizing

We know for sure that Dutch students can master the schematizing technique reasonably well when it is taught according to the Mirande and van Bruggen scenario of a 6-week course. A really apt and flexible application of the technique is to be acquired by practice, in a process that certainly has not yet reached its conclusion at the end of the course. We have indications of a positive correlation between qualitative mastery of the technique during the course and remaining active schematizers after the course. We also have found that the course, LbS, together with the scenario, form a well-functioning test-bed for research into schematizing. Students tend to accept the necessity of integrating research activities with the course and adhere reasonably well to the experimental constraints.

We also know that it takes a well-motivated and self-organized student to learn the technique in a self-study format. Because this type of student is unlikely to volunteer for a study skills course, we can safely say that schematizing should be taught via our scenario, which includes an experienced instructor, relatively small groups, and a lot of supervised practice.

We also have found that students typically experience a period during the process of learning to schematize when it is very tempting to quit. This is the so-called "schematizing crisis," and it generally appears after the fourth session. It frequently takes some forceful convincing by the instructor to overcome this crisis.

Immediate Effects

The findings on the immediate or relatively short-term effects of schematizing are the least conclusive. We do know that students feel positive about schematizing at the end of a course, but we have not been able to show any objective effects. For example, we have not been able to demonstrate that students are better text-comprehenders after the course, nor do they report extensive changes in the structure of their study behavior.

In this regard, our expectations may have been unreasonable. Given that (1) schematizing is a way of approaching longer segments of complex text and takes a fairly long time to develop proficiency, (2) students have strong doubts about their competence right after the course, and (3) students claim to be hampered rather than helped by the obligation to study by schematizing at the final testing session; it is quite unlikely that any positive, objective effects would be observed immediately after the course. Clearly, if all these conditions hold, a fair test of the effectiveness of schematizing must allow it time to settle, so that it is performed without being an extra (and time-consuming) activity. The data for longer-term effects are consistent with this interpretation.

Longer-Term Effects

Taking medium and long-term effects together, we cannot escape the conclusion that either potentially successful students are attracted to schematizing, or that students become successful students after they have learned schematizing. This is very clear in the data from the 1978 education group, and is consistent with the data from the 1977 education group. We examine each of these alternatives.

Are the students who volunteer for the schematizing course in some respects special students? We have found no indication for this to be the case. They do not differ demonstrably from their nonvolunteer counterparts, in terms of deficiencies in previous education. They may be expected to differ in motivation, although this appears to be a moot point. Students who voluntarily take study skills courses may be bright students who take their studies seriously, or they may be slow students who know that they need to take advantage of every opportunity for improvement. In the 1977 group, the experimental students lagged behind the controls by 1.8 credit points after their first few months of study, thereby suggesting that they may have been of the second variety. The students of Study 6 (the longitudinal series) for the most part also belonged to this latter category, and substantive differences were found between treatment groups, as well as between treatment groups and the controls.

Because it is unlikely that students who take two courses are very much more motivated than students who take one course, we are left with the conclusion that we have no indication that those students who take the course in schematizing are likely to be successful anyway. That leaves the other possibility: schematizing does something to students that makes them substantially more successful students. The evidence tends to support this proposition. For example, the credit-point advantage of the treatment group equates to roughly one ½-year of study over a period of 3 years. As far as we know, only rearranging curricula into the format of the Personalized System of Instruction and its variants, and (on a different scale) computer-assisted instruction have claimed effects of this magnitude. No studies of study skills courses that report effects of this magnitude are known to us.

WHAT DO WE NOT KNOW ABOUT SCHEMATIZING?

We know schematizing is effective, but we do not know *how* its effects are derived. Breuker (Chapter 2, present volume) proposes a text comprehension model and presents a plausible way for schematizing to fit this model. Our research, however, has not been addressed to questions of *how* schematizing influences the way people comprehend texts. Here also is probably the major flaw in our project: the lack of sufficient integration between the development of theoretical models and the actual research performed. The difficult circumstances under which this research must be performed (being "field research") are real, but form a poor excuse. Where attempts were made to examine the processes of text comprehension and the differential effects of schematizing for subjects with different cognitive abilities, the efforts were performed in a way that, in retrospect, could not possibly have produced the desired results. The main reason for this, as pointed out, is that objective measurements were administered at an inappropriate time. The most important thing we know is that, in general, schematizing does positively influence the text comprehension process.

HOW CAN WE GET TO KNOW MORE ABOUT SCHEMATIZING?

Three approaches should be emphasized in future research on the effectiveness of schematizing. The first approach would be to analyze in detail those process aspects in text comprehension that schematizing may be hypothesized to influence, according to the lines suggested by Breuker in Chapter 2, present volume. Laboratory experimentation to test out those hypotheses is essential to determine not only that schematizing is effective, but also *why* and *how*.

Second, it would be a sensible thing to make schematizing widely available, to broaden the research base. We have (1) a course in schematizing,

(2) a scenario for administering the course, and (3) a set of research instruments with known properties. Research into schematizing by other research groups would broaden the base. We are currently looking into ways of making the entire package available to interested researchers.

Third, the findings presented in this chapter do, of course, leave room for doubt. The last approach then would be to replicate the long-term effectiveness study of schematizing, with better experimental control. The most important improvement, although not a cure-all (cf. Holley & Dansereau, 1981), would be assigning subjects randomly to conditions.

We have done substantial groundwork with the schematizing method, and have been generally pleased with our results. A plethora of substantive research questions remains to be investigated. Future efforts by ourselves and, hopefully, other researchers will be directed toward examining these issues. Pragmatically, schematizing and other spatial strategies such as networking and mapping are effective aids to text processing; while we can theorize why this is so, it needs to be determined empirically.

ACKNOWLEDGMENTS

The research reported in this chapter was conducted while both authors were with the Center for Research into Higher Education at the University of Amsterdam. We are indebted to Alman Metten and Frank van Balen, Department of Education, University of Amsterdam, for kindly allowing us to analyze and report on the data they collected in their long-term study of education students.

REFERENCES

Balen, F. van, & Metten, M. (in press). *Effecten van studievaardigheidsbevordering en studiebegeleiding op studievoortgang* [Effects of reading-study skills promotion and counseling on study progress.] Amsterdam: Pedagogisch-Didactisch Instituut, University of Amsterdam.

Bruggen, J. M. van (1980). *Vaardig Leren Studeren; een literatuuronderzoek naar de effekten van studievaardigheidskursussen* [Learning to study effectively: A review of the effects of reading-study skills courses] (COWO Report). Amsterdam: University of Amsterdam.

Bruggen, J. M. van (1981a). *Verkenningen rond het schematiseren* [Surveys in schematizing]. Amsterdam: Vakgroep Onderwijskunde.

Bruggen, J. M. van (1981b). *Graphentheorie en schema's* [Theory of graphs and schematizations] (COWO Report). Amsterdam: University of Amsterdam.

Camstra, B. (1979). *Empirical research with "learning by schematizing."* Paper presented at the EARDHE International Conference, Klagenfurt.

Camstra, B., Metten, A., & Mirande, M. (1979). *Effektonderzoek van een studievaardigheidscursus* [Effect study of a study skills course] (COWO Report). Amsterdam: University of Amsterdam.

Cook, T. D., & Campbell, D. T. (1979). *Quasi-experimentation: Design and analysis issues in field settings*. Chicago: Rand McNally.

Daalder, M. (1976). *Organiseren van leerstof* [Organizing subject matter]. Congresboek Onderwijs Research Dagen, Groningen.

Driesum, R. van, Frankenhuizen, G., Quast, J., van Schuppen, S., Veen, S., Mirande, M., & Camstra, B. (1978). *Handboekbegeleiding met schema's* [Guided textbook study with schematizations] (COWO Report). Amsterdam: University of Amsterdam.

Elshout, J. J. (1976). *Karakteristieke moeilijkheden in het denken*. Unpublished doctoral dissertation, University of Amsterdam.

Entwisle, D. R. (1960). Evaluation of study skills courses: A review. *Journal of Educational Research, 53*, 243–251.

Fairbanks, M. M. (1974). The effect of college reading improvement programs on academic achievement. In P. L. Nacke (Ed.), *Interaction, Research and practice for college-adult reading, 23rd Yearbook of the National Reading Conference*. Clemson: NRC.

Frijda, N. (1977). Memory processes and instruction. In A. M. Lesgold, J. W. Pellegrino, S. D. Fokkema & R. Glaser (Eds.), *Cognitive psychology and instruction*. New York: Plenum Press.

Grosveld, F., & Hoof, G. van. (1976). *Hoe studeren studenten?* [How do students study?] (COWO Report). Amsterdam: University of Amsterdam.

Guilford, J. P. (1967). *The nature of human intelligence*. New York: Academic Press.

Holley, C. D., & Dansereau, D. F. (1981). Controlling for transient motivation in cognitive manipulation studies. *Journal of Experimental Education, 49*, 84–91.

Kunst, H. (1978). *Cognitie van Semantische Systemen*. Unpublished doctoral dissertation, University of Amsterdam.

Mirande, M. (1981). *Studeren door Schematiseren* [Study by schematizing]. Utrecht: Het Spectrum.

Mirande, M., & Bruggen, J. M. van (1981). *De schematiseercursus; draaiboek voor het geven van de cursus "Studeren door Schematiseren"* [The schematizing course; Scenario for conducting the course "Study by schematizing"] (COWO Report), Amsterdam: University of Amsterdam.

Mirande, M., & Camstra, B. (1978). *Schematiseren als leerstrategie* [Schematizing as a learning strategy]. Paper presented at Onderwijs Research Dagen 1978, Utrecht.

Santeusanio, R. O. (1974). Do college reading programs serve their purposes? *Reading World, 13*, 258–271.

CHAPTER 9

Mapping: Representing Informative Text Diagrammatically*

BONNIE B. ARMBRUSTER   *THOMAS H. ANDERSON*

INTRODUCTION

Mapping is a technique for representing ideas in text in the form of a diagram. Mapping was designed specifically to represent informative text, the type of prose found in textbooks and other materials used primarily in school learning situations. The technique was originally developed by a team at the Center for the Study of Reading, University of Illinois, in 1978, as part of a project on studying strategies funded by the Advanced Research Projects Agency and the National Institute of Education. In addition to its use as a study technique, mapping has other instructional and research applications (see Surber, Chapter 10; and Schallert, Ulerick, & Tierney, Chapter 12). The purposes of this chapter are to (1) define and illustrate the technique of mapping, (2) discuss general mapping strategies in terms of current cognitive theory, and (3) suggest some applications of mapping.

A basic assumption of mapping is that text is structured hierarchically.

*The research reported herein was supported in part by the National Institute of Education under Contract No. HEW-NIE-C-400-76-0116.

SPATIAL LEARNING STRATEGIES
Techniques, Applications, and Related Issues

Relationships and Symbols Used in Mapping

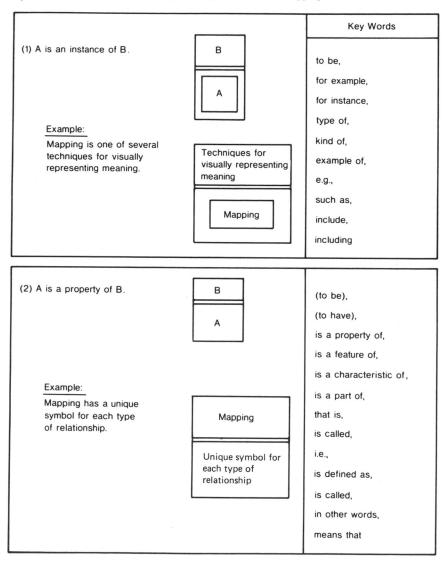

FIGURE 1. Relationships and symbols used in mapping.

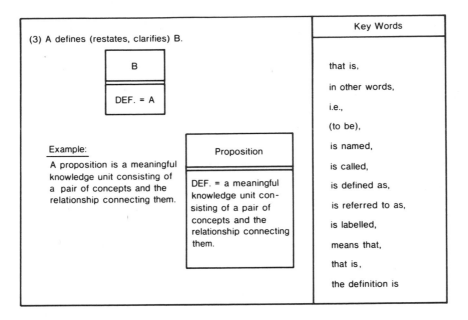

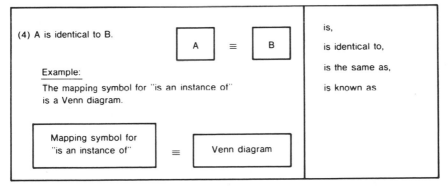

FIGURE 1. (*Continued*)

(5) A is similar to B.

A ≈ B

Example:

Mapping is similar to Networking.

Mapping ≈ Networking

Key Words

like,

likewise,

is similar,

similarly,

in the same way or manner

(6) A is not similar to B.

A ⧣ B

Example:

Mapping is different from outlining

Mapping ⧣ Outlining

is different from

(7) A is greater than B.

A > B

A is less than B.

A < B

Example:

The number of relationships recognized in mapping is greater than the number of relationships recognized in networking.

Number of relationships recognized in mapping > Number of relationships recognized in networking

more,

greater,

larger,

less,

smaller

FIGURE 1. (*Continued*)

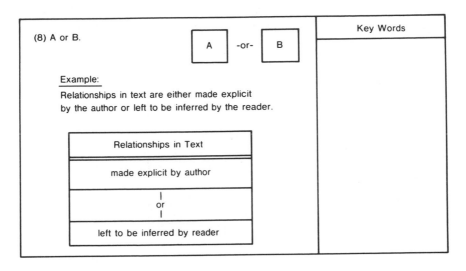

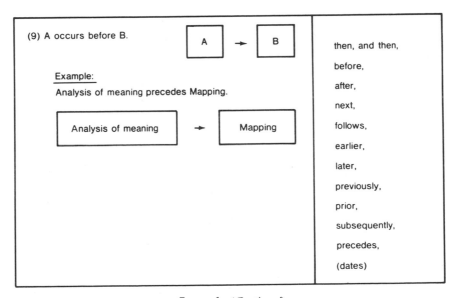

Figure 1. (*Continued*)

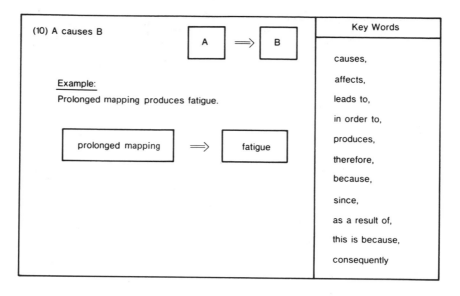

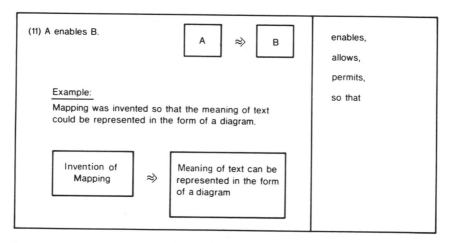

Fɪɢᴜʀᴇ 1. (*Continued*)

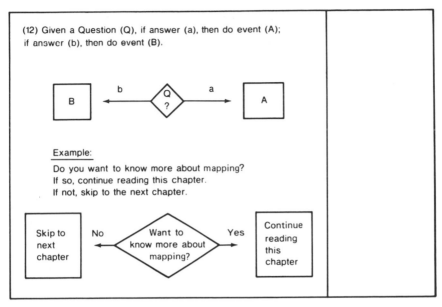

FIGURE 1. (*Continued*)

Mapping recognizes three major levels in the text hierarchy. From lowest to highest, these levels are the proposition, the text unit, and the frame. Each of these levels is defined and illustrated in turn.

THE PROPOSITION

The proposition is the basic building block of the text hierarchy. For purposes of mapping, the *proposition* is defined as a meaningful knowledge unit consisting of a pair of concepts and the relationship connecting them. In mapping, each possible relationship is represented by a unique symbol. Figure 1 presents the relationships used in mapping, the corresponding symbols for representing these relationships, and the words and phrases that commonly express these relationships in text. Note that the symbol X can be used to negate any relationship, although it is illustrated in Figure 1 only with the similarity relationship. Also, although mapping uses the logical relationships *or, and,* and *but;* only the use of *or* is illustrated; *and* and *but* are used analogously.

Propositions are connected in various ways to form the structure of text. The structure of text is determined by the author's purpose. This purpose can be thought of as a question the author is addressing. In other words, the form of text follows its function. Two basic kinds of text structure are recognized in mapping: text units and text frames.

TEXT UNITS

In addressing many topics in many subject matter areas, authors appear to be guided by a few basic purposes or questions. The structure of the responses to these questions constitute the basic components of content area text. We call these basic structures *text units*. Table 1 represents some of the general author purposes or questions, the name of the structure (text unit) corresponding to each, and the map of each text unit (unit map). Note that each text unit contains a typical proposition or combination of propositions. Examples of text units from actual textbooks and their corresponding unit maps are given in Table 2.

Note that some of the text unit maps are similar to other, more familiar, diagrammatic techniques. The descriptive map of the text about batholiths resembles an outline that a student might generate from that passage. Rather than requiring the students to place numbers and letters in front of the proposition about batholiths, mapping requires that the propositions be separated from one another by horizontal lines.

Mapping also resembles flowcharting, a technique made prominent by computer programmers. The map that depicts the process of building a sod house looks similar to a flowchart. These temporal sequencing maps can become more elaborate when logical connectives, such as *and* and *or,* and conditional questions (illustrated as Relationship 12 in Figure 1) are included.

The compare–contrast map is similar to the double-entry tables used in many textbooks—the classification of traits of two or more named entities. The major feature that mapping adds to the typical table is the facility of recording the precise relationship between the various traits. For example, in the map comparing and contrasting P-waves and S-waves, one of the trait differences is that in *P-waves,* particles vibrate back and forth while in *S-waves* particles move up and down. This difference is clearly signalled by the symbol ⚹.

Finally, Venn diagrams, a technique often used in Boolean algebra, is found in the mapping representation of *examples*. The map about deciduous trees gives several examples: oak, hickory, beech, and maple. These examples are subsets of the total set of deciduous trees and are represented as embedded boxes within the larger box labeled deciduous trees.

TABLE 1

TYPES OF GENERAL AUTHOR PURPOSES AND THE CORRESPONDING TEXT UNITS AND UNIT MAPS

Examples of Author Purposes or Questions

Imperative Form	Interrogative Form	Text Unit	Unit Map

Define A.
Describe A.
List the features—
characteristics—
traits of A

What is A?
Who is A?
Where is A?

Descriptions

Trace the develop-
ment of A

Give the steps in A

When did A occur
(in relationship to
other events)?

Temporal sequences
(processes, procedures,
chronologies)

Explain A.
Explain the cause(s) of A.
Explain effect(s) of A.

Draw a conclusion about A

Why did A happen?
How did A happen?

What are the causes/
reasons for effects/
outcomes/results of A?

Explanations

(continued)

TABLE 1 (*Continued*)

Examples of Author Purposes or Questions		Text Unit	Unit Map
Imperative Form	Interrogative Form		
Predict what will happen to A. Hypothesize about the cause of A.	What will be the effects—outcomes—results of A?	Explanations (cont'd.)[a]	
Compare and contrast A and B.	How are A and B alike and/or different?	Compare–Contrasts	[b]
List the similarities and differences between A and B.			
Define and give examples of A.	What is A, and what are some examples of A?	Definitions—examples	

[a] ⟮↑↑↑≋⟯ denotes that any of the three relationships may apply.

[b] Any of the relationships of comparison (≈ , ≭ , ⟨ , ⟩ , ≡) might apply.

TABLE 2

Examples of Text Units and Corresponding Unit Maps

Description[a]

    Batholiths are the largest igneous rock bodies. They may form several kilometers below the surface of the earth. They are 50 to 80 kilometers across and extend for hundreds of kilometers in length. Batholiths are too thick for their lower surfaces to be seen. They are exposed at the earth's surface only when the overlying rock has been removed by erosion. Most batholiths are great masses of granite. They form the cores of the world's mountain systems.

Batholiths
largest igneous rock bodies
may form several kilometers below the surface of the earth
50-80 kilometers across
extend for hundreds of kilometers in length
too thick for lower surfaces to be seen
exposed at earth's surface only when overlying rock has been removed by erosion
most are great masses of granite
form the cores of the world's mountain systems

    [a]Bishop, M. S., Sutherland, B., & Lewis, P. G. (1981). *Focus on earth science*. Columbus, OH: Charles E. Merrill, p. 330.

Temporal Sequence[b]

    Sod houses were usually built on a slight rise or hillside to escape flooding. First, a floor space was leveled out with spades. This was wet and tamped down until solid. The next step was to cut bricks from the sod. Then the bricks were laid to make the walls. When the walls were about three feet high, simple wooden frames for the door and windows were put in place. Finally, the roof, made with cedar beams and sod bricks, was put on.

(*continued*)

TABLE 2   (*Continued*)

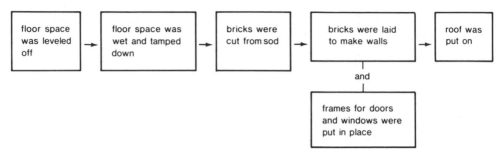

[b]Aaron, I. E., Jackson, D., Riggs, C., Smith, R. G., & Tierney, R. (1978). *Workbook to accompany racing stripes.* Glenview, IL: Scott, Foresman, p. 64.

Explanation[c]

In cold or mountainous regions, rocks are often subjected to the action of freezing water because of daily changes in the temperature. During the day, when the temperature is above the freezing point of water (0°C), rainwater or melted snow or ice trickles into cracks in the rocks. During the night, when the temperature falls near the freezing point of water, the trapped water expands as it changes into ice.

As freezing water expands, the expanding ice pushes against the sides of the cracks with tremendous force, splitting the rocks apart. In this way, large masses of rock, especially the exposed rocks on the tops of mountains, are broken into smaller pieces. Frost often has the same effect on the paved streets of our cities. During the winter, water trapped in cracks in the pavement freezes into ice. The ice may expand enough to crack and loosen the pavement. Potholes develop from such cracks.

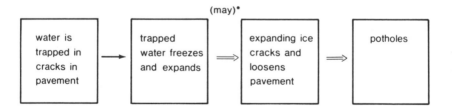

* Note relationship qualified with a word in parentheses.

[c]Lesser, M., Constant, C., & Wisler, J. J. (1977). *Contemporary Science,* Book I. New York: Amsco School Publications, pp. 282–283.

Compare–contrast[d]

Body waves are of two kinds. The *P-wave,* or primary wave, travels forward in a horizontal direction. Rock particles vibrate back and forth. They are pushed close together, then move apart to their original positions. A slinky toy, held at one end, then given a slight jerk, shows the P-wave motion. The *S-wave* or secondary wave, vibrates at right angles to the P-wave. Particles move up and down, but the wave itself travels forward. The S-wave motion is like that of a rope fixed at one end and moved up and down at the free end.

TABLE 2   (*Continued*)

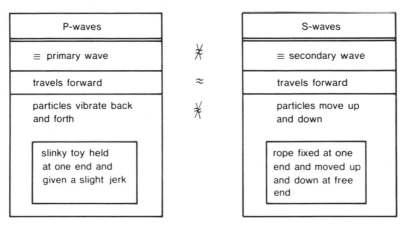

[a]Bishop, M. S., Sutherland, B., & Lewis, P. G. (1981). *Focus on earth science*. Columbus, OH: Charles E. Merrill, p. 292.

Definition—example[e]

    In this forest biome, you would notice many deciduous trees. *Deciduous trees* grow leaves in the spring, which fall from the trees in autumn. Oak, hickory, beech, and maple are deciduous trees.

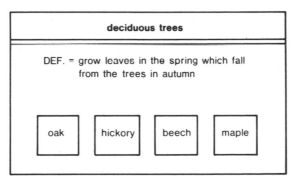

[e]Sund, R. H., Adams, D. K., & Hackett, J. (1982). *Accent on science*. Columbus, OH: Charles E. Merrill, p. 142.

TEXT FRAMES

    Each discipline or content area has an associated set of fundamental or generic concepts. For example, some of the generic concepts associated with biology are *systems, structures,* and *biological processes,* whereas the generic concepts of physical geography include *climate, landforms,* and *geological processes.* Each of the generic concepts of a discipline has a set of features or attributes. For example, typical features of a biological system, such as the digestive system, are *function of the system, component parts, function of the component parts,* and *process* (how it works). An additional feature of interest may be *problem–solutions* (problems that can occur with the system and ways to prevent the problem from occurring, or solving it after it has occurred).

A *text frame* is the structure of text that responds to questions about the generic concepts of a discipline. A text frame is thus a generic text structure within a particular content domain. A frame has *slots* for the features associated with the generic concept. The slots of a frame are assumed to constitute the main ideas of the concept or the most important information connected with a topic. Each slot has its own structure, which may be a single proposition but is more often a text unit.

An author instantiates a text frame with information in response to implicit questions about a specific instance of the generic concept. For example, authors of introductory biology textbooks usually try to answer for the reader the implicit question, What is the digestive system? as a specific instance of the generic concept of biological systems. In order to respond to this question, the author answers implicit questions about the component features of the generic concept. In other words, the author fills in the slots associated with the frame. For example, in order to answer adequately the question, What is the digestive system? the author answers the subquestions "What is the function of the digestive system? "What are the component parts of the digestive system? What are the individual functions of the component parts? How does the digestive system work? and perhaps What are some problems that can occur with the digestive system? How can these problems be prevented or solved? Note that some of these questions can be answered with a single proposition (for example, the function of the digestive system: It enables food to be broken down into particles that can be absorbed by the cells), whereas other questions require a response in the form of a text unit (for example, explaining the process of how the digestive system works).

Text frames can be represented diagrammatically as *frame maps.* The next sections present some text frames and their corresponding frame maps.

THE GOAL AND PROBLEM–SOLUTION FRAMES

Elsewhere we have written about some text frames and frame maps appropriate for explanations in history (Armbruster & Anderson, 1982a). Here we present a brief summary of these frames and maps.

The most basic frame, which we call the *goal frame,* is depicted in the following frame map: The goal frame is a simple structure that can be used to explain events in terms of the goal-directed behavior of individuals, groups,

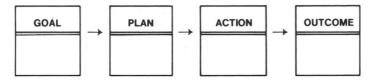

FIGURE 2. The form of a goal frame.

and nations. The slots of the frame are assumed to constitute the main ideas of the explanation of an historical event. The slots can be instantiated to any desired level of detail.

An example of an instantiation of a goal frame is an explanation of English settlements in the New World in the seventeenth century. According to several sources, the goal of those who invested in the settlements was to make a profit. The plan was to have settlers in North America raise some of the products England would otherwise have to import. The action was to establish colonies along the East Coast of North America. The outcome was that the investors failed to make a profit from the colonies.

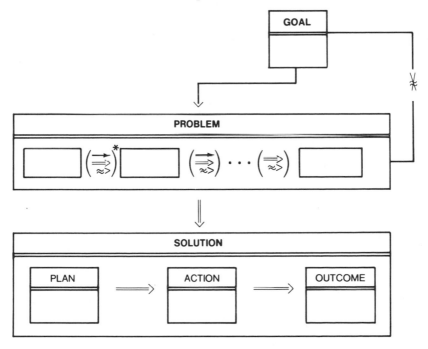

$*\left(\begin{smallmatrix}\longrightarrow\\ =>\\ \approx>\end{smallmatrix}\right)$ denotes that any of the three relationships may apply.

FIGURE 3. The form of a problem–solution frame map.

A variation of the goal frame is what we call the *problem–solution Frame.* A problem–solution frame map has the form illustrated in Figure 3.

The *problem* is an event, a condition, or a series of events or conditions resulting in a state that is an obstacle to the attainment of the goal. The problem prompts a *solution,* which takes the form of the *plan, action,* and *outcome* of the goal frame. The outcome of the solution either solves or fails to solve the problem. In other words, the outcome either satisfies or fails to satisfy the goal.

An example of an instantiation of a problem–solution frame is an account of the voyages of discovery. Such an account usually begins with a statement of the *goal*—the desire of Europeans for silks, spices, and other goods from the Far East. The account goes on to explain the problem of obtaining goods from the East, including the difficult and dangerous journey, the high fees charged by middlemen, and the small total amount of goods delivered. The account continues with the solution: the plan to find an all-water route to the Far East, the action of the actual voyages, and the outcomes of early disappointments in the attempt fo find an all-water route, as well as the resulting discoveries of the explorers.

THE SYSTEMS FRAME

We have already mentioned a text frame for biological systems. The same frame is applicable to technological systems, for example, the hydraulic brake system of an automobile or the flushing mechanism of a toilet. The systems frame map has the form illustrated in Figure 4.

The *function–uses* slot depicts the proposition that the system enables the performance of a particular general function or functions or has a particular use or uses. The *parts and their functions* slot may include a description of each part of the system and the function enabled by the part. The *explanation of how it works* slot is an explanation text unit that explains how the system works. The *problem–solution* slot is composed of a frame similar to the problem–solution frame already discussed, except that there is no human agent with goals and plans. The problem consists of a series of events that prevent the performance of the function or that result in a function that is in some way inferior to the optimal function of the system. The solution consists of a series of events leading to a condition different from the problem condition; this new condition in turn enables the system to function or to function better.

As an instantiation of the system frame, consider a treatise on the hydraulic braking system. The text might state that the function of the system is to stop the vehicle. The treatment of parts and their functions may include

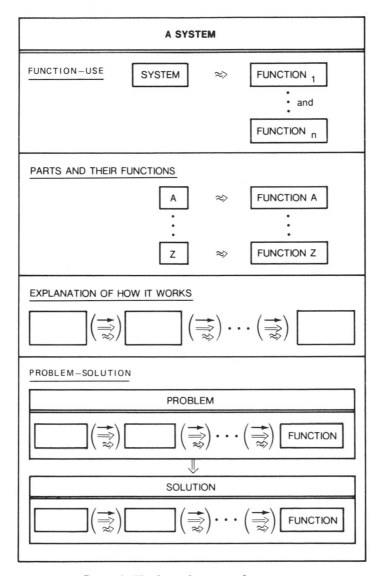

Figure 4. The form of a systems frame map.

descriptions of master cylinders, brake lines, brake fluid, pistons, wheel brake assemblies, brake drums, brake shoes, retracting springs, and brake pedals, and the function performed by each of these parts. The explanation of how it works might consist of an account of what happens with each of the parts from the time the driver pushes down the brake pedal to the time the brake fluid returns to the master cylinder. The problem–solution slot consists of explaining how insufficient brake fluid or worn brake shoes would prevent the brakes from working, or working well, and how replacing these would restore the function of the braking system.

In the preceding part of the present chapter, we define three levels in a hierarchy of text structure—the proposition, the text unit, and the text frame—and show how each can be represented diagrammatically using the mapping technique. In the next section we discuss two basic strategies for mapping.

STRATEGIES FOR MAPPING

In discussing mapping strategies, we draw on an analogy from a theory of reading comprehension. According to schema-theoretic views of reading comprehension (see Breuker, Chapter 2; Goetz, Chapter 3, present volume), information processing proceeds in two basic modes: bottom-up and top-down. *Bottom-up,* or *data driven, processing* proceeds from lower to higher levels of linguistic analysis. The processing begins with an analysis of letter features, combines words to construct meanings of phrases and sentences, and so on through increasingly comprehensive levels of interpretation and integration. In terms of schema theory, bottom-up processing starts from the lowest level schemata and gradually builds higher-order schemata.

Top-down, or *conceptually driven, processing* proceeds in the opposite direction. Based on some minimal knowledge of the text (for example, a title, illustration, or topic sentence), the reader forms an expectation or hypothesis about the meaning of the text. Reading then consists of a search for information to either support or refute the hypothesis. In terms of schema theory, the reader first activates higher-order schemata and then seeks information in the text to fit the schemata.

In schema-theoretic accounts of reading comprehension, text processing involves both top-down and bottom-up processing simultaneously. That is, through bottom-up processing the reader finds the information needed to fill out the higher-order schemata and through top-down processing the reader can find and assimilate information in an efficient manner (Adams & Collins, 1977).

Mapping can proceed in two basic modes, which are analogous to the bottom-up and top-down modes of text processing. In bottom-up mapping, the mapper begins by mapping individual propositions, then tries to integrate the propositions into a text unit map, and perhaps finally attempts to integrate the text units into a text frame. In top-down mapping, the mapper begins with a hypothesized text frame map, and then instantiates the slots of this frame map with text unit maps and proposition maps. As with text processing, mapping involves both bottom-up and top-down modes. However, in any given mapping situation, we think one type of mapping will predominate as a function of three major variables: the mapper's prior knowledge, the clarity or "considerateness" of the text (Kantor, Anderson, & Armbruster, 1983), and the mapper's purpose.

First, the mapper's prior knowledge about the content or topic of the text influences the choice of mapping mode. Mappers can only use top-down mapping, starting with the text-frame map, if they know the appropriate text frame for the content. Novice learners who do not yet know the basic frames of the content area but who do know something about basic text structures might still be able to use top-down mapping beginning at the level of the text unit. Without knowledge of text frames or text units, mappers are able only to map from the bottom up.

Second, the structure, coherence, or clarity of the text itself influences whether mapping will proceed top-down or bottom-up. Some informative text is so obscure or complex that deciding on a best frame and trying to instantiate the frame map with content from the text may be more trouble than it is worth. For such texts, mapping down from the text unit level or mapping up from the proposition level may be the only options. Indeed, the maps of such texts may never progress further up the hierarchy than the level of the proposition, or an occasional isolated text unit, because the higher-order integrating structure is missing from the text and impossible to infer.

Finally, the choice of top-down or bottom-up processing depends on the purpose of the mapper. Top-down mapping would be the preferred mode if the mapper's purpose was to cull out of the text the main ideas or important understandings about a particular topic. For example, students who are preparing for an essay exam in history, given constraints of time and energy, may only want to study the most succinct explanation of any given historical event. In such a case, the student might map only minimal information pertaining to the goal, plan, action, and outcome. This highest-order frame map could be further elaborated by embedded-text unit maps and proposition maps to reflect the degree of the mapper's interest in elaborations of the main ideas of the basic frame map. On the other hand, bottom-up mapping would be the preferred mode if the mapper's purpose is to analyze, to understand, or to remember the text at the level of propositions or of text units. For example, if students are mapping text in preparation for a test on facts or details, they might wisely limit their mapping to the levels of propositions or text units.

APPLICATIONS OF MAPPING

The effectiveness of mapping as a studying technique has been evaluated in only one study (Armbruster & Anderson, 1980), in which 11 eighth-graders were taught to map short expository prose passages during approximately 12 hours of instruction. Although the results tended to support mapping as a studying strategy, the authors pointed out limitations of the technique, including the time required to map all ideas in a text and the low motivation of students to expend the effort. Armbruster and Anderson have concluded that mapping may be most reasonable as a studying strategy if students represent only major concepts and relationships (for example, using a frame map) and/or if they map text that is particularly difficult to learn or hard to remember.

Despite the possible limitations of mapping as a studying technique, mapping has other applications. For example, Armbruster and Anderson (1982b) have suggested ways that top-down and bottom-up mapping could be incorporated into exercises used by classroom teachers to help students understand and remember what they read in textbooks. Mapping could also be used as a tool in the teaching of writing. Because of the correspondence between the shape of maps and the structure of text, filled-in maps could serve as the basis for writing exercises. That is, students could be given information in mapped form and asked to translate the map into prose. Mapping could also be used in the planning stage of writing in much the same way traditional outlines are used. That is, students could be encouraged to organize their ideas and notes into a map before writing a first draft.

We have suggested a few ways that mapping might be used. Indeed, the potential applications are limited only by imagination. What we do not yet know is which of the ideas are good ones; the answer to this question awaits further research.

REFERENCES

Aaron, I. E., Jackson, D., Riggs, C., Smith, R. G., & Tierney, R. (1978). *Workbook to accompany racing stripes* (p. 64). Glenview, IL: Foresman.

Adams, J. J., & Collins, A. (1977). *A schema-theoretic view of reading* (Tech. Rep. No. 32). Urbana: University of Illinois, Center for the Study of Reading. (ERIC Document Reproduction Service No. ED 142 970)

Armbruster, B. B., & Anderson, T. H. (1980). *The effect of mapping on the free recall of expository text* (Tech. Rep. No. 160). Urbana: University of Illinois, Center for the Study of Reading. (ERIC Document Reproduction Service No. ED 182 735)

Armbruster, B. B., & Anderson, T. A. (1982a). *Structures for explanation in history textbooks: Or,*

So what if Governor Stanford missed the spike and hit the rail? (Tech. Rep. No. 252). Urbana: University of Illinois, center for the Study of Reading. (ERIC Document Reproduction Service No. ED 218 595)

Armbruster, B. B., & Anderson, T. H. (1982b). *Idea-mapping: The technique and its use in the classroom: Or, simulating the "ups" and "downs" of reading comprehension* (Reading Ed. Rep. No. 36). Urbana: University of Illinois, Center for the Study of Reading.

Bishop, M. S., Sutherland, B., & Lewis, P. G. (1981). *Focus on earth science* Columbus, OH: Merrill, pp. 292, 330.

Kantor, R. N., Anderson, T. H., & Armbruster, B. B. (1983) How are children's textbooks inconsiderate? Or, of flyswatters and alfa. *Journal of Curriculum Studies, 15*(1), 61–72.

Lesser, M., Constant, C., & Wisler, J. J. (1977). *Contemporary science* (Book I). New York: Amsco School Publications, pp. 282, 283.

Sund, R. H., Adams, D. K., & Hackett, J. K. (1980). *Accent on science* Columbus, OH: Merrill, p. 142.

PART III

Related Applications of Spatial Strategies

CHAPTER 10

Mapping as a Testing and Diagnostic Device

JOHN R. SURBER

DIAGNOSIS OF LEARNING
THROUGH TEST ERRORS

Some years ago Clinchy and Rosenthal (1971) asserted that a correct response from a student may well be less informative to an instructor for evaluating a student's understanding than an incorrect response. They argued that a correct response may be a lucky guess or an ambiguous indication of a partial understanding whereas an incorrect response can be an important clue to the nature of a student's misunderstanding. Instruction can then be aimed at the misunderstanding. The assumption that errors are a reflection of mental organization is not particularly new. For example, Piaget made use of children's erroneous responses in arguing that there are qualitative changes in children's thinking.

As a first step toward a systematic study of students' errors, Clinchy and Rosenthal provided a classification of types of errors and, in addition to giving numerous examples of error types, suggested possible lines of remediation for each type of error. More recently, Gropper (1974, 1975) proposed a comprehensive approach to analyzing dimensions of student re-

SPATIAL LEARNING STRATEGIES
Techniques, Applications, and Related Issues

sponses—both correct and incorrect. Although this approach was developed from a behavioristic perspective, it does not seem to have stimulated any systematic research. In part, the lack of research may be a result of the failure to develop a systematic method for assessing errors.

The most extensive empirical work on error analysis comes from a program that has focused on a particular area of procedural knowledge—simple arithmetic problems. Brown and Burton (1978) looked for patterns in children's solutions to a large number of addition and subtraction problems. They discovered that many of the errors that children made could be described by application of incorrect rules. By producing a complete model of the production system necessary for solving the problems, Brown and Burton were able to identify the deviations or bugs in children's production systems for adding or subtracting. At that point they were able to construct a sequence of problems that would permit identification of which bug or bugs were present in any particular child's procedural knowledge.

The work of Brown and Burton is important in a number of respects. First, it documents the systematic basis for many of the errors made in the process of learning to solve arithmetic problems. Second, their work provides a model for an approach to using errors to discover the nature of a learner's misunderstanding. Finally, they demonstrate that this approach can lead to systematic diagnosis of misunderstanding. Notably, this approach has been pursued by others (Klein, Birenbaum, Standiford, & Tatsuoka, 1981; Tatsuoka & Tatsuoka, 1981).

Despite the importance of errors in assessing knowledge, they have been neglected by traditional methods of achievement testing. With multiple-choice testing an experienced teacher may attempt to select as distractors common misconceptions about the concept being tested. Nevertheless, the final result of this type of testing is typically a score based on percentage correct, with no attempt to diagnose misunderstanding by using a pattern of incorrect responses.

INADEQUACIES OF TRADITIONAL TEST FORMATS

There are three major drawbacks of traditional tests that render them unsuitable for diagnosis of misunderstanding: (1) insensitivity to structure, (2) intrusions and distortions, and (3) errors of omission. In this section, a brief summary of these issues is presented. For a more detailed discussion, see Surber and Smith (1981).

Insensitivity to Structure

Traditional tests are generally insensitive to the structure of the subject matter that is being tested. Any particular *discipline* (a subject of study or topic) is not merely a collection of lists of concepts. A discipline is recognized as such because of the interrelationships of its concepts. Some concepts are central and some more peripheral, some general and some quite specific. Relationships such as class inclusion, causality, and temporal sequence tie concepts together into an organizational framework. To assess adequately a student's knowledge, a text must be capable of testing the interrelationships among concepts.

A mundane example of the importance of interrelationships of concepts is a "restaurant script"—our knowledge of what takes place when a person dines at a restaurant. The concepts of being greeted at the door, shown to a table, ordering food, and so on, are tied together as a well-rehearsed temporal sequence of events, not just a random list of concepts. It has been demonstrated that understanding the general structure of dining at a restaurant can increase the memorability of specific instantiations of that total structure (Anderson, Spiro, & Anderson, 1978). The nature of individual items of a multiple-choice test make it difficult to test the learner's knowledge of the general structure of the domain.

Intrusions and Distortions

The traditional alternative to this drawback of multiple-choice tests is the use of a test format that requires extended constructed-response questions (short answer or essay). Essay questions may require the student to describe the interrelationships of concepts, but this format has its own drawbacks. Problems associated with scoring are among the most frequently cited (e.g., Gronlund, 1981). However, for the present discussion there is the more important problem—how to deal with erroneous knowledge—intrusions and distortions.

In an essay test, important information may be distorted or information that was not part of the instruction (correct or erroneous) may be given as part of the response. This is a prime example of a test format in which there is no general method of dealing with declarative knowledge errors in terms of scoring or for diagnostic purposes. Unlike the program approach developed by Brown and Burton (1978), these error responses do not lead to a better understanding of what the learner knows. In short, an essay test does not permit the systematic diagnosis of a learner's misunderstanding.

ERRORS OF OMISSION

A third drawback of traditional test formats is the failure to distinguish between a lack of knowledge and erroneous knowledge. An incorrect response on a multiple-choice test may reflect either a misunderstanding on the part of the learner (of the information questioned) or a failure to learn. Additionally, these same shortcomings may be present with a correct response but are obscured by a "lucky guess." An omission on an essay test suggests a failure to have acquired the appropriate information. More importantly, when a student does lack information, there is no systematic way to assess the importance of the missing knowledge. Multiple-choice tests usually weigh all items equally. Missing a key characteristic that is necessary for discriminating one concept from another is viewed in the same way as missing a relatively less important characteristic that is common to both concepts. Errors of omission need to be evaluated in the context of their importance in the understanding of the topic or concept being tested.

The bulk of the present chapter focuses on an alternative form of testing which is intended to address the problems discussed above. Because the alternative test format is based on spatial representation of text, the discussion of the test format is preceded by a brief section discussing text maps.

TEXT MAPS AND MAP TESTS

The specific method of spatial representation of text from which we developed our test format is based on the text map scheme developed at the University of Illinois by Armbruster and her colleagues (see Chapter 9, present volume, for more details of this approach). Alternative spatial representation strategies such as networking (see Holley & Dansereau, Chapter 4) or schematizing (see Mirande, Chapter 7, present volume) could probably be used in the same manner. Mapping was chosen as the basis for testing largely because we were more familar with that approach. At the time we started investigating map tests, there were seven basic symbols for describing interrelationships between topics or concepts: (1) definition, (2) characteristic or property, (3) example, (4) temporal sequence, (5) causal sequence, (6) similarity, and (7) greater-than or less-than comparisons. In addition, a symbol to mark particular importance and a symbol for negation of the seven basic symbols were included in the system. Although Armbruster and Anderson have made some additions and modifications in the above list, we have continued to work with the same basic set of symbols with only a minor modification which will be described below.

Figure 1 lists the symbols and their associated relationships, and illustrates their use in mapping the topic, "Composting Toilets." Although this particular map was generated from information in my own memory, it basically represents what might have been an article describing composting toilets—their characteristics and advantages—and contrasting composting toi-

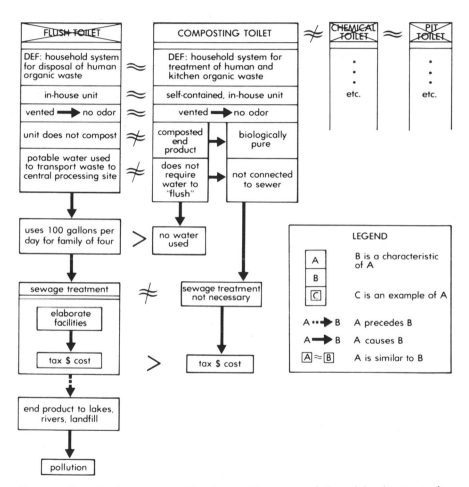

FIGURE 1. Example of a master map. Key: Boxes with one rectangle (containing A) over another equivalent rectangle (containing B) show that B is a characteristic of A. Boxes with one rectangle (containing B) inside another rectangle (containing A) show that B is an example of A. A single arrow from A to be shows that A precedes B. A double arrow from A to B shows that A causes B. Boxes with *approximately equals* signs connecting them show that the concepts within them are similar.

lets with three noncomposting examples. The full topic is fleshed out by
making visually explicit the relationships among related bits of information
and the topic.

The basic procedure for creating a map test consists of taking a completed map for the topic to be tested, such as the one in Figure 1, and deleting
portions of this completed or *master map*. In effect we are creating cloze
(Anderson, 1974) tests from master maps. Figure 2 illustrates what we refer
to as a cloze–content test. The test has been generated from the master map
by deleting portions of the text information but leaving the entire structure of

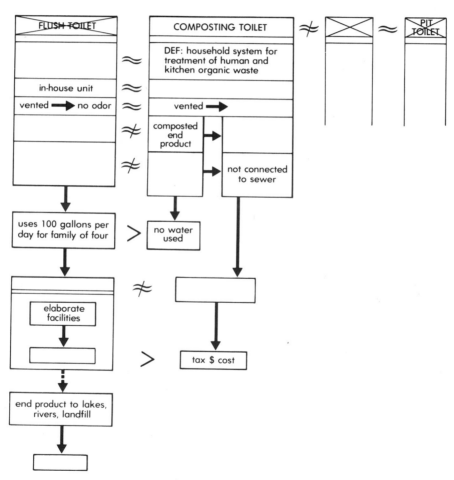

Figure 2. Cloze–content map test derived from master map in Figure 1.

the map (all the symbols) intact. Figure 3 is an example of a cloze–relationship test where both relationship symbols and text content have been deleted. A variation of this test can be constructed by giving the student a list of information that should be included; instructions may indicate that the list is not exhaustive. An extreme form of the test exists when the student is simply given a topic and told to map the entire topic from memory of the original text.

In all cases, map tests are cued recall tests with a considerable amount of control regarding the degree and type of cuing. For example, the cloze–con-

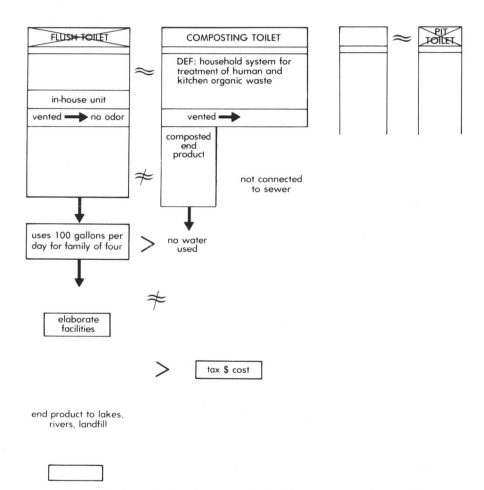

FIGURE 3. Cloze–relationship map test derived from master map in Figure 1.

tent type of test is similar to free recall in terms of the amount of information required of the student, but the map structure cues or constrains the kind of information (with respect to its relationship to the topic) that *should* be supplied by the student. By appropriate instructions to the student, it may be indicated that the map structure cues the minimum amount of information that should be supplied and that the student may add to the overall map. This would allow more flexibility in assessing additional information that the student deems relevant to the topic.

Diagnosis of errors or misunderstanding will depend to some extent on the particular type of test or extent of cuing present. If most of the content is listed and the student is required only to indicate the relationships among the given elements of information (cloze–relationship test) there is less demand for the student to have discriminated more important from less important information when studying the topic being tested. Such a test does go beyond a traditional matching type of test format in that the student must indicate not only what goes together but also *how* the information fits together. Nevertheless, such a test seems to measure a fairly primitive level of comprehension and would probably only discriminate between relatively minor misunderstanding of details and gross failure in learning.

In a more complete version of Figure 1, specific examples of composting toilets could be given with comparisons of their characteristics. This information is less critical for understanding the main topic and, in general, there tends to be a decrease in importance as one goes from top to bottom on a map. Exceptions may be causal or temporal chains, as is the case with the causal chains in Figure 1. The lack of sewage treatment is a key point for understanding the advantage of composting toilets over flush toilets. In this case the first three properties, common to both flush and composting toilets are less important than the differentiating sequence in the bottom half of the map.

On the other hand, if a student were given "chemical toilet" or "pit toilet" and classified these as examples of a composting toilet, this would indicate a basic failure to understand the concept. This misunderstanding could be pinpointed by examining the characteristics given for pit and chemical toilets to see if "composting," "biologically pure end product," or some similar property were listed; or if the property "composting" were given for these nonexamples; or if this critical feature (processing of waste) was omitted from all types of toilets. The point is that diagnosing misunderstanding involves looking at a pattern of responses, not just a response to a single item. An omission of a single property may account for a pattern of related errors, such as incorrect classification of example. Additionally, an intrusion of an inappropriate characteristic may likewise result in a pattern of related errors that reflects a larger misunderstanding.

RESEARCH ON MAP TESTS

The goals of the initial exploratory work on map tests were to (1) develop training procedures to teach students to take map tests, (2) explore various training procedures to teach students to take map tests, (3) explore various forms of map tests, (4) develop scoring procedures for map tests, and (5) study the technical characteristics of map tests. Although the primary purpose of map testing is assessing students' comprehension of and memory for prose, the four preceding goals are prerequisite to this major purpose.

TRAINING STUDENTS TO TAKE MAP TESTS

In our initial testing we used junior college students enrolled in a basic chemistry course; however, most of the subsequent data were collected on students enrolled in basic study skills classes at the university level. With each population, all testing corresponded in both content and time to the regular course testing. In other words, topics tested with the map tests were part of the subject matter of the courses in which the testing was conducted, rather than experimental prose passages.

For the first phase of testing, a 23-page instruction manual was prepared. The manual introduced first the symbol for mapping a concept and its definition, then the symbol for mapping properties or characteristics of a concept, and then the symbol for examples. Following a brief explanation of each symbol, one or more examples were given. Exercises in reading maps and constructing maps from short paragraphs also followed each symbol. After the first three symbols were introduced there was a set of exercises combining all three symbols. Then other symbols were introduced, followed by exercises of increasing complexity.

Initially we used two to three 50-minute class sessions for the training. In each session, students worked exercises. Project staff guided discussion and gave feedback during these sessions. Based on what we learned from the first phase of training, we revised the manual extensively. We removed most of the exercises on reading maps and increased the number of exercises on constructing maps. In addition, we added a final exercise in which students were required to read a four and one-half page article on the Caribbean Islands as a homework assignment. Then, in the following session, they were asked to construct a map of the passage from memory. This exercise was added to simulate the actual testing session in which students would be mapping topics from their course, from memory. These changes also increased the training time to five 50-minute class sessions. However, the basic format of guided reading, completion of exercises in the manual, and discussion of mapping solutions remained basically the same throughout three phases of training and testing (corresponding to three semesters).

CONSTRUCTING MAP TESTS

In the construction of traditional test formats, independence of the individual items is an issue of concern. Specifically, it is felt that the failure to respond correctly to one item should not cause the test taker to fail subsequent items (and vice versa). With map tests, failure to correctly supply a major topic or concept would likely result in failure to correctly give the definition, examples, or other subordinate information for that topic. However, because the purpose of map tests is diagnosis of student errors, this lack of independence is not necessarily a problem. To use the preceding example, if the student gives pit toilet as an example of composting toilet, it is necessary to look at the characteristics or properties given for pit toilet to locate the source of the misunderstanding. The properties are not independent of the erroneous classification but are, nevertheless, useful information. To prevent students from going on lengthy tangents, we took some steps to decrease dependence of responses. This is subsequently discussed in greater detail.

The master map for a typical test topic was about twice as long as the map in Figure 1. As a result, the typical test was two to three pages for each topic, to allow the students room for their responses. The most demanding (least cued) test form that we have used consists of a blank outline for a map; that is, the symbol for the major concept of a topic was given at the top of the first page, with five to eight related concepts or examples listed on a cover–instruction page. In the first testing phase, we used a test where only the major topic was given, and we were concerned about students going off on a completely irrelevant tangent. To deal with this possibility, we used what we called a *progressive frame* approach. This procedure required the student to map approximately one half-page in response to the topic. Then he or she turned the page and got feedback in the form of a correct map of the first part of the topic. Next, on the same page as the feedback, the student continued to map his or her response. This routine was continued until the map was completed. As it turned out, this form of testing was entirely too confusing for students to understand, so the progressive frame approach was dropped in subsequent testing.

After our initial experimentation, we primarily used three test forms: (1) a blank map with a short list of content to be included (cued recall); (2) a complete map structure with all symbols and relationships indicated (but with no filled-in content) and five to eight items of content listed (cloze–content); and (3) a map, like Figure 3, with partial structure and some content included but no additional content list (cloze–relationship). For creating a cloze–relationship test, we developed a rough set of deletion rules to apply to the master map:

1. Omissions will be made from the bottom up.
2. Either the relationship or the content will be given for each of the major concepts.
3. Placement of content and symbols will be such that more room is allowed for student responding than existed in the master map.
4. Symbols of each type will be deleted roughly in proportion to their representation in the master map.

The map tests were administered as closely as possible in time to the regular classroom tests that covered the same content. Each test had a cover sheet with instructions and, for some forms, a list of content to be included. If content was given on the instruction page, it was also stated that the list was incomplete and the student should supply additional information about the topic. In addition to the test and instruction page, each student was also given a one-page symbol-summary sheet. This sheet depicted each symbol and gave a brief explanation of its use, and students were encouraged to refer to it, as needed, throughout the test. The time needed to complete the test varied with form, topic, and student but the test generally took 20 to 45 minutes.

SCORING MAP TESTS

Because one of our goals on this project was to determine the technical characteristics of map tests, we needed a scoring system that would produce scores that could be used to determine reliability and validity. Although we have experimented with several scoring systems, the one given in Figure 4 has served as the basis for most of the analyses to date. Because there are two categories of response (topic content and relationship) on a map test, each of these has been represented as a dimension of the matrix in Figure 4. There are three possible outcomes with relationship information: a relationship can be indicated correctly, incorrectly, or omitted. If a particular test form includes a particular relationship as a given, it can be used correctly or incorrectly but not omitted.

There are four possible outcomes with content information. First, the content is correct with respect to the master map from which the test was taken. In this case, scoring would include paraphrases or gist except where a verbatim statement is necessary (e.g., a chemical formula). Second, the student includes information that appropriately fits with the topic of the map

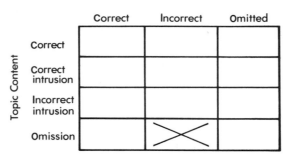

FIGURE 4. Scoring categories for map tests—relationship type by content category.

tests but was not an explicit part of instruction (or not explicitly represented in the master map). This allows for a rather broad range of inferences, additional details or examples, and corollary information. Third, the student includes information that is not relevant to the topic being tested. This response is categorized as an incorrect intrusion. A useful aspect of map tests is that the student must make explicit, by using the relationship symbols, how he or she thinks the incorrect intrusion relates to the topic. This permits a systematic approach to the diagnosis of students' misunderstandings. Fourth, the student omits information that is contained in the master map and was judged necessary for a full understanding of the particular concept being tested.

By using the two-dimensional array of Figure 4 it is possible to classify 11 different types of responses. Cell (4,2), content omitted–relationship incorrect, makes little sense. One might also suppose that Cell (4,1), content omitted–relationship correct, would be of little use; however, there are instances where students have produced a symbol without indicating any content. For example, a student may recall that a concept has three important properties yet remember only two and indicate with an additional line that another property should be given.

The next step in scoring the map tests was the development of a standard set of rules that could be applied to the students' responses to make reliable judgments about the category into which a particular response should be placed. In order to develop these rules, two different scorers each scored a set of map tests. Then the separate scores were compared and the disparities were discussed. The tests with the greatest disparities in scores were independently rescored and compared again. This process continued until the scorers felt they had reached a high degree of agreement. The result of this "score–compare–discuss" process was a set of written rules that both scorers felt represented thoroughly the decision process they used in scoring the map tests.

After the scoring roles had been refined, both scorers scored all the tests from our first phase of data collection. Reliability for these data is discussed in a later section of the present chapter.

Because the scoring rules were an outcome of extensive discussion between two scorers, it was felt that a further check on the adequacy or sufficiency of these rules should be made to determine how much (or how little) experience or training was necessary for a person to be able to apply the rules. The person selected for this task was trained to map, using the same materials that had been used with subjects participating in the research. Then she was given score sheets (copies of the matrix in Figure 4), an earlier draft of the scoring rules, and brief verbal instructions. The results of this test of the scoring rules were quite satisfactory. The third scorer was able to complete the task without difficulty and had interrater correlations with the first two scorers of .71 and .76. As a result we feel that we have a scoring system that can be taught to others relatively easily and applied with a respectable degree of reliability. This communicability of test scoring procedures is important to the extent that it increases the likelihood and feasibility of the use of this type of test in nonresearch, educational settings.

PATTERNS OF RESPONSES

For purposes of comparison across testing occasions or across topics, it would be desirable to report scores as proportions. Although this is possible for some of the categories, it is not possible for others. For example, the total number of correct or incorrect intrusions is not fixed. Although these response types could be taken as a proportion of total responses for a subject, there is a problem in deciding which of the omit categories should be counted as a response—certainly not omit—omit, but why not correct content–relationship omitted? As a result we have worked primarily with cell frequencies.

Table 1 gives the mean cell frequencies for the 11 categories of responses from our second phase of data collection. These means are computed across different forms of the test (e.g., cloze–content, cloze–relationship), which have differing numbers of responses required for an exact match to the master map. This was done because there were too few students responding to each test form. However, the number of responses for an exact match to the master map ranged from a minimum of about 20 to a maximum of about 40.

As can be seen from Table 1, the highest frequency of responses is in the omit–omit category. The next highest frequency is in content omitted–relationship correct. In most cases, though not all, this occurs when a symbol has been included on the test form and the student has failed to respond to it. There were a number of instances in which the student actually

TABLE 1

Mean Response Frequencies for Map Test Subscores

Topic content	Map relationship		
	Correct	Incorrect	Omitted
Correct	3.62	2.65	0.82
Correct intrusion	3.37	1.49	0.69
Incorrect intrusion	1.05	0.66	0.10
Omitted	4.50	—	17.28

included a symbol but failed to include the content information. The next three highest cell frequencies are content correct–relationship correct, content correct–relationship omitted, and correct intrusion–relationship correct. We take this general pattern, together with relatively low frequencies in the other cells, as an indication that students can, with relatively little training, respond successfully to map tests.

However, there are a number of interesting questions that cannot be answered from this scoring scheme. For example, what proportion of the frequencies in each cell represents the student responding to listed information or given symbols versus recalling this information or producing a symbol? To answer this question, as well as others, we have been experimenting with an alternative scoring scheme. However, most of our investigation of the technical characteristics of map tests are based on the 11-cell scheme, and discussion of the alternative scoring procedure is here deferred until after the presentation of analyses based on the 11-cell method.

TECHNICAL CHARACTERISTICS OF MAP TESTS

From the outset of our research on map tests, we have been concerned with the technical aspects or psychometric properties of these vehicles. In this section, I discuss our findings on the reliability and validity of these tests.

RELIABILITY

Of the several types of reliability, our first concern was with the rater or scorer reliability. Following the aforementioned development of our scoring

TABLE 2

CORRELATIONS BETWEEN TWO SCORERS FOR MAP TEST SUBSCORES

Topic content	Map relationship		
	Correct	Incorrect	Omitted
Correct	.98	.83	.56
Correct intrusion	.98	.93	.89
Incorrect intrusion	.93	.91	.82
Omitted	.93	—	.94

scheme, we generated a set of rules for categorizing responses. Because there was a considerable amount of interrater discussion of the scoring procedures for the first data set, reliability was spuriously high. A better test of scorer reliability is possible with our second data set where there was relatively little discussion prior to scoring the tests. Table 2 presents the correlations between two scorers for each of the 11 score categories or cells. With the exception of Cell (1,3), all coefficients are above .82 and most are above .90. For our first set of data we also computed generalizability coefficients (Cronbach, Glesser, Nanda, & Rajartnam, 1972) for each of the 11 subscores. With five raters, the second subscore (Cell [1,2]) is .50, while all other scores ranged from .75 to .97. In general, it appears that our scoring procedures are quite reliable.

A second, informal, type of reliability was also investigated. In this case the concern was with the agreement among experienced "mappers" in constructing the master map. Four experienced mappers mapped a seven-page passage on medical applications of lasers. The total number of content entries on these maps varied from 30 to 69. Of those entries, 14 appeared to be the minimum necessary for describing the major concepts of the passage. This includes the topic itself, three major properties, three examples of laser types, and their associated applications for medical use. Of these 14 entries, three mappers included all 14 and the fourth included 13. For the 13 units mapped by all four people, there was 87% agreement on the way they should be mapped. For the three people who mapped all 14 units, there was 98% agreement on how these units should be mapped. As is obvious from the variance in the total number of units mapped, the major source of disagreement concerns the amount of detail to include in the map.

We also intended to look at reliability across testing occasions. However, we only had multiple testing occasions in our first phase of data collection and subject attrition was too high to make any such analyses reasonable.

Validity

From the 11 subscores that are produced by the scoring matrix, two composite scores were computed for each subject. The composites were intended to approximate logically the "total number correct" score that is obtained on traditional objective tests. These composites were then used to obtain the index of validity of the map tests by correlating the composites with the score obtained from the instructor's course exam (the criterion).

Composite 1 comprised Subscores 1, 3, 4, and 5 (Cells [1,1], [1,3], [2,1], and [2,3]) from the scoring matrix. These scores represent instances in which the response involved correct topic content and either a correct map relationship symbol or an omitted symbol. Subscores 2 and 6 were not used because, although they represent correct content responses, the relationship used was not correct.

Composite 2 comprised Subscores 7, 8, 9, and 10. This composite represents all instances in which the content was incorrect (regardless of the relationship response), combined with situations in which the topic was omitted although the correct symbol had been given on the test form.

The criterion used in the first phase of data collection was the classroom unit test on matter in the basic chemistry course. This test was constructed by the course instructor and consisted entirely of brief fill-in type items requiring students to recall a concept, given the definition; an element name, given the symbol; an element number, given the name; and so on. Any response that was misspelled was counted as an error for purposes of the chemistry class. No rescoring was done when the test was used as a criterion in the analyses reported here.

The correlations ($N = 36$) were .42 between the criterion and Composite 1, .10 between the criterion and Composite 2, and $-.13$ between Composites 1 and 2. The low correlation between the two composite scores suggests that correct responses (Composite 1) are not simply an outcome of a high rate of responding; that is, students who made many correct responses were not necesarily the same subjects who made many errors. The lack of a strong negative correlation also indicates that, unlike traditional tests, there is no inverse relationship between correct and incorrect responses. It is possible for a student to make many correct responses *and* many incorrect responses, thereby allowing one to examine error patterns of high-scoring students (measured by Composite 1) as well as low-scoring students.

The correlations between the composite scores and the criterion are about what one would expect. The criterion and Composite 1 exhibit some overlap; this should be expected because both are measures of number of correct responses. However, the scores also contain variance that is not in common, and this is due to several factors: (1) spelling was not scored on the map tests, (2) relationship understanding was demanded on the map tests, (3) list responses were a part of Composite 1, and (4) mapping ability played a role in Composite 1. Given the rather different nature of the two tests, we feel that the degree of relationship between Composite 1 and the criterion measure is well within the range of acceptability. Indeed, a relationship much higher than $r = .75$ would have suggested that map tests may not be sufficiently different from traditional tests to warrant the additional effort.

In our most recent phase of data collection, we have attempted a more stringent test to see if the information provided by map tests could be obtained more easily by a multiple-choice test. In this case we were given permission to construct the multiple-choice tests that would serve as both the required classroom exam and as our criterion. The multiple-choice items were worded in such a way as to test as closely as possible the information used in the map tests. For example, items were written which asked about *characteristics* of concepts, *examples* of concepts, which *concept* approximately went with a particular example, what the next step in a (*temporal*) sequence was, and so forth. In other words, an attempt was made to create a multiple-choice test which, by using the language of maps (though not the structure), tested the same knowledge as the map tests. As nearly as possible we also attempted to write distractors that were similar to the kinds of errors made on map tests.

On this testing occasion we had two distinct topics that were being tested—topics which were mapped separately. Though the items for the two topics were combined on the multiple-choice test, we scored the map tests separately. As before, composite scores were created from the map tests to produce a general correct score and a general incorrect score. In Table 3 these composites are labeled C+ and C−, respectively, and the two topics are distinguished by the labels Map 1 and Map 2. As before, the (1,1) response derives from the cell in the scoring matrix and represents a correct content–correct relationship response. MC Total is the total number correct on the multiple-choice test.

The correlations among the variables described above are presented in Table 3. In three of the four correlations between MC Total and positive responses on the map tests—Map 1 (1,1), Map 1 C+ and Map 2 C+—the correlations are moderately low. The relationship between the two negative composite scores and MC Total is functionally zero. The pattern is similar to the results previously discussed here and provides some support for the validity of the approach. That is, positive responding on map tests is related to correct responding on the multiple-choice test and error responses are not related to the scores on the multiple-choice test.

Other correlations in Table 3 appear to be fairly straightforward. The responses in Cell (1,1) show a high relationship to their respective positive composite scores and a negative or null relationship to the negative com-

TABLE 3

Correlations between Multiple-Choice and Map Test Scores

Variables	MC total[a]	Map 1[b] (1,1)	Map 2 (1,1)	Map 1 C+	Map 2 C+	Map 1 C−
MC Total						
Map 1 (1,1)	.11					
Map 2 (1,1)	.32	.36				
Map 1 C+	.29	.89	.42			
Map 2 C+	.33	.53	.94	.54		
Map 1 C−	−.08	−.36	−.25	−.50	−.28	
Map 2 C−	.03	−.36	−.02	−.36	−.05	.45

[a]Total number correct on multiple-choice test.

[b]Map 1 and Map 2 refer to the mapping test scores for the two topics; (1,1) is a cell in the map scoring matrix; C+ and C− are the composite correct and incorrect mapping scores, respectively.

posite scores. Although each Cell (1,1) score shows a moderate correlation with the composite score for the other topic tested, the correlation with its corresponding composite is much higher. Because mapping ability is constant across topics, the higher correlation of Cell (1,1) score with its corresponding composite score is presumably due to knowledge of the subject matter particular to that topic only.

As discussed above, the distractors for the multiple-choice test were written to represent the kinds of errors that we had been scoring on the map tests. Although an attempt was made in constructing the foils to represent the full range of possible errors (i.e., the other 10 cells of the scoring scheme) the only foils that were chosen with sufficient frequency to make analysis possible were correct intrusion–incorrect relationship (Cell 2,2) and incorrect intrusion–correct relationship (Cell 3,1). The correlations between MC (2,2) and Map 1 (2,2) and Map 2 (2,2) are −.04 and .13, respectively. The correlations between MC (3,1) and Map 1 (3,1) and Map 2 (3,1) are .21 and .05, respectively. It is clear from these correlations that the multiple-choice foils are not measuring the same thing as the responses on the map tests.

MC (2,2) did show a fairly high relationship ($r = .66$) with MC (3,1), suggesting that to some extent these are measuring the same thing. Furthermore, the correlation between these two variables and MC Total was quite high ($r = .95$ and $r = .82$, respectively). A possible explanation for the correlations with the MC (2,2) scores is that subjects are selecting foils that contain concepts or key words–phrases related to the topic tested, particularly with regard to the relationship to the topic. For the correlation between MC Total and MC (3,1) it might be that students are confusing content from one study skills topic with the other topic, because some of the (3,1) foils (incorrect intrusion–correct relationship) for Topic 1 were taken from Topic 2 and vice versa. In short, the multiple-choice foils may simply measure an ability to recognize key words–phrases that were associated with the topics studied. This same recognition memory strategy would result in many correct responses on the multiple-choice test as well. This problem with multiple-choice items, which bears a close relationship to wording in instruction (i.e., verbatim items), has been discussed extensively elsewhere (Anderson, 1972).

TENTATIVE CONCLUSIONS

The intent of map tests is to diagnose "bugs" in declarative knowledge. However, the major thrust of data collection and analysis to date has been to explore questions of reliability and validity and the possibility of obtaining the same information by more conventional means. Concern over the relationship between map tests and traditional test formats arises from the fact that formats such as multiple-choice are the established standard. Therefore, it is important to understand the differences between map tests and more traditional formats (although it should be noted that the differences among traditional formats such as multiple-choice and essay are not well understood). An obvious source of difference is one that is usually conceptualized as the differences in memory demands (e.g., retrieval processes) between recognition memory (multiple-choice) and cued recall (short essay or fill-in tests), although this distinction is not always accurate (i.e., higher-order multiple-choice questions can test more than recognition memory). Because, on its face, the map test format seems to correspond more closely to cued recall, future research on map tests might well compare them with short essay questions. The essay responses could be mapped to obtain scores that would permit comparison with the map tests. Scoring of the map tests appears to have a distinct advantage over typical scoring of essay tests, particularly in terms of interrater reliability.

Diagnosis of errors seems to call for a different scoring scheme than the one we have been using. As mentioned earlier, we are currently experimenting with an alternative scheme, but results so far are tentative. It appears that error diagnosis could best be accomplished by repeated testing for each subject. This could be accomplished more easily in a more traditional laboratory-type setting where subjects who are trained to map take a number of map tests over a period of time on a range of subject matter that is carefully chosen to represent the full range of mapping relationships. Then the data could be inspected for each individual, rather than by using aggregate data which may obscure the presence of consistent error patterns. That is, one student may have a problem with causal relationships, whereas another may have no problem with causal relationships but confuses properties and examples, and a third student may have no major problems. The data from such hypothetical students, when averaged, would reveal no consistent pattern. The recent work of Harnish and Linn (1982) and Tatsuoka and Tatsuoka (1982), dealing with S-P charts and related notions, have direct bearing on this issue and should be considered a viable possibility for identifying such patterns.

Related to this issue of comprehension problems, it would be interesting to compare maps of good and poor students. In this case the maps could be constructed open-book rather than from memory. This approach to investigating comprehension problems might well reveal some of the weak links in the study behavior of less successful students (see Anderson, 1979).

REFERENCES

Anderson, R. C. (1972). How to construct achievement tests to assess comprehension. *Review of Educational Research, 42,* 145–170.

Anderson, R. C., Spiro, R. J., & Anderson, M. C. (1978). Schemata as a scaffolding for the representation of information in connected discourse. *American Educational Research Journal, 15,* 433–440.

Anderson, T. H. (1974). Cloze measures as indices of achievement comprehension when learning from extended prose. *Journal of educational measurement, 11,* 83–92.

Anderson, T. H. (1979). Study skills and learning strategies. In H. F. O'Neil & C. D. Spielberger (Eds.), *Cognitive and affective learning strategies.* New York: Academic Press.

Brown, J. S., & Burton, R. R. (1978). Diagnostic models for procedural bugs in basic mathematical skills. *Cognitive Science, 2,* 155–192.

Clinchy, B., & Rosenthal, K. (1971). Analysis of children's errors. In G. S. Lesser (Ed.), *Psychology and educational practice.* Glenview, IL: Scott, Foresman.

Cronbach, L. J., Glesser, G., Nanda, H., & Rajartnam, N. (1972). *The dependability of behavioral measurements: Theory of generalizability for scores and profiles.* New York: Wiley.

Gronlund, N. E. (1981). *Measurement and evaluation in teaching* (4th ed.). New York: Macmillan.

Gropper, G. L. (1974). *Instructional strategies.* Englewood Cliffs, NJ: Educational Technology Publications.

Gropper, G. L. (1975). *Diagnosis and revision in the development of instructional materials.* Englewood Cliffs, NJ: Educational Technology Publications.

Harnish, D. L., & Linn, R. L. (1982). Analysis of item response patterns: Questionable test data and dissimilar curriculum practices. *Journal of Education Measurement, 18,* 133–146.

Klein, M. F., Birnbaum, M., Standiford, S. N., & Tatsuoka, K. K. (1981). *Logical error analysis and construction of tests to diagnose student "bugs" in addition and subtraction of fractions*

(Research Rep. 81–6). Urbana, IL: University of Illinois, Computer-Based Education Research Laboratory.

Surber, J. R., & Smith, P. L. (1981). Testing for misunderstanding. *Educational Psychologist, 16*, 163–174.

Tatsuoka, K. K., & Tatsuoka, M. M. (1982). Detection of aberrant response patterns and their effect on dimensionality. *Journal of Educational Statistics, 7*, 215–232.

Tatsuoka, K. K., & Tatsuoka, M. M. (1981). *Item analysis of a test designed for diagnosing bugs; item relational structure analysis method* (Research Rep. 81–7). Urbana, IL: University of Illinois, Computer-Based Education Research Laboratory.

CHAPTER 11

The Representation of Knowledge: Curricular and Instructional Implications for Science Teaching

JAMES H. STEWART

INTRODUCTION

It is common to envision a curriculum as that which is to be learned by students—curriculum developers intend that students' knowledge, skills and attitudes will change in anticipated directions as the result of instruction based upon a curriculum. This perspective can be identified in the writings of Bobbitt (1918, 1924) and Tyler (1950). More recently Johnson (1967, 1977) has been very specific on this point. To him a curriculum is "a structured series of intended learning outcomes" (ILOs) (1967, p. 130). Johnson's definition is adopted here.

Johnson's definition of a curriculum as a series of ILOs can be applied to instructional sequences of varying length—including entire courses, units of study within a course, or a single lesson. The development of curricula at any of these levels is a difficult activity, given the complexity of even introductory high school science subject matter and the diversity of learners' backgrounds and interests with respect to such content. Consequently, techniques that

235

make what is to be learned more obvious and more coherent, for both teachers and learners, have important practical implications for science education. In this paper, techniques for presenting knowledge will be discussed in the context of science curriculum development. The techniques fall into two categories: (1) those that can be used to represent conceptual knowledge (concept maps and active structural networks), and (2) those that can be used to represent procedural knowledge (flowcharts). These techniques can assist the curriculum planner in surveying disciplinary knowledge, selecting curricular content, and sequencing the selected content.

The general value of knowledge representation for curriculum developers has been outlined by Greeno (1976):

> The goal of instruction is that students should acquire knowledge and skills of various kinds. A rich set of concepts has been developed in scientific psychology that can be applied to analyze the structure of knowledge and cognitive skills. Thus it should be possible using these concepts to carry out analyses of knowledge and skill that are desired as outcomes of instruction. It may be expected that the explicit statement of instructional objectives based on psychological theory should have beneficial effects both in design of instruction and assessment of student achievement. The reason is simple: we can generally do a better job of accomplishing something and determining how well we have accomplished it when we have a better understanding of what it is we are trying to accomplish [p. 123].

KNOWLEDGE REPRESENTATION AND SCIENCE CURRICULA

In representing ILOs in science courses, traditional linear listing is possible, but because of the inherent limitations of lists, it is difficult to convey the conceptual interrelatedness that exists in any semantically rich science discipline. Philosophers of science such as Hempel (1966) have written about this integrity when discussing the role of concepts (meanings of symbols) in science. The limited but central meanings of the symbols are usually specified by definitions, but the extended and more complete meanings of the symbols are formed by combinations of concepts with relational terms in a network of propositions. According to Hempel (1966), concepts are "the knots in the network of systematic interrelationships in which laws and theoretical principles [i.e., propositions] form the threads" (p. 64).

In science education attempts have been made to represent knowledge in two dimensions, thus getting away from the linear nature of lists (e.g., Bogden, 1977; Pines, 1978; Stewart, Van Kirk, & Rowell, 1979). Stewart et al. (1979) termed these representations concept maps and argued that, unlike outlines, they could be used to express the recognizable patterns of organization in science disciplines. In describing concept maps Stewart *et al.* (1979) employed the following analogy:

> An analogy can be made between concept maps and roadmaps, with concepts corresponding to cities. An outline will only provide a one-dimensional list of cities: it might list them in some order (e.g., by population, north-to-south, alphabetically); it can demonstrate certain relationships such as class inclusion (e.g., names of suburbs can be shown to be subheadings of cities); but it cannot give the reader an adequate view of the geography of the area it is trying to portray. A non-linear two-dimensional concept map, on the other hand, can be thought of as a scheme including not only cities, but a charting of the major highways (propositions) which link them. Further, not all cities are of the same population density; neither will the concepts on a map be of identical explanatory density or power. These differences can be easily portrayed on a concept map through utilization of the vertical dimension, which usually represents a continuum from general to specific: the most general concepts appear at the top of the map. As a reader of the map proceeds downward, more specific subordinate concepts, with less explanatory power, are encountered. Finally, at the bottom of the map are found specific, often interchangeable examples that will be used to illustrate the concepts above them [p. 172].

Figure 1 is an example of a concept map used by Stewart *et al.* (1979). Concept maps can help focus the curriculum developer's attention on the teaching of concepts and on the distinction between curricular and instructional content—that is, between content that is intended to be learned versus that which will serve as a vehicle for learning.

An obvious shortcoming of these example concept maps is the lack of specifications concerning the nature of the relationships connecting concepts. However, researchers in artificial intelligence and information processing psychology who have been addressing the same problem of the representation of meaning use more specific methods (Anderson & Bower, 1973; Frederickson, 1975; Kintsch, 1974; Lindsay & Norman, 1977; Norman & Rumelhart, 1975; Winograd, 1973). An important feature of many of these representations is that unlike concept maps, they make explicit relationships between concepts.

One such technique is the *active structural network* of Norman and Rumelhart (1975). In these networks, meaning is specified in terms of *predicates:* "A predicate is a general function that specifies the relations that might exist among some set of concepts" (p. 41). Predicates correspond closely to verbs, adjectives, and adverbs, and take nouns as arguments. These predicates, however, *underlie* meanings of the parts of speech listed above. For instance, Norman and Rumelhart have identified four classes of primitive predicates that underlie verb meanings:

> The *stative* component of a verb conveys the fixed relationship that holds among its arguments for a specified period. The *change* component tells simply that a change of

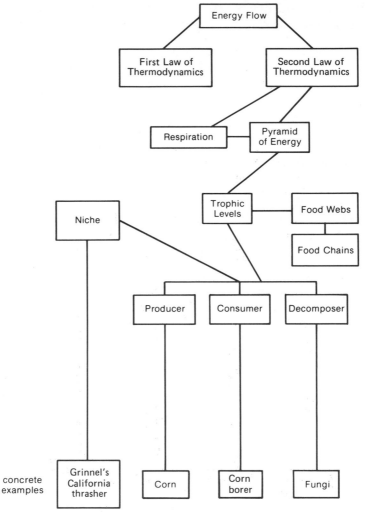

FIGURE 1. A general concept map for ecology (from Stewart, Van Kirk, & Rowell, 1979; reprinted with permission).

state has occurred. The *causative* component communicates the sources of, or reason for, the change. The *actional* component describes the behavior involved in the performance of the action specified by the verb. All verbs seem to contain at least one of these primitive components and a single verb may contain all of them [p. 47].

Figure 2 is an active structural network representing meiosis, a process of cell division that produces either sperm or egg cells. The representation is

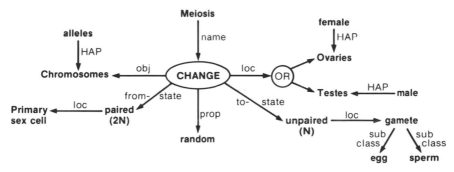

FIGURE 2. A general representation of meiosis (from Stewart, 1982; reprinted with permission).

at a very general level. As with many representations of science knowledge, it makes use of the CHANGE predicate. From Figure 2 it can be seen that:

1. The name of the CHANGE is meiosis.
2. The objects of the CHANGE are chromosomes (the bearers of the hereditary material—alleles).
3. The objects (chromosomes) CHANGE from a paired (2N) state to an unpaired (N) state.
4. The objects (chromosomes) are located in the ovaries of females or testes of males.

Although this network does not identify all of the components of a single meiotic division, it does contain the major ones—the change in chromosome state from a 2N primary sex cell to an N gamete, and the location in the organism (ovaries or testes) where the change takes place. A great deal of information is represented in Figure 2 at a "low magnification."

Figure 3 is a representation of a specific component of meiosis: the replication of chromosomes and the eventual reduction of the number by half prior to the maturation of the sperm or egg. In contrast to the representation in Figure 2, Figure 3 is a "higher magnification" and thus has a more restricted field of view. It would also be possible to take a more macro view than Figure 2 or a more micro view than Figure 3. For example, the more micro view might include a representation of the duplication and subsequent two divisions—not at the level of chromosomes, but at the molecular level of deoxyribonucleic acid (DNA). In addition, it would be possible to connect either of the illustrated networks to networks of Mendelian genetics, because the reduction of chromosome number leading to the production of sperm and egg serves as the basis for genetic continuity. With networks it is possible to represent the conceptual structure of a discipline at varying levels of complexity and to relate structures via their shared concepts. Active structural

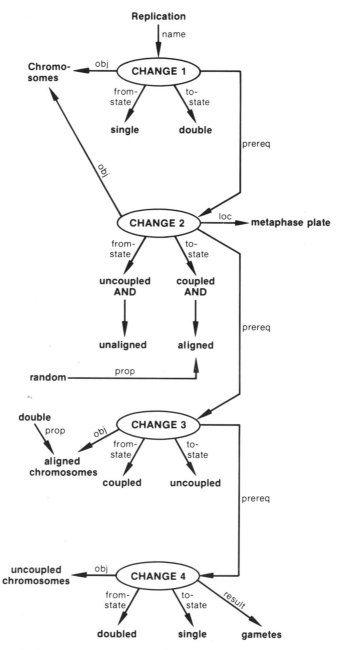

FIGURE 3. A detailed representation of meiosis (from Stewart, 1982; reprinted with permission).

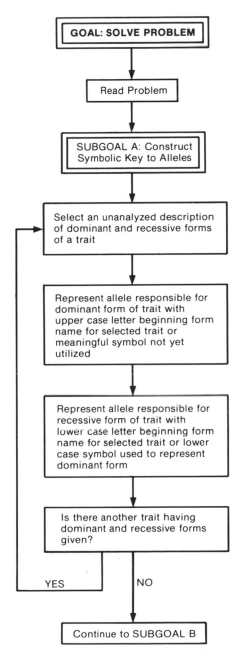

Figure 4. Subgoal A: Construction of a symbolic key to alleles (from Stewart, 1982; reprinted with permission).

networks have been discussed in the context of science curriculum development by Finley and Stewart (1982).

Concept maps and active structural networks, although useful in representing conceptual knowledge, do not encompass all that science teachers want their students to know following instruction. In addition, teachers normally expect their students to learn to use that knowledge (Stewart, 1982). One common activity in which students are expected to use their conceptual knowledge is the solving of problems. (Greeno [1976] has dis-

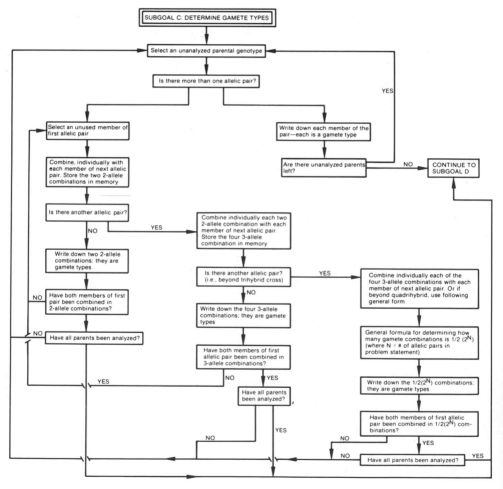

FIGURE 5. Subgoal C: Procedural knowledge in the determination of gamete types (from Stewart, 1982; reprinted with permission).

TABLE 1

A Sample Dihybrid Problem

In humans, six-fingeredness is under the control of a dominant allele and five-fingeredness is under the control of a recessive allele. The ability to curl one's tongue is under the control of a dominant allele and the lack of such ability is under the control of a recessive allele. What are the offspring genotype and phenotype possibilities for the children of one parent who is heterozygous for both number of fingers and the ability to curl the tongue, and a second parent who is five-fingered and heterozygous for tongue curling?

cussed a similar point with respect to conceptual knowledge and problem solving in mathematics). Curriculum developers, including teachers, need to pay explicit attention to the procedural knowledge (i.e., knowledge of the steps involved) in the execution of a problem solution. Generally it is possible to view problem-solving steps as a series of subgoals in the attainment of a goal—the solution to the problem (see Newell & Simon, 1972). The outcome of the execution of each subgoal will serve as input to the subsequent subgoal.

One approach to representing the algorithmic aspects of procedural knowledge is to use flowcharts. Such an approach is illustrated in Figures 4 and 5, which are flowchart representations of the procedural knowledge commonly employed in the solution of a class of genetics problems. The procedures (essentially algorithms) are appropriate to the solution of monohybrid (one-trait) through n-hybrid (multitrait) problems in which it is stated in the problem which alleles (forms of a gene) are dominant and which are recessive. Figure 4 is the first of six subgoals involved in solving the problem and Figure 5 represents the procedures involved in the generation of all possible gamete (sperm and egg) types. In Figure 5 (Subgoal C) meiosis and genetics are conceptually interrelated. Table 1 contains a sample from this class of problems.

CONCEPTUAL KNOWLEDGE REPRESENTATION

Conceptual knowledge representations (Figures 2 and 3) can be constructed using the guidelines of Lindsay and Norman (1977), Norman and Rumelhart (1975), and Stewart and Van Kirk (1981). As was the case with procedural knowledge representations, the curriculum developers must be very familiar with the subject matter to be represented. Stewart and Van Kirk (1981) have commented on the level of detail that is to be included in a representation, depending upon the intentions of the curriculum developer:

> In preparing to develop a representation, the question of the level of representation should be addressed—should one portray every sentence, every example? Should only the most general concepts and relationships appear in the network? Or should the network represent something in between these two extremes? Only a particular researcher or instructional developer working on a particular project can answer these questions. A rigid system of analysis and representation would be of little use to educators. One of the most important advantages of the semantic content analysis techniques . . . is their flexibility [p. 177].

The first step in the construction of the representation is to list all of the important concepts (e.g., gene, chromosome, allele) and their meanings, as well as important propositions. These are usually generalizations such as "Alleles segregate (separate) from each other during gamete formation." The next step is to take what seems to be the most basic proposition in the list and use it as a starting point for the construction of the network. Additional ideas are then added to this core, thus building up a network of concepts that are connected to one another by labeled relationship lines. When this step is completed the curriculum developer then checks the network to insure that important concepts and generalizations are included. Subject matter experts should validate the final product.

PROCEDURAL KNOWLEDGE REPRESENTATION

The development of a representation of procedural knowledge should be based on knowledge of the problems that students are expected to solve—for example, dihybrid-cross problems in high school genetics. The first step in the construction of such a representation might be an examination of how texts describe the steps involved in a solution. For instance, in high school biology (as in other science and mathematics) texts, the primary approach to teaching genetics problem solving is through the use of sample problems. Often texts describe only the high points of a solution, leaving out many details. For example, the representations in Figures 4 and 5 are essentially the same as the sample genetics problem solutions in high school biology texts, but they are more explicit about the steps in each subgoal. In addition to analyzing texts one could also watch teachers, in lectures and discussions, teach a set of problem-solving steps. The information obtained probably would be very similar to that found in high school texts. As with texts, teachers are apt to cover major points, students being expected to deduce and fill in the details.

An additional and most important step for the curriculum developer interested in representing procedural knowledge is to work through the solution to a sample problem, recording what is done at each step. This should be done in as detailed and explicit a manner as possible, without overlooking any components of a subgoal. This approach will provide a more complete set of steps than typical text or teacher presentations. In genetics where mono- through n-hybrid problems can be solved following essentially the same algorithm, the steps will have to include a means of cycling back through earlier steps to solve more complex problems. Examples of decision points where cycling is possible can be found in Figures 4 and 5.

The final step in a procedural construction is to have experts in the subject area validate the representation.

CURRICULAR IMPLICATIONS
FOR KNOWLEDGE REPRESENTATION

As indicated earlier, the general value of knowledge representation for curriculum developers has been outlined by Greeno (1976). In addition, Posner (1978) and Posner and Rudnitsky (1982) have described curricular uses of conceptual knowledge representation. Posner (1978) states that knowledge representation may be of assistance in carrying out three tasks faced by curriculum developers: (1) surveying the knowledge that constitutes a discipline (e.g., ecology, transmission genetics), (2) selecting from such knowledge those subsets appropriate for students to learn, and (3) sequencing the selected content in a meaningful way. Sources for a discipline survey for a high school course would probably include college-level texts, other professional texts, journals, and discussion with discipline experts, as well as the curriculum developer's own appropriate knowledge. Guidance for selecting from the available discipline knowledge would come from what has been chosen for presentation to similar groups of students, from tradition, and from the curriculum developer's own experiences. The sequence or organization of the discipline survey is modified by those factors affecting the content selection phase, particularly the experiences of the curriculum developer. Representations of both procedural and conceptual knowledge could play a role in each of these activities—surveying, selecting, and sequencing.

SURVEYING DISCIPLINE CONTENT

The outcome of the curriculum developer's survey of knowledge in a discipline is often represented by a set of notes in outline form or even more simply as lists of propositions which serve as the basis for the selection process. However, there are advantages to representing the outcomes in network format, so that the organization of the knowledge in a discipline is more systematically portrayed. High school and university faculty members with extensive subject matter knowledge who have tried mapping knowledge in their disciplines have felt that they have benefited from it. Mapping makes the overall organization of the content and the extensive relationships that exist among the concepts very explicit. For example, it may point out areas in which the expert assumes relationships that students in fact might not know or suspect.

Conceptual connections, which might otherwise be overlooked, are identified as the result of this systematic mapping. It is worthwhile to think of two classes of relationships: those that exist within narrowly focused content units (for example between dominance, recessiveness, genotype, and phenotype in Mendelian genetics) and those that connect two of the more focused content units, such as basic Mendelian genetics and meiosis. Posner (1978), using the vocabulary of cognitive psychologists, has termed these within- and between-schema relationships. Just as two schemata at one level may be joined to form a higher-level unit of knowledge, so can two higher-level units be linked. This embedding schemata view, in addition to being consistent with many cognitive psychologists' depiction of human long-term memory, also can assist a curriculum developer to "see" a hierarchical organization in the subject matter that is less easily portrayed by lists of propositions.

From the results of the discipline survey, a representation such as an active structural network or flowchart can be made. These representations of conceptual and procedural knowledge than serve as the input to the selection process.

SELECTING AND ORGANIZING CONTENT FOR INSTRUCTION

Even with extensive representations of discipline knowledge, the importance of selecting from that content cannot be overstated. The results of this selection serve three interrelated and important functions: (1) the selections, when sequenced, form the cognitive (as opposed to affective and psychomotor) ILOs; (2) they serve as guides for the development of the instructional activities; and (3) they serve as the basis for the evaluation of student achievement. The selection phase of curriculum development places additional demands on the curriculum developer: she or he must be concerned with maintaining the integrity of a discipline, as well as insuring that the selected content is potentially meaningful for students.

Knowledge representations are important in selection of curriculum content for two related reasons. First, having a discipline survey represented in network (or flowchart) format helps to insure that the knowledge base for the selection procedure is extensive and conceptually coherent (rich in relationships among concepts). Second, network or flowchart representations of the selected content (the intended learning outcomes for students) increase the likelihood that the instruction received by students will be conceptually coherent.

As Finley (1981) has pointed out, science curricula (as evidenced by observation of instruction) is often not conceptually coherent. He has indicated that a common characteristic of even what seems to be very good science instruction is that the conceptual integrity of the content is neither complete nor explicit. Even so, what students learn is not solely a function of curricular organization; students do not come to instruction as blank slates to be written upon. They have conceptions that they see as relevant to the new learning situation. Many of these conceptions may be in the form of alternative conceptions such as a Lamarckian view of evolution or an Aristotelian or impetus view of motion. Because a student is actively involved in constructing meaning from the knowledge presented in instruction, the lack of an explicit treatment of the ways concepts or schemata are related is an open invitation for students to construct meaning solely within the framework of their alternative conceptions—it is difficult to Newtonize an Aristotelian.

Although network representations in themselves do not alleviate the problem of students' alternate conceptions influencing what they learn, representations may be valuable in two ways. First, the process of mapping content as selected from the discipline survey has value in that it is suggestive of trouble spots that students experience when learning. Teachers who have been involved in representing science knowledge for curriculum purposes frequently comment on the range of difficulties they experience when working on a single map. Some areas are simple to represent, but others may take much time and thought. The areas that teachers find difficult to map are most often the areas that their students have difficulty learning. The possibility that mapping helps teachers to anticipate areas where students will have learning difficulties is intriguing.

With respect to the second factor which might influence student learning—the coherence of the curricular and instructional content—networks can be of great assistance. Constructing networks of the knowledge students are expected to learn increases teacher understanding of the structure of their objectives, and it may increase the degree to which they attempt to assist students in seeing the interrelated whole.

When selecting content from the discipline representation it is likely that it will be both complete (the necessary relationships among concepts will be present) and explicitly treated. By having the curriculum or ILOs both complete and explicit increases the likelihood that the instruction based on the ILOs will share the same features.

The preceding discussion is focused on the value of representing conceptual knowledge. A similar case may be made for analyzing and representing the procedures that are commonly employed to solve important classes of problems. In carrying out such an analysis and representing the results as a flowchart, the procedural steps might become more explicit in the mind of the curriculum developer, and some empathy for novice problem solvers might emerge as well. Probably the most significant consequence of this effort would come from the integration of conceptual and procedural representations, thereby leading to instruction in which it is obvious that the procedures are not executed for their own sake, because the conceptual knowledge in the discipline provides meaning to the procedures. Conversely, science teachers rarely expect students to possess only conceptual knowledge. The value of having conceptual knowledge is that it provides a basis for the exploration of nature—a basis for action (exploration in science comprises three broad categories: description, explanation, and prediction).

Figure 6 gives one possible format for representing conceptual and procedural knowledge simultaneously. It represents a subgoal for the solution of a genetics problem in flowchart form and a network representation of the conceptual knowledge that is necessary to execute the steps in the subgoal.

The likelihood that knowledge representation will be as important to sequencing decisions as it is to surveying and selecting content is small. Representations will most likely be useful in sequencing when they can be used to make the relationships between content "chunks" more explicit. For example, in genetics teaching the normal sequence is meiosis, basic Mendelian genetics, extensions of basic transmission genetics, and molecular genetics. One value of mapping in this case is that the attention of the curriculum developer might be focused on ways by which the various units could be conceptually related, thus increasing the coherence of the content for students. The question of networks as an aid in curriculum organization decisions has been addressed by Posner (1978). He too suggests that networks may have some value in deciding how to relate various parts of a course: "Network construction obviously does not make planning decisions for the course designer but the networks certainly serve as one guide in these sorts of decisions" (p. 28).

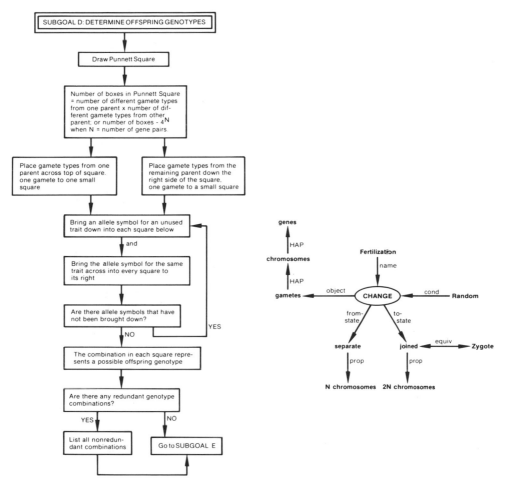

FIGURE 6. Subgoal D: Determination of offspring genotypes (from Stewart, 1982; reprinted with permission).

RELATED USES OF NETWORK REPRESENTATIONS IN SCIENCE EDUCATION

There are additional uses of networks which may be important, even though they are not curricular in terms of Johnson's (1967) definition of curriculum. Two of these are: (1) instructional applications in which students are directly involved in constructing and using networks, and (2) evaluation of student achievement.

There have been at least two different instructional uses of knowledge representations reported in the science education literature. Bogden (1977) has described using concept maps as an aid in discussion sections of a college-level genetics course. He used the maps to assist students in understanding the interrelationships among the many concepts presented during each week's lectures and laboratories. While he did not report on the effect of map use on student achievement, he did indicate that many of the students found the maps useful as a review technique that assisted them in organizing the genetics content. Dansereau has used a similar approach, with similar results, in teaching a graduate-level statistics course (see Holley & Dansereau, Chapter 4, present volume).

I have similarly used semantic networks while teaching a nonmajors university lecture and lab biology course. As in many laboratories, the students were so busy executing laboratory procedures that they often did not have time to reflect on the conceptual underpinnings of what they were doing or how the laboratory was tied to the lectures. In order to alleviate this problem, the instructors set aside the last 20 minutes of laboratories for review, using active structural networks. The function of the networks (to provide an organized overview of the content), as well as how to read them, was explained to students, who subsequently experienced little difficulty in using and understanding them. Students were given networks and shown how each laboratory activity related to the conceptual organization of the course. Self-reported results for two groups of students were mixed. One group viewed networks as another level of content to be learned rather than as an aid to organizing the biology content. A second group felt that the networks were doing for them what had been intended—increasing their understanding of the organization of the content. Unfortunately, no empirical studies have been reported in the science education literature on the influence of representations on student achievement.

Novak (1980, 1981) has made a preliminary report on another use of representations. In his study, seventh-grade students were taught to construct basic networks, which included concepts and labeled relationship lines. Following this training, students were expected to construct networks of their science instruction. Although Novak has not reported on the effect of this in terms of conceptual gains, he has found that it is feasible to expect seventh-grade students to be able to construct their own knowledge representations.

A second noncurricular use of knowledge representation is in the evaluation of student learning. To date, the most prevalent use of networks in evaluation has been in research situations (Stewart, 1980; also, see Surber, Chapter 10, present volume). In a classroom setting the maps of conceptual knowledge may be used to guide test construction because they represent the major conceptual organization that students are expected to learn from instruction. Teachers could compare test questions against the network to ensure that:

1. The knowledge necessary to answer the question was explicitly developed in the instruction.
2. The question is focused on the conceptual forest rather than on the example trees.
3. Students are evaluated on their knowledge of why they execute steps in a problem-solving situation rather than on their ability to execute the steps.
4. Foils in a test question have some close connection to the correct answers and to the question.

CONCLUSION

In this chapter suggestions have been made as to how the representation of conceptual and procedural knowledge may function in the development of curricula in instructional settings, and as an aid to evaluating student learning.

It should be kept in mind that the knowledge representations described in this chapter serve a single purpose—to assist the curriculum developer and teacher to better organize the conceptual knowledge in a discipline. Therefore, networks function with respect to only one type of objective. Good science teaching will undoubtedly include many other objectives. For example, teachers will generally be quite concerned with the affective development of their students, including attitudes about science as well as feelings of self-worth. Although these aspects of science teaching were not discussed in this chapter, this does not mean that they are unimportant in science curricula. Rather, it indicates that knowledge representation is not as clearly appropriate for these tasks as it is for representing conceptual and procedural knowledge. (However, see Holley and Dansereau [Chapter 4] for some preliminary work on mapping in the affective domain.)

Additionally, it is important to recognize that representations are, in the final analysis, only tools. Although they may assist a teacher or a student in understanding the organization of a discipline, they should not be given too central a role in instruction. Education involves more than providing students with a view of a particular organization. Students should also be aware of what competing organizations look like and above all what empirical data there are that make the structure we provide reasonable. If representations are seen as tools to sharpen the curriculum developer's knowledge of a discipline's conceptual organization and the interrelation of the conceptual with the procedural, they can be valuable. If we are able to increase the coherence of the design, the probability of increasing the clarity with which students organize such knowledge is also increased.

REFERENCES

Anderson, J. R., & Bower, G. H. (1972). *Human associative memory.* New York: Wiley.

Bobbitt, F. (1918). *The curriculum.* Boston: Houghton.

Bobbitt, F. (1924). *How to make a curriculum.* Boston: Houghton Mifflin.

Bogden, C. A. (1977). *The use of concept mapping as a possible strategy for instructional design and evaluation in college genetics.* Unpublished Masters' thesis, Cornell University.

Finley, F. N. (1981). A philosophic approach to describing science content: An example from geologic classification. *Science Education, 65,* 513–519.

Finley, F., & Stewart, J. (1982). Representing substantive structures. *Science Education, 66,* 593–611.

Frederickson, C. H. (1975). Representing logical and semantic structure of knowledge acquired from discourse. *Cognitive Psychology, 7,* 371–388.

Greeno, J. G. (1976). Cognitive objectives of instruction: Theory of knowledge for solving problems and answering questions. In D. Klahr (Ed.), *Cognition and instruction.* Hillsdale, NJ: Erlbaum.

Hempel, C. G. (1966). *Philosophy of natural science.* Englewood Cliffs, NJ: Prentice-Hall, 1966.

Johnson, M. (1967). Definition and models in curriculum theory. *Educational Theory, 17,* 127–140.

Johnson, M. (1977). *Intentionality in education.* Albany, NY: Center for Curriculum Research and Services.

Kintsch, W. (1974). *The representation of meaning in memory.* Hillsdale, NJ: Erlbaum.

Lindsay, P. H., & Norman, D. A. (1977). *Human information processing: An introduction to psychology (2nd ed.).* New York: Academic Press.

Newell, A., & Simon, H. A. (1972). *Human problem solving.* Englewood Cliffs, NJ: Prentice-Hall, Inc.

Norman, D. A., & Rumelhart, D. E. (1975). *Explorations in cognition.* San Francisco: Freeman.

Novak, J. (1980). Learning theory applied to the biology classroom. *The American Biology Teacher, 42,* 280–285.

Novak, J. (1981). Applying learning psychology and philosophy of science to biology teaching. *The American Biology Teacher. 43,* 12–16.

Pines, A. L. (1978). *Scientific concept learning in children: The effect of prior knowledge on resulting cognitive structure subsequent to audio-tutorial instruction* (Doctoral dissertation, Cornell University, 1977). *Dissertation Abstracts International, 38,* 7806314.

Posner, G. J. (1978). *Cognitive science: Implications for curriculum research and development.* Paper presented at the Annual Meeting of the American Educational Research Association, Toronto.

Posner, G. J., & Rudnitsky, A. N. (1982). *Course design* (2nd ed.). New York: Longman.

Stewart, J. (1980). Techniques for assessing and representing information in cognitive structure. *Science Education, 64,* 223–235.

Stewart, J. (1982). Two aspects of meaningful problem solving in science. *Science Education, 66,* 731–749.

Stewart, J., & Van Kirk, J. (1981). Content analysis in science education. *European Journal of Science Education, 3,* 171–182.

Stewart, J., Van Kirk, J., & Rowell, R. (1979). Concept maps: A tool for use in biology teaching. *The American Biology Teacher, 41,* 171–175.

Tyler, R. W. (1950). *Basic principles of curriculum and instruction.* Chicago: University of Chicago Press.

Winograd, T. A. (1973). A procedural model of language understanding. In R. C. Shank & K. M. Colby (Eds.), *Computer models of thought and language.* San Francisco: Freeman.

CHAPTER 12

Evolving a Description of Text through Mapping

DIANE L. SCHALLERT   *SARAH L. ULERICK*

ROBERT J. TIERNEY

PROBLEMS IN THE ANALYSIS OF INFORMATIVE DISCOURSE

Open a high-school level textbook. Nearly any text will do, although a science or social studies text is most likely to support our point. Now turn to the third page, say, of Chapter 4. There, you are likely to find a great deal of print, words arranged in sentences and paragraphs, with some of the words in bold print and some diagram or illustration breaking up the print. Now pretend that you are a diligent and relatively successful student, approaching the text in response to a class assignment. Read the page.

What do you know now about the topic discussed on page 3 of Chapter 4? If you have performed the task we assigned you sincerely, you should know a number of concepts associated with the topic of the chapter and how these concepts are related to one another. It is unlikely that you remember the exact wording or phrasing or that you noted the style of the prose. It is also

SPATIAL LEARNING STRATEGIES
Techniques, Applications, and Related Issues

unlikely that you found yourself pursuing to any great extent elaborations and ramifications from the text. What you have learned are some facts and how these are organized in relation to the topic.

Now, pretend that you are a researcher interested in discourse processes and have decided to analyze the same page of prose. Nearly any text analysis system you might choose will serve our point. Read the page again. If you perform this task sincerely, you find that you read much more slowly. In fact, you may stop reading altogether as you struggle with the myriad decisions inherent in any text analysis. As you move haltingly from word to word, you are likely to wish the text were many words shorter and did not contain quite so many of those interesting facts and relationships that you, in your guise of student, enjoyed moments before.

At this point, we hope that the tasks we assigned have made clearer the problem we have been struggling with for the past 3 years. The problem has been to analyze the language found in textbooks—a variety of discourse that is relatively common, has its own unique characteristics, and plays a role in an important setting, the classroom. As part of that setting, textbooks are intended to teach students new concepts and to have them consider know-ledge, systems of information, and ways of knowing as veridical transactions with the world. In our research with students learning from textbooks, we needed to describe what it was they were expected to learn. We needed a system that, like the students, would identify the essential information that the textbook's author intended to present in his or her prose. Although the major clues to the author's intended message are the actual words used, the message *is* the ideas and relationships between ideas that the author hoped students would learn about the topic.

To locate the focus of our system from a different perspective, consider the reader–author transaction in informative text. The author is usually an expert on the topic of the text and brings to the writing task an extensive knowledge base about the topic, coupled with some knowledge of the read-ing audience. The topic knowledge consists of facts, concepts, and relation-ships organized in a relatively permeable and flexible structure which reflects the author's preferred way of approaching the topic. The author does not, in most cases, know everything about every concept related to the topic but knows how and where to find needed information within the framework he or she has developed. In writing for the benefit of other experts, the author faces the task of selecting a focus, imposing an organization on concepts, and choosing the exact wording and phrasing, all with the goal of leading the expert reader to comprehend the message.

Writing a textbook imposes an additional set of constraints on the expert author. He or she must not only convince the audience of the validity of his or her claims, but must also *teach* them the claims and the basis upon which they rest. The decisions of organization, syntax, wording, and even whether to include certain subconcepts must be made while keeping in mind a reader who, to begin with, is much less sophisticated about the topic and who will likely be tested in some detail on the information presented. Thus, textbook language becomes a particular (peculiar?) mixture which reflects what the expert knows about a topic, how he or she believes that knowledge should be expressed to a less knowledgeable reader, and how that expression can serve the purpose of providing the reader with a knowledge base that can be measured (tested in a classroom setting). How successful the author–reader transaction will be depends in large part on how accurately the author has gauged the knowledge base of the potential readers, and how well he or she has chosen the words to highlight the concepts and relationships between concepts that students are intended to know after having read the text.

In pursuing our goal of describing the text that students were expected to learn, we considered available text analysis systems. There were several that recommended themselves by virtue of their flexibility in representing discourse and of their respected empirical bases. For example, the analysis systems of Kintsch (1974; Kintsch and van Dijk, 1978; Turner and Greene, 1977), Meyer (1975), and Frederiksen (1972, 1975) have been used extensively to describe informative texts. In these systems, a text is analyzed into smaller components called *propositions* (after Fillmore, 1968) that represent pieces of text bigger than a word and smaller than a clause or sentence. Propositions can be further identified and classified. In addition, these systems have the potential of describing whole-text patterns of propositions. However, where these systems have been most useful in the description of the ongoing process by which a reader takes the print on the page and constructs a meaning for it piece by piece, we needed a system that would describe what a reader is expected to learn from a text. Although it is theoretically crucial to determine how readers process print, it is also important to focus on the more permanent changes in readers that might occur as they encounter print. Furthermore, the latter is an important instructional goal: to have students not only understand what they read, but change their conceptions of the world as a result of their contact with an author's (or teacher's) message.

Thus, we developed *relational mapping,* a system of text analysis particularly suited to describing the concepts and relationships between concepts intended by the author, and which readers should learn when they approach informative discourse in an instructional setting. The system borrows from Armbruster and Anderson (see Chapter 9, present volume) the same limited list of relationship categories and the same grapho-symbolic representation of these relationships. The maps we produce, as a first step in our text description, reflect an underlying assumption that the author intended everything stated about a topic to form a coherent whole. From the graphic map, we derive relationship propositions that are rated for explicitness and embeddedness. These propositions can be used in a number of ways, such as in scoring recall protocols, deriving test questions, and preparing students to learn from the text.

RELATIONAL MAPPING

In this section, we describe in detail the parts and process of relational mapping. Our goal is to provide detail sufficient for anyone interested in the system to apply it and to know when its use would be appropriate. In subsequent sections we discuss the technique's problems and potential.

THE PIECES

There are two major, independently useful products of relational mapping—the map and the list of relationship propositions. The map is a graphic representation of the concepts and relationships that we, as text analysts, identify as the intended message of the author. It is constructed by identifying the concepts (ideas, facts, topics) in the text and then graphing (mapping) the relationships that hold the concepts together to form a coherent whole. Concepts are somewhat loosely defined in the system and their scope varies with the level needed for research or instructional purposes. In a very detailed map, for example, concepts may be single adjectives or prepositional phrases related as properties of a superordinate concept. In more general mapping, as when a chapter or 1-hour lecture is mapped, whole sentences and sometimes paragraphs or chapter units may serve as concepts. The specificity of a map depends on what the researcher or teacher expects the learner to derive from the text.

Three major assumptions guide the mapping process. The first, alluded to earlier, is that the text forms a coherent discussion of the topic. That is, we make the assumption that everything the author states is somehow relevant and related in some way to the topic. This assumption becomes the basis for inferences we make, and for implied concepts and relationships we bring into the map to make all its parts cohere.

The second assumption is that the concepts presented by the author are organized and are subsumed (embedded) by their relationship to the topic of the text. Thus the graphic representation of the text shows by its structure the set membership, property, comparison, and process relationships that hold the concepts together. The first and second assumptions work together when we, as text analysts, find a place in the developing map for every concept presented by the author.

The third assumption is that a relatively limited set of relationship types will be adequate in representing all of the ways in which two concepts can be related to each other in informative discourse. The relationship types come from a rhetoric tradition and identify Concept B as defining Concept A, as being a property of Concept A, as being an example of Concept A, as being similar or not similar to Concept A, as being greater than or less than Concept A, as occurring before Concept A, or as causing Concept A. The relationship types as well as the graphic symbols used to represent the relationships are presented in Figure 1.

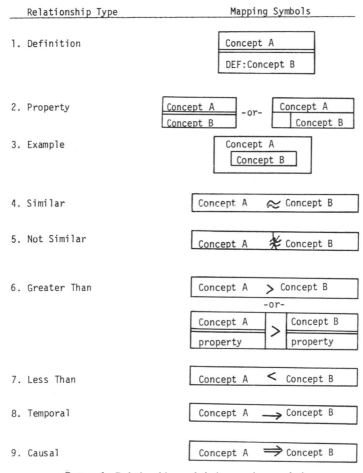

FIGURE 1. Relationships and their mapping symbols.

Note that we occasionally group the *similar, not similar, greater than,* and *less than* relationships and call them *comparison* relationships. Similarly, we refer to the *temporal* and *causal* relationships as *process* relationships because they both indicate the steps in a chain of events (or reasoning). The *definition* and *property* relationships are closely related by giving *characteristics* of concepts, whereas the *example* relationship gives *set membership* information.

The last of the preceding assumptions forces the text analyst to make a certain kind of categorical decision about each potential relationship identified in a text. Any relationship between two concepts must be one of the nine types possible within the system. The three assumptions of mapping, working together, lead the text analyst to show the structure and embeddedness of ideas within a text in terms of one or more of the nine possible relationship types. Thus, for example, Concept A may cause Concept B and this relationship may be a property of an example of the main topic of a text.

Once a map is produced, the list of relationship propositions can be derived. This simply involves making an explicit verbal statement of how Concept A is related to Concept B. Each relationship proposition is then compared to the original text and a decision is made about how explicit the author was in indicating the concepts and the relationship that make up the proposition. Finally, the level of embeddedness of each relationship proposition is determined by counting the number of steps that are needed to connect it back to the main topic of the text. Thus, the relationship propositions yield three products: type of relationship, rated explicitness, and level of embeddedness.

THE PROCESS

In this section we describe the process by which we arrive at a map of a text and derive its associated list of relationship propositions. The discussion is subdivided into four categories: the map, the relationship list, level of embeddedness, and rated explicitness.

The Map

In mapping a text, we begin by reading the whole passage, keeping in mind the level of detail that the map will need to reflect, given our established purpose. The following text, extracted and adapted slightly from a high school level biology textbook, serves to illustrate the process of mapping.

Sharks, Rays, and Skates
Sharks, rays, and skates belong to the class *Chondrichthyes*. This means "cartilage fishes." It is thought that they developed early in the Devonian period. Of the

fishes that lived in the ancient seas, many cartilage fishes have survived relatively unchanged in great numbers.

Sharks are similar to true fishes in many ways. But they have certain differences which place them in a separate class. Sharks have *placoid scales* which have the same origin as the shark's teeth. The mouth is a horizontal slit on the ventral side of the head. The jaws of the shark are very strong and lined with razor-sharp, pointed teeth. The teeth are placed in several rows. When a tooth is lost, another one may move forward to replace it. The teeth slant backward to hold the food securely in the mouth. This, combined with great strength, makes the shark a fearsome hunter.

Water enters the mouth, where it passes over the gills on either side of the head. The water is then forced out through separate pairs of gill slits. The gills are the respiratory organs of the fish. (Otto & Towle, 1977, p. 423.)

As the map develops, the three assumptions previously described guide the decisions we make in representing the text: (1) the relationship between any two concepts must be one of the nine types recognized by the system; (2) all concepts must be to related the main topic through embedding; and (3) concepts and relationships, even though not mentioned explicitly by the author, must appear in the map if they are needed to make the whole text coherent.

After reading the text, our first task is to identify the main topic of the passage. This is not always an obvious choice. In the preceding passage, there are several possibilities. One is the heading, which proclaims that the text will be about "sharks, rays, and skates." The first sentence tells us that these three organisms belong to the superordinate class Chondrichthyes, and characteristics of the class as a whole are then provided in the first paragraph. Perhaps, "class Chondrichthyes" is the topic. However, most of the text is a discussion of sharks and perhaps, by a virtue of the extent of discussion, "sharks" should be considered the topic.

We have found that two guidelines can be used to establish the topic of a text. The first is primacy in the presentation of concepts in the text. As much as possible, in mapping we try to adhere to the serial order of concepts presented and thus, we often identify an "early" concept as the topic of a text. The second guideline applies to situations in which two concepts compete to be chosen as the topic, but one is the logical superordinate of the other. Our text author claims that sharks, rays, and skates are *examples* of the class Chondrichthyes, and, thereby, makes these concepts subordinate terms. In such a situation, the superordinate term automatically becomes the topic. In this case, both guidelines support the same decision, because the concept "class Chondrichthyes" represents a superordinate term and also occurs near the beginning of the text.

The main topic is represented graphically by writing it on the map, drawing a double line under it, and placing a large—and for the moment, empty—box around it (see Figure 2). The box will eventually be filled with

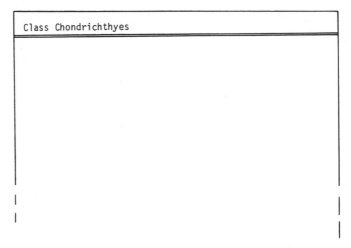

FIGURE 2. First-stage map of the sample text.

the concepts presented in the rest of the text, all structurally tied in some fashion to the main topic.

In proceeding through the text, similar decisions are made. What is a concept? How is it related to other concepts? Where does it go on the map? These questions are answered simultaneously with the selection and placement of each succeeding concept, and revisions of the developing map are often necessary. Consider our sample text. In the first paragraph, the author has presented some information about "class Chondrichthyes" as a group of fishes. We want these items placed close to the main topic in the map and subordinate to it. (We ignore for the moment the first sentence.) The author states in the second sentence, "This means 'cartilage fishes.'" We make the inference that "this" refers to our main topic and we take the word "means" as a marker for the relationship of definition. As the next concept placed on the map, we write below the double line "DEF: cartilage fishes," and draw a line across the map underneath the definition (see Figure 3).

We then proceed to the next sentence to see if it presents concepts related to the main topic. The sentence describes when the cartilage fishes probably developed. We judge this information to be a property or descriptor of the main topic, and as representing just one instructional concept. Accordingly, the whole sentence is mapped as a property of "class Chondrichthyes." Evidently, the author is not willing to state the concept as a fact but qualifies it with "It is thought that." This qualifier may or may not be instructionally important. It may reflect the author as scientist reverting to the careful style meant for other scientists. At this point, we choose to include it in the map, but only as part of the same instructional concept it qualifies (see Figure 3).

```
┌─────────────────────────────────────────────────────────────┐
│ Class Chondrichthyes                                         │
├─────────────────────────────────────────────────────────────┤
│ DEF: cartilage fishes                                        │
│ thought to have developed early in the Devonian period       │
├─────────────────────────────────────────────────────────────┤
│ are among the fishes of the ancient seas                     │
│ many have survived relatively unchanged in great numbers     │
│                                                              │
│                                                              │
│                                                              │
│                                                              │
│                                                              │
└                                                             ─┘
```

FIGURE 3. Partial map of sample text.

The final sentence of the paragraph is more complex than the preceding ones. Two more properties of cartilage fishes are presented: They live in ancient seas, and many have survived. The former property is actually a less precise restatement of the information about the Devonian period, although the author is not clear on this equivalence. Because that inference is not essential to understanding the text as a coherent whole, it is not mapped as such. A sophisticated reader might also infer from the property that there were *other* fishes in ancient seas. This inference is also probably true but, again, provides nonessential elaboration of the content. We feel less certain that the author intended for students to infer that meaning; therefore, we leave it out. To this point, the map of the text would appear as it is presented in Figure 3.

The remainder of the passage is concerned solely with sharks and their various characteristics. Sharks are related to the main topic, class Chondrichthyes, by "belonging to it," along with rays and skates. Thus, we pick up the information from the first sentence and indicate that sharks, rays, and skates are all examples of the class. Examples are mapped as concepts enclosed in boxes within the big box that represents the whole text. "Rays" and "skates" become one-word boxes because the author does not say anything more about them. "Sharks," by contrast, heads a large box to be filled with concepts that are related specifically to sharks. Figure 4 depicts the completed map of the sample text.

Before describing other aspects of relational mapping, we need to make a few comments about sections of the "sharks" box. All of the properties of sharks do not have equivalent embedding. The author has described several properties: they have scales, a mouth, and jaws. For each of these, additional information is given; for instance, the jaws have teeth and the teeth are razor-sharp, pointed, and come in several rows. To represent these properties of properties, we indent successively embedded properties to show which concepts are connected.

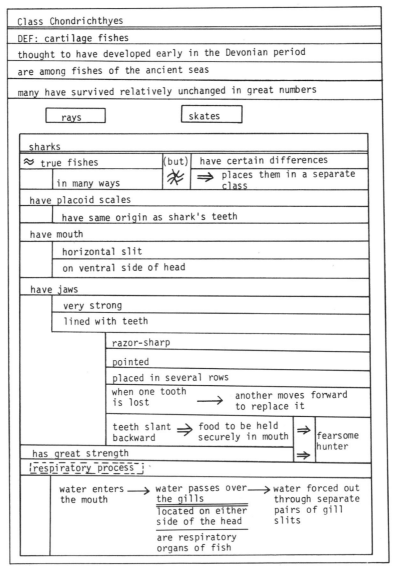

FIGURE 4. Final map of the sample text.

Toward the end of the second paragraph, the author includes concepts that are related temporally and causally. The temporal relationship is cued by the word "when." It is shown on the map by a single arrow ($\rightarrow$) between two concepts. After one tooth is lost, the author states, another may move forward to take its place. First one event occurs and then the other. This entire relationship is represented as a property of "teeth." Relationships of causality are featured in the remainder of the second paragraph. The slant of the teeth causes food to be held securely and this, in turn, contributes to making the shark a fearsome hunter. Causal relationships are indicated by double arrows ($\Rightarrow$) on the map.

The final paragraph of the text presents a special problem. It begins with the phrase, "Water enters the mouth." The term "shark" is not used and, in fact, only in the last word of the paragraph do we find explicit mention of fish. "Mouth" has not been mentioned for several sentences. How then is this section of the text to be related to the rest, if we are to assume that the text is coherent? It is in such a situation that essential inferences must be made. In this case, several are needed. First, we assume that the paragraph must be presenting more information about sharks. This assumption is based on another assumption we make about text; that is, if a major topic change were occurring, the author would tell us. By default, in this case, new information must be continuing the development of a previously introduced topic. Second, we infer that the temporal chain of events describing the flow of water must refer to some feature or property of the shark. The property needed is one that can serve as a superordinate concept to the process of water circulating over the gills and gill slits of the fish. What that superordinate property might be becomes clearer in the last sentence when the author states, "The gills are the respiratory organs of the fish." Respiratory organs must be playing a role in a process, and a superordinate process label is exactly what we need for this section of the map. Thus, we infer that sharks have a respiratory process and we tie the final paragraph to the map through this inferred property of sharks. The dashed lines around the concept "respiratory process" indicate that it is implied rather than explicitly stated in the text.

Thus, we complete our map of the sample text. Two further notes need to be added to explicate some conventions we have found useful. When describing a text at a relatively detailed level, we make it a practice to render on the map any concept or relationship that the author mentions explicitly, even though occasionally this may mar the simplicity of the ideal structure being developed. Also, we have used the "not similar" symbol ($\divideontimes$) whenever the author either explicitly states a contrast relationship or implies one by the use of connectors such as "but" or "however."

The process so far described yields a graphic summary of the concepts and relationships that we, as text analysts, perceive the author to be communicating to potential learners. As such, the map could be used as a glorified outline for instructional purposes. In text description research, the map is particularly compelling in its display of the pattern of ideas, the extent of elaboration of particular subtopics, and the types of connections that the author is inviting. However, by itself, the map is difficult to use in describing what readers are actually expected to learn from the text. To that end, we derive the list of relationship propositions.

The Relationship List

Every concept on the map is tied to some other concept by a relationship. The list of relationship propositions is derived by a simple and fairly mechanical process of verbalizing what the map presents graphically, Concept A—Relationship—Concept B. The list presented in Table 1 is derived from our "Sharks, Rays, and Skates" passage.

Although the process of deriving the list is relatively mechanical, we have found a number of conventions necessary when dealing with certain mapping situations:

1. The definition, property, example, or effect in a causal relationship (or second event in a temporal relationship) is always identified as Concept B in the list. Note that we have used the verb *precedes* to indicate the temporal relationship.

2. Whole relationship propositions may serve as concepts in a later proposition. For example, Propositions 9, 12, 24, 28 and 33 in the list shown in Table 1 represent such cases. Proposition 12 is particularly complex; it restates two properties of sharks mentioned in previous propositions, one of which (11) causes the shark to be placed in a separate class. These two properties are now concepts in Proposition 12 and are related to each other by a contrast relationship ("not similar").

3. The order in which propositions are listed is not crucial. Usually, all properties and examples of a concept are given before that concept is tied to another concept by a comparison, temporal, or causal relationship.

4. Occasionally, a temporal, causal, or comparative relationship coexists with property relationships. In such cases, a vertical line appears on the map, separating the concept that is a property of a main concept from the temporal, causal, or comparative symbol. Note the differences in the sections of the map (Figure 4) relevant to the following excerpt from our sample text: "When a tooth is lost, another moves forward to replace it. The teeth slant backward to hold the food securely in the mouth. This, combined with great strength, makes the shark a fearsome hunter." The relevant propositions are numbers 24 through 31 (Table 1). The first sentence depicts a fact or concept about teeth. That fact is a property of teeth (see Proposition 24). The concept itself breaks down into a temporal relationship between two subconcepts (see

TABLE 1

LIST OF RELATIONSHIP PROPOSITIONS FOR THE SAMPLE TEXT

Proposition number	Embeddedness[a]	Concept A[b]	Relationship[b]	Concept B[b]
		1	1	1
1	1	Class Chrondrichthyes	Definition	Cartilage fishes
		1	1	1
2	1	Class Chrondrichthyes	Property	Thought to have developed early in the Devonian period
		1	1	1
3	1	Class Chrondrichthyes	Property	Are among fishes of ancient seas
		1	1	1
4	1	Class Chrondrichthyes	Property	Many have survived relatively unchanged in large numbers
		1	1	1
5	1	Class Chrondrichthyes	Example	Rays
		1	1	1
6	1	Class Chrondrichthyes	Example	Skates
		1	1	1
7	1	Class Chrondrichthyes	Example	Sharks
		1	1	1
8	2	Sharks	Similar to	True fishes
		1	1	1
9	3	Sharks are similar to true fishes (#8)	Property	In many ways
		1	1	1
10	2	Sharks	Property	Have certain differences
		1	0	1
11	3	Have certain differences	Causes	Places them in separate class
		1	1	1
12	4	Sharks are similar to true fishes (#8)	Not similar	have certain differences places them in a separate class (#10, 11)
		1	1	1
13	2	Sharks	Property	Have placoid scales
		1	1	1
14	3	Placoid scales	Property	Have same origin as shark's teeth
		1	0	1
15	2	Sharks	Property	Have mouth
		1	1	1
16	3	Have mouth	Property	Horizontal slit

(*continued*)

TABLE 1   (*Continued*)

Proposition number	Embeddedness[a]	Concept A[b]	Relationship[b]	Concept B[b]
		1	1	1
17	3	Have mouth	Property	On ventral side of head
		1	1	1
18	2	Sharks	Property	Have jaws
		1	1	1
19	3	Have jaws	Property	Very strong
		1	1	1
20	3	Have jaws	Property	Lined with teeth
		1	1	1
21	4	Lined with teeth	Property	Razor-sharp
		1	1	1
22	4	Lined with teeth	Property	Pointed
		1	1	1
23	4	Lined with teeth	Property	Placed in several rows
		1	1	1
24	4	Lined with teeth	Property	When one tooth is lost precedes another moves forward to replace it (#25)
		1	1	1
25	5	When one tooth is lost	Precedes	Another moves forward to replace it
		1	1	1
26	4	Lined with teeth	Property	Teeth slant backward
		1	1	1
27	5	Teeth slant backward	Causes	Food to be held securely in mouth
		1	0	1
28	6	Teeth slant backward causes food to be held securely in mouth (#27)	Causes	Fearsome hunter
		1	1	1
29	2	Sharks	Property	Has great strength
		1	1	1
30	3	Has great strength	Causes	Fearsome hunter
		1	1	1
31	2	Sharks	Property	Fearsome hunter
		1	0	0
32	2	Sharks	Property	Respiratory process
		0	0	1
33	3	Respiratory process	Property	Water enters the mouth precedes water passes over gills, precedes water forced out through sepa-

TABLE 1 (*Continued*)

Proposition number	Embeddedness[a]	Concept A[b]	Relationship[b]	Concept B[b]
				rate pairs of gill slits (#34, 37)
		1	1	1
34	4	Water enters the mouth	Precedes	Water passes over gills
		1	1	1
35	5	Gills	Property	Located on either side of head
		1	1	1
36	5	Gills	Property	Are respiratory organs of the fish
		1	1	1
37	5	Water passes over gills	Precedes	Water forced out through separate pairs of gill slits

[a]Embeddedness refers to the hierarchical level of the proposition.
[b]The numeral above the concept (relationship) identifies it as being either explicit (1) or implicit (0) in the passage.

Proposition 25). Each of these subconcepts does not seem to have independent status as properties of the concept "teeth." By contrast, the next sentence differs in that "slanting backward" *is* a property of teeth (see Proposition 26) and also a cause of "holding food securely in the mouth" (see Proposition 27). However, this last concept, by itself, is not a property of teeth and thus, a vertical line does not appear on the map immediately after the causal arrow. The vertical line just before "fearsome hunter" indicates that a relationship proposition is needed to show the direct relationship between "shark" and "fearsome hunter" (see Proposition 31).

Level of Embeddedness

Once the list of relationship propositions is produced, the level of embeddedness of each proposition can be determined. Embeddedness refers to the number of ties that are needed to connect any concept to the main topic of a text. Concepts that are further from the main concept have higher embeddedness numbers. For example, in Table 1 the propositions in which the topic of the text, class Chondrichthyes, appears as Concept A (see Propositions 1 through 7) have levels of embeddedness of 1. Proposition 28 is the most embedded idea and requires six steps before it is connected to the main topic.

The construct of embeddedness in mapping is related to the hierarchies of propositions which are produced using Kintsch's (Kintsch & van Dijk, 1978) or Meyer's (1975) systems of analysis and, like theirs, corresponds to an intuitive or rated sense of the importance of concepts in a passage. In a study in which we attempted to test this notion directly (Schallert & Tierney, 1982), we asked students to rate the importance of sentences written directly from the propositions of a sample of texts. We examined whether information more closely tied to the main topic (low levels of embeddedness) received higher importance ratings than information further from the main topic (high levels of embeddedness). The results confirmed this expectation. In addition, results of a study in which high school students recalled passages taken from their textbooks indicated that the relationship propositions that were highly embedded were recalled less frequently (Schallert & Tierney, 1982). Thus, our formal system of indicating the hierarchy of concepts, embeddedness, seems to be related to the intuitive concept of importance.

A caution is needed, however. Level of embeddedness is a by-product of the structure decisions made during mapping, and, to some degree, of the order of presentation of concepts within the text. In some cases, seemingly trivial concepts, used to introduce the topic of a text, show up as Level 1 propositions, because they are connected directly to the main topic. For this reason, levels of embeddedness cannot be equated in every case with an intuitive concept of importance, although a high degree of correspondence can be expected, as previously noted.

Rated Explicitness

As described earlier, concepts and relationships occasionally must be inferred in order to produce a coherent representation of the text. It is reasonable to expect that these items may cause difficulties for students who are reading the text. To test notions of whether, and where, authors remain implicit in presenting information, and of how students respond to such processing demands, we needed a method of indicating in our relationship list which parts of propositions were inferred in the process of representing the text. We have found that judgment decisions regarding these notions work very well, in that independent raters typically agree with each other, or reach consensus, on most such decisions. The procedure involves taking each part of each proposition (Concept A, relationship, Concept B), comparing it to the original text, and deciding whether the author has given an explicit indicator of that part of the proposition in the text. In Table 1, the "0's" above the words indicate implicit information and the "1's" indicate explicit information. In comparison to other texts we have analyzed, the sample text used here is unusually explicit in rendering its structure.

We have found that explicitness decisions are fairly easy to make for the concept parts and for most of the relationships. Some difficulty occurs with the property relationship. Whereas for other relationships, a fairly strict criterion of requiring an explicit marker of the relationship works well; "property," we have found, is very seldom indicated explicitly. We have decided to rate property relationships as being explicit whenever the connection between two concepts was fairly obvious. Compare Proposition 15 to Propositions 13, 14, 16, and 17 (Table 1). Verbs of possession mark the connection between the two concepts in Propositions 13, 14, and 16. The concepts of Proposition 17 are still relatively explicitly connected by being presented consecutively in the same sentence. Proposition 15 represents the property relationship that holds "sharks" to "mouth." We judge the relationship to be implicit because the concept, mouth, is given without introduction and without directly mentioning that the author is writing about a feature of sharks. Still, the decision is a relatively less assured one, as indicated by the fact that two raters working independently came to different decisions and then arbitrated a rating of implicit.

Considering a relationship proposition as a single idea, varying types or degrees of explicitness are possible, ranging from a totally explicit relationship proposition (1–1–1) to a totally implicit one (0–0–0). By rating each part of the relationship proposition separately, this method can identify cases where only the relationship has been inferred from the text (1–0–1) or where one or both of the concepts have been inferred (0–1–1, 1–1–0, or 0–1–0). In 30 (300-word) passages we analyzed, which were taken from high school biology and history textbooks, the most commonly implicit component was the relationship between the concepts (1–0–1).

PROBLEMS WITH RELATIONAL MAPPING

For any given concept in a text, relational mapping indicates how it relates to other concepts, how explicitly the text states the concept and its relationships, and how embedded the concept is within the overall text structure. There are two major problems with the system we have developed. First, it is very dependent on the subjective judgment of the text analyst. Subjectivity is involved in deciding what is a concept, what is the major topic of a text, what are the main structural relationships presented by the author (what is the overall shape of things), and what is explicitly stated in the text. Granted we have developed guidelines to increase the consensuality of analysis. And, granted we take our cue as much as possible from what the author is explicitly saying about the topic. However, the process is not a formal system in the way that Kintsch's micropropositional analysis approximates. Relational mapping provides a picture of what the text analyst understands to be the message of the author, and at best, that picture will be fairly reliable from one expert reader–analyst to the next.

The second major problem derives from the first and is related to the issue of alternate maps for the same text. In our analysis of naturally occurring pieces of discourse, we frequently found that two text analysts working independently represented the same text in somewhat different ways, and occasionally, in radically different forms. When this occurred, a discussion session usually would result in consensus about the map that "felt right" to both analysts. However, we were fairly often struck by how ambiguous authors were in, say, indicating that they wished the reader to contrast two concepts rather than to simply describe them. In addition, we found that even when authors were relatively clear and simple in their presentation, a reader (or analyst in this case) could easily produce a very different map simply by approaching the text with a special question or purpose that differed from the author's organization.

This last problem may turn out to be a virtue of relational mapping, reflecting its flexibility in describing text. As many have claimed, a text is not an object to be described apart from a comprehender (see Pichert & Anderson, 1977). What makes a text a text is its coherent representation first in the author's and then in the reader's mind. The meaning and structure of a text are not inherent in the print but are invited by the author and imputed to the text by the reader. Our system is compatible with this view and assigns responsibility to the text analyst to decide what representation best reflects the author's intended message. In a sense, relational mapping is not so much a *text* analysis system as it is a *conceptual* analysis system. Although there is a great potential for error whenever one proposes to describe what another person might have meant by an utterance, interpretation can come closer to the mark, when dealing with informative text (particularly the textbook variety), by using relational mapping. The latitude of equally adequate meanings is narrower with such text, since textbook authors are rarely intentionally polysemous. Thus, we believe that despite all the problems with subjectivity, our goal of describing what a textbook author intends to be learned by students is reasonable and our system is a reasonable tool in meeting this goal.

POTENTIAL OF RELATIONAL MAPPING

By the very nature of its process, relational mapping provides a description that is one step removed from the surface representation of a text. This feature makes it ideal for representing what a reader might produce as a summary of a text or what a learner might extract from a text. Although there is an obvious danger associated with attempting to describe the ideal summary and the ideal knowledge representation acquired from a text, the danger is no greater than that, say, associated with the choices and expectations reflected in a teacher's use of a content-area textbook. Teachers show what they have decided students should learn from their textbooks both directly (e.g., by listing objectives) and indirectly (e.g., by asking certain questions about the content, and basing classroom lectures and discussions on the concepts and organization presented in the textbooks). What teachers do selectively and intuitively, we do systematically and extensively in producing a map of a text.

To the extent that we are successful in capturing in our maps the key concepts and relationships in the discourse, our system will be useful in describing the intended message in informative text. In particular, relational mapping should prove useful whenever researchers and authors need to ascertain what students have (should have) learned from informative discourse. For example, mapping can (1) make explicit the basis for asking questions, (2) depict graphically where authors differ in the presentation of the same concepts, due to different high-level clusterings, (3) provide a scoring basis to determine what students have learned from a text, and (4) be used to describe lecture as well as written material, chapters as well as paragraphs, and implicit as well as explicit content. Its overall potential is the flexibility it affords in describing how well learners have been able to meet the intent of informative discourse.

REFERENCES

Fillmore, C. J. (1968). The case for case. In E. Bach & R. Harms (Eds.), *Universals in linguistic theory*. New York: Holt.

Frederiksen, C. H. (1972). Effects of task-induced cognitive operations on comprehension and memory processes. In J. B. Carroll & R. O. Freddle (Eds.), *Language comprehension and the acquisition of knowledge*. Washington, D.C.: Winston.

Frederiksen, C. H. (1975). Representing logical and semantic structure of knowledge acquired from discourse. *Cognitive Psychology, 7*, 317–458.

Kintsch, W. (1974). *The representation of meaning in memory*. Hillsdale, N.J.: Erlbaum.

Kintsch, W., & van Dijk, T.(1978). Toward a model of text comprehension and production. *Psychological Review, 85*, 363–394.

Meyer, B. J. F. (1975). *The organization of prose and its effects on memory*. Amsterdam: North-Holland.

Otto, J. H., & Towle, A. (1977). *Modern Biology*. New York: Holt.

Pichert, J. W., & Anderson, R. C. (1977). Taking a different perspective on a story. *Journal of Educational Psychology, 69*, 309–315.

Schallert, D. L., & Tierney, R. J. (1982). *Learning from expository text: The interaction of text structure with reader characteristics*. Final report to the National Institute of Education, NIE-G-79-0167.

Turner, A., & Greene, E. (1977). *The construction and use of a propositional text base* (Tech. Rep. 63). Boulder, CO: The University of Colorado, Institute for the Study of Intellectual Behavior.

CHAPTER 13

Graphic Postorganizers:
A Spatial Learning Strategy

RICHARD F. BARRON   *ROBERT M. SCHWARTZ*

INTRODUCTION

The present chapter presents a form of spatial learning strategy that has been termed a graphic postorganizer. The procedure requires learners to manipulate the vocabulary of a learning task in order to create a diagram or schematic representation that depicts relationships among the terms.

The chapter begins by providing an operational definition for constructing and implementing a graphic postorganizer. We anticipate that this will prove useful to other instructors or investigators who wish to study the device or contrast its effects with other types of spatial learning strategies.

Next, we place the process in historical perspective and review in detail two research studies we have undertaken to assess its effects. The first (Barron & Stone, 1974) was the initial, graphic postorganizer study. It demonstrated a small, statistically significant effect for graphic postorganizers in a short-term, school-like learning task. The second investigation (Barron & Schwartz, 1980) demonstrated large statistical and practical effects for the device in a long-term, complex learning task, involving an entire course of study.

275

SPATIAL LEARNING STRATEGIES
Techniques, Applications, and Related Issues

Finally, we discuss implications of the research cited and suggest directions for future investigations.

AN OPERATIONAL DEFINITION

A *graphic postorganizer* is a learning task that follows initial instruction in a subject area. Learners are required to manipulate vocabulary to schematically depict subordinate, parallel, and superordinate relationships among the terminology. The term postorganizer has been adopted to distinguish the process from similar strategies that require presentation or manipulation of vocabulary *prior to,* or as an initial phase of, instruction.

The following operational definition is presented as a series of steps to be followed by a teacher or researcher who is attempting to implement the strategy. The steps are listed in sequence and, where appropriate, additional commentary has been inserted.

1. *Analyze the vocabulary of the learning task and list all the terms you feel are important for the students to understand.*

2. *Arrange (re-arrange) the list of words into a schema or diagram which depicts relationships among the terms.*

3. *Add to the schema terms you believe are understood by the learners and that clarify relationships among terms and the course or discipline as a whole.*

These initial steps require an instructor or investigator to construct a personal graphic organizer. In long-term or complex learning tasks, such as those embodied in an entire course of study, it is often necessary to prepare a series of related graphic postorganizers rather than a single large one. For example: One organizer might divide the discipline into several branches, with subsequent organizers depicting conceptual relationships within each branch. Here, a caution is in order. The structure of a subject or discipline is often discussed as though this were an entity with a form about which various individuals might agree. However, this is rarely, if ever, the case. We have noted that colleagues who attempt to use the strategy often become stymied in the initial series of steps due to excessive concern about the correctness of the relationships depicted. The graphic postorganizer should depict relationships as the teacher or researcher perceives or has taught them.

4. *Determine a mode of presentation for the learners' (re)construction of the graphic postorganizers.* This will vary according to several factors, such as the number of students who will engage in the process and the nature of the facilities in which the procedure will take place. In large lecture situations,

the students should be provided with a separate list of the terms to be used. They should also be given one or more partially completed graphic postorganizers. Depending upon the nature and complexity of the content, the diagram may show the placement of several terms. The remaining word slots are to be depicted by blank lines, five to eight spaces in length. The learners' task is to insert terms from the word list into appropriate slots or spaces on the diagram. It is best if the students work with pencil and eraser since, initially, they will make numerous false starts and modifications.

In smaller classes or groups, where seating occurs at large desks or tables, the learners may be given the vocabulary terms, typed separately, on index cards. This allows them to manipulate the terms directly without erasing the diagram each time they wish to modify a word placement or category.

5. *Introduce the students to the process with an example.* Prior to undertaking the actual strategy, it is helpful to define the task for the students with an example. There are several ways to initiate this introduction. One way is to present a list of simple terms, such as animal, carrot, gold, horse, mineral, bean, silver, dog, matter, and vegetable. Inform the students that all the terms are related and that relationships can be visually depicted by arranging the words into a diagram. Ask the group if they can see a term or terms that are broader or more inclusive than the others. As they respond, a diagram similar to Figure 1 can quickly be developed at the blackboard or via an overhead projector. Then inform the learners that a similar process can be undertaken to enhance learning, using the terminology from the course.

6. *Organize the students into groups consisting of two or three individuals and distribute the (first) list of terms and partially completed organizer to each person.* Although engaging in the strategy on a group basis may make for a less than ideal treatment implementation in a research study, we believe it is pedagogically sound. An important part of the process is the discussion, occasional disagreement, and interaction derived from the group work.

7. *As the students engage in the activity, circulate from group to group to provide assistance.* The amount of support necessary varies according to the type of students involved, as well as the difficulty or complexity of the con-

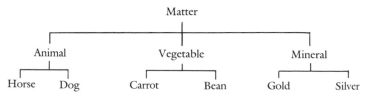

FIGURE 1. Graphic postorganizer example for introducing the strategy.

tent being learned. Less mature learners and difficult content usually require considerable assistance the first time or two that the process is used. However, as a general rule, it is advisable that the instructor not become involved in a particular group's discussion, except as the result of a direct request for aid from a group or one of its members. In most instances, the students will become involved in working through the activity if the instructor or investigator does not interfere.

8. *Terminate the activity and provide feedback.* The amount of time necessary to complete a particular graphic postorganizer usually cannot be specified in advance. Rarely will all groups finish at the same time. Furthermore, depending upon the complexity of the task and the number of terms to be used, a point may be reached at which certain groups find that they can proceed no further. One learns to sense when to stop the procedure based upon drops in the level of discussion, the quantity of questions or requests for assistance, or digressions in conversation that are not associated with the postorganizer.

In providing feedback to the learners, two approaches have been found useful. In one, the entire class develops the graphic postorganizer, or the series thereof, at the blackboard under the direction of the instructor. In the second approach, the teacher or investigator presents his or her own graphic postorganizer(s), explaining why the terms were arranged in a certain fashion. It should be noted that with either approach, disagreement may develop. However, the additional discussion generated is desirable and it should be considered an integral part of the strategy.

In conclusion, this section presents an operational definition for graphic postorganizers. In the next section, the developmental history for the strategy is reviewed.

HISTORICAL PERSPECTIVE

Graphic postorganizers were originally developed as part of a larger set of strategies for guiding reading–learning in content subjects at Syracuse University's Research and Demonstration Laboratory under the direction of H. L. Herber. As initially conceived, the device had a much different purpose and process.

Originally, the procedure had its roots in the theory of *meaningful reception learning* (Ausubel, 1963, 1968). Ausubel claimed that a major variable in new learning in a subject matter field is one's existing knowledge or cognitive structure. He maintained that new meanings in a discipline are acquired only in relation to a previously learned background of relevant principles and concepts. Thus, if existing cognitive structure is clear, stable, and organized, new learning should be enhanced. Conversely, if existing cognitive structure is unclear and disorganized, new learning will be impeded. Following this line of reasoning, Ausubel argued that learning and retention could be facilitated by strengthening relevant aspects of a learner's existing cognitive structure.

Ausubel proposed the use of *advance organizers* as one means of strengthening existing cognitive structure. These devices took the form of introductory prose passages written at a higher level of generality, abstraction, and inclusiveness than the actual learning material. Advance organizers, it was claimed, "provide ideational scaffolding for the stable incorporation of the more differentiated material in the learning passage" and "increase the discriminability between the new material and similar or conflicting ideas in cognitive structure" (1968, p. 148).

In an early set of papers (Barron, 1969; Earle, 1970; Estes, Mills & Barron, 1969), it was proposed that schematic presentations of vocabulary assumed the logical properties of advance organizers. Initial research investigations, as well as correspondence with Ausubel, supported this contention. The procedure was labeled a *structured overview*.

Subsequently, three related studies (Barron, 1972, Barron & Cooper, 1973; Estes, 1972) were undertaken to determine whether or not the two types of advance organizers were of practical utility in classroom instruction. These studies were directed toward the general question, When, if ever, might a teacher be advised to implement a prose advance organizer or a structured overview? They assessed the effects of the devices relative to three learner variables judged to be easily identified by classroom teachers and potentially useful as a means of differentiating instruction. The three learner variables were (1) grade level, (2) general reading ability as measured by a standardized test, and (3) passage-specific reading ability as measured by a cloze readability test on the learning passage.

The results of these three studies have been reported elsewhere (Barron, 1981) and are not discussed here in detail. None of the investigations demonstrated significant differences between students who received advanced organizers or structured overviews and students who received no introduction to the learning passage.

These negative findings caused a reformulation in the application of the device. We had been treating structured overviews as something a teacher did *for* students: organizing their knowledge before embarking upon a new learning task. In debriefing sessions with students in the aforementioned studies, it became apparent that in instances where the device seemed to enhance learning, this may not have been due to its effect upon cognitive structure variables, but to an effect upon reading or learning processes. That is, students who reported a belief that the device aided their learning also informed us that they consciously attempted to relate the new specific information from the learning passage to the introductory presentation. However, the majority viewed the device as having no effect upon their learning. These students appeared to treat the structured overviews or prose organizer and the learning passage as separate, discrete pieces of information. They seemed to make no attempt to integrate or interrelate the devices to the learning passage.

Thus, the question became how can one encourage learners to more actively participate in the process of integrating new, less familiar content presentations with their existing knowledge base? It appeared that this could be accomplished by having them construct their own graphic postorganizers on a postlearning basis, rather than presenting an organizer to them as a readiness activity. In the section that follows, we review two investigations undertaken for this purpose.

RESEARCH RESULTS

In this section, two studies on the effects of graphic postorganizers are reviewed. The results suggest that the procedure is most effective when undertaken as a culminating activity in large-scale, complex learning tasks such as those involving an entire textbook or course of study, rather than with individual lectures or text assignments.

STUDY 1: THE EFFECT OF GRAPHIC POSTORGANIZERS ON LEARNING OF VOCABULARY RELATIONSHIPS IN A PASSAGE OF SOCIAL SCIENCE CONTENT

Barron and Stone (1974) studied the effects of graphic postorganizers on the learning of vocabulary relationships in a passage of social science material. Subjects were 141 tenth- and eleventh-grade students, classified as "above average" to "superior" according to their school's tracking system. They were randomly assigned to three treatment conditions: graphic advance organizer (GAO), graphic postorganizer (GPO), and control (C). In all treatments, subjects were required to read a 3000-word passage about mental health. The content of the passage was judged to be unfamiliar to the students and its readability was placed at the eighth-grade level.

Treatment was scheduled over a 2-day period. In the GAO condition, subjects received an experimenter constructed graphic advance organizer and read the learning passage on the first day. On the second day, they were asked to recall the organizer from memory and instructed to reread the learning passage.

In the GPO treatment, subjects read the learning passage on the first day. The following day they were provided with a copy of the learning passage and asked to construct a graphic postorganizer according to the following procedure. First, they were given a short demonstration of how to construct a graphic postorganizer. Next, they were randomly placed into triads and provided with a copy of the learning passage and a set of index cards. Each index card contained a term or group of terms from the learning passage. Finally, subjects were instructed to arrange the index cards in the manner described in the earlier demonstration, to depict relationships among the terminology. After approximately 30 minutes, the experimenter stopped the activity. Feedback was provided by showing subjects the organizer presented in the GAO condition.

In the control condition, subjects read the learning passage on the two successive days.

Outcome Measure

The outcome measure was a vocabulary relationship test (VRT) based on the content structure of the mental health passage. The instrument was patterned after a device proposed by Cronbach (1943). It consisted of 25 items, each containing four terms; three of these terms were related in some fashion, based on their presentation in the learning passage. The subjects' task was to indicate which one of the terms was unrelated (or less directly related) to the other three terms. A similar vocabulary relationship measure was utilized in Study 2, which is discussed later. However, in Study 2 the test required that subjects make conceptual distinctions regarding the reading process and the teaching of reading. The importance of the distinctions between the two tests, in terms of their effect on practical decision making, is discussed in a subsequent section of this chapter.

Results

For the total sample, scores on the VRT ranged from 4 to 24, with a mean of 13.33 and standard deviation of 3.06. Means and standard deviations for each of the three treatment groups are presented in Table 1.

Two planned comparisons were undertaken. The first contrasted achievement on VRT between GAO and GPO. It yielded a significant difference ($p < .05$, one-tailed) in favor of GPO. The second comparison contrasted the performance between GAO and the control group, and was not statistically significant.

TABLE 1

Means and Standard Deviations for Vocabulary
Relationship Test, Study 1

Treatment	$\bar{X}$	SD
Graphic postorganizer (GPO)	14.52	3.30
Graphic advance organizer (GAO)	13.10	2.86
Control (C)	12.38	3.02

The results supported the hypothesis from prior research, demonstrating that a facilitative outcome for graphic advance organizers is due, in part, to the effect upon students' reading or learning processes rather than to manipulation of background knowledge or cognitive structure variables. It was concluded that in the learning of vocabulary relationships, it is more effective to have students manipulate their knowledge of vocabulary than to have teachers attempt to conduct this manipulation for them.

Study 2: The Effect of Graphic Postorganizers on Learning of Vocabulary Relationships in a Complex, Long-Term Learning Task

Barron and Schwartz (1980) conducted a study to determine whether graphic postorganizers facilitated the learning of vocabulary relationships in a complex, long-term learning task. Subjects in the study were 64 graduate students, selected randomly from a larger group, who were enrolled in sections of an introductory reading methods course. Most of these individuals were teachers enrolled in Master's degree programs in Reading–Language Arts or Learning Disabilities. Their teaching assignments ranged from first grade to high school, and their experience as teachers ranged from less than 1 to more than 18 years. The course was scheduled to meet in weekly 3-hour-and-50-minute blocks of time for a period of 14 weeks.

The major course content was transmitted during the first 9 weeks. Topics included reading readiness–beginning reading, word recognition processes, vocabulary development and word meaning skills, comprehension theory and practice, group appraisal processes, and individual diagnosis and remediation.

All class meetings followed a similar format. The instructor began with a lecture averaging approximately 90 minutes. Following a short break, students engaged in highly structured, small group discussions related to the content of the lecture, using various types of guide materials (Herber, 1978).

The instructor then elaborated upon these guide materials. Following this, some students were dismissed while others chose to remain for an optional group question–answer period. Individual conferences were scheduled after every class meeting.

All class sessions were supplemented by various kinds of assignments. For example, "one-point papers" required the application of instructional procedures introduced in class, and "simulations" required the interpretation of contrived group test data. At the end of 9 weeks, the major course requirement was undertaken: Students conducted an individual diagnosis for a child who was experiencing reading difficulties and constructed a set of hypothetical instructional plans for remediating the problem.

Forty-two of the 64 students were enrolled in the same section of the course. This allowed the establishment of three treatment conditions. The instructed experimental (IE) group consisted of individuals who took the course and completed a graphic postorganizer treatment. The instructed control (IC) group took the course simultaneously with the IE group, but did not construct graphic postorganizers. The uninstructed control (UC) group was composed of students enrolled in another section of the course. Students in this group were administered the criterion measure as a pretest prior to receiving any course content.

Subjects in the experimental class were randomly assigned to the IE and IC conditions. Treatment for both groups occurred in separate meetings held at the end of the semester, ostensibly as review sessions for the final examination. These meetings lasted approximately 90 minutes.

The IE group was given four partially completed graphic postorganizers. Their task was to complete each postorganizer by inserting terms from an appended list of words into appropriate spaces on the organizer. Subjects were assigned to pairs and given varying periods of time to complete each organizer. At the end of each time period, the instructor displayed the completed organizer on an overhead projector. Subjects were not allowed to take notes and all the experimental materials were collected at the conclusion of the treatment.

The IC group was presented with the four lists of words used in the IE treatment. The instructor defined each of the terms and elaborated upon these definitions.

Outcome Measure

The outcome measure was similar to the one described in the previously discussed study. It was termed the reading vocabulary relationship test (RVRT) and consisted of 30 multiple-choice items which were related to reading concepts from the course. Each item contained four words, and the

TABLE 2

Means and Standard Deviations for Reading
Vocabulary Relationship Test, Study 2

Treatment	$\bar{X}$	SD
Instructed experimental (IE)	21.35	4.21
Instructed control (IC)	14.45	4.13
Uninstructed control (UC)	10.55	2.74

subjects' task was to indicate the word that was unrelated, or least related, to the other three. The criterion measure was administered 1 week after treatment and it was presented as one portion of a larger final examination.

Results

For the total N, scores on the RVRT ranged from 4 to 29 with a mean of 15.27 and a standard deviation of 5.77. Means and standard deviations for each of the experimental groups are presented in Table 2.

Two comparisons were conducted to evaluate differences among treatment groups. The first comparison contrasted the achievement of students who had constructed the graphic postorganizers with that of the instructed control group (IE versus IC). This comparison indicated a significant difference ($p < .01$) in favor of the postorganizer treatment. The second comparison tested the difference between the instructed and uninstructed control groups (IC versus UC). This test also yielded a significant difference ($p < .01$) in favor of those who had received the course content.

An overall estimate of the strength of the relationship between the treatment conditions and the RVRT yielded an ω^2 value of .58 (Hayes, 1963). Keppel (1982), however, cautions that the inclusion of an uninstructed control in this type of analysis tends to overestimate the relationship between the independent and dependent variables. Recalculating the ω^2 value for just the I–E and I–C groups resulted in $\omega^2 = .35$ (i.e., 35% of the variance in the vocabulary relationship measure is accounted for by the difference between these groups). The experimenters concluded that construction of graphic postorganizers can have a far-reaching effect upon students' understanding of vocabulary relationships in a complex, long-term learning task.

DISCUSSION

Theoretical conceptualizations about learning as it occurs in school-type instructional situations indicate that a critical factor in the acquisition and retention of new understanding is related to the clarity, stability, and organization of one's background knowledge, cognitive structure, or schema. However, prior information variables are not, in our opinion, sufficient to explain the extremely strong effects of the graphic postorganizer treatment in the Barron and Schwartz (1980) study. Why did a treatment lasting approximately 90 minutes produce such large achievement differences when the two groups of students had equal experience with course content in direct instruction amounting to over 40 hours?

This situation may be explained in part by Ausubel's (1968) conception of two types of learning sets. Under conditions of a *meaningful learning set,* the learner is consciously and actively attempting to relate and incorporate the newer, less familiar material into an existing background of information. Under conditions of a rote-learning set, information is processed but this occurs on a more arbitrary, less substantive basis. New meanings are less directly linked with existing knowledge and one's rate of forgetting is more rapid (see Goetz, Chapter 3, present volume).

An analogy regarding the difference in levels of processing may be drawn from Simon and Chase (1973), who investigated strategies employed by expert and novice chess players while studying board positions arranged in a game situation versus a random pattern. An individual with limited background knowledge about chess is inclined to adopt a rote set even though potentially meaningful relationships exist among the pieces. Thus, the effect of spatial learning strategies in general, and graphic post organizers in particular, may be due in part to the possibility that they assist or "force" learners to adopt a meaningful learning set. New meanings—in this case, related to vocabulary concepts—are projected into and integrated with a larger conceptual network, rather than existing as isolated, arbitrary entities.

With respect to the research cited in this chapter, it is not surprising that the effects of graphic postorganizers were magnified in the more complex learning situation. This was due, in all likelihood, to the nature of the course and its overall meeting structure. That is, instruction was distributed over a period of 14 weeks and compartmentalized into smaller, more isolated topics. It is likely that most students only partly mastered particular content and associated terminology from week to week. As the semester progressed, varying degrees of forgetting occurred and concepts introduced earlier were not integrated with those from previous course meetings. Involvement in the graphic postorganizer procedure may have overcome these problems by providing a structure whereby students simultaneously reviewed and relearned vocabulary concepts and integrated them into a larger conceptual network.

One reservation which has been raised regarding the research cited in the present chapter involves the selection of an outcome measure. In both studies, the criterion measure involved a test of the learner's understanding of vocabulary relationships. Is this an important or viable learning outcome relative to the content with which we have conducted our research? Is it more valuable than a test of propositional understanding? This may be an appropriate question for future research, but for now we believe an argument for the criterion can be made on logical grounds. With respect to the content of Study 2, involving the teaching of reading, we believe that incomplete semantic or conceptual networks may have a deleterious effect upon one's instructional practices. For example, relatively large numbers of teachers enter the course with an incorrect understanding of the term *word recognition*. They consider it the equivalent of *phonics*. Typically, when such an individual encounters a child who is experiencing reading difficulties due to overattention to phoneme–grapheme correspondence, the teacher provides the child with more phonics instruction, rather than recognizing the need to teach utilization of syntactic and semantic cues.

Similarly, a teacher who has no semantic representation for "directed reading–thinking activity" (Stauffer, 1969), or who cannot dissociate the procedure for postreading comprehension strategies, is unlikely to be able to make use of this excellent pedagogical tool.

Numerous avenues exist for future research. One probable outcome of the present volume is that it will spur a number of investigations designed to compare the effects of various types of spatial learning strategies. We find two areas of contrast particularly interesting. One concerns the effect of different forms of spatial learning strategies upon learners' macroprocessing. The second involves transfer of training.

Tobias (1982) has defined macroprocesses as "the frequency and intensity with which students cognitively process instructional input" (p. 5). He suggests that when a particular teaching method produces differential learning outcomes, this may be due to the stimulation of different macroprocessing behavior on the part of the students. Additionally, he argues that instructional research has focused primarily upon external differences among methods, thereby obscuring important similarities and differences in learners' macroprocessing.

The various forms of spatial learning strategies introduced in this text certainly display a number of external differences. For example, graphic postorganizers appear to have a more limited structure and function than Holley and Dansereau's (Chapter 4, present volume) networking strategy. That is, in networking the student is taught to analyze prose into node–link diagrams using a set of six instructor or experimenter-provided links. The nodes contain paraphrases and images of key ideas or concepts, whereas the links specify relationships among key ideas. The networking process emphasizes the identification of hierarchies (type–part), chains (lines of reasoning–temporal ordering–casual sequences), and clusters (characteristics—evidence—analogies). These specific structures are then embedded into a broader hierarchical framework. In the graphic postorganizer procedure, on the other hand, the links between nodes or concepts are unspecified. The relationships learners identify are primarily parallel, subordinate, and superordinate in nature and must be inferred and supplied by the students (see Vaughan, Chapter 6).

On the surface, it may appear reasonable to assume that such external differences may produce different macroprocessing behaviors. However, this may not prove to be the case. That is, both procedures may similarly stimulate students to actively comprehend material, relate it to their prior experiences, and organize what is learned with what has been organized previously. This question is, in our opinion, an interesting topic for additional research.

A second avenue of future research concerns transfer of training. In our own research we are interested in investigating whether or not spatial learning strategies affect procedural as well as declarative knowledge. According to Ryle's (1949) conceptualization, declarative knowledge involves "knowing that" (e.g., that Columbus is generally credited with discovering America, that an isoceles triangle has two equal sides) whereas procedural knowledge involves "knowing how" (e.g., how to ride a bicycle, how to conduct a directed reading lesson). Declarative knowledge can be verbalized and can be acquired relatively quickly through viewing, hearing, or reading. Procedural knowledge, on the other hand, cannot be verbalized and is acquired only by engaging in the skill or process to be mastered over extended periods of time.

We suspect that the graphic postorganizer process, although it appears declarative in nature, may transfer to procedural knowledge, such as conducting a reading diagnosis. That is, it seems logical to assume that the better structured a teacher's knowledge about various types or classifications of reading disabilities and procedures appropriate for remediating such problems, the more able she or he would be to interpret test data and plan a corrective instructional sequence. The next step in a line of research designed to assess this question would appear to involve development and validation of transfer tests dealing with diagnostic interpretations. It might be of value to conduct a similar type of assessment in other disciplines or fields, such as medical education or computer technology.

CONCLUSION

This chapter has presented a spatial learning strategy that has been termed a graphic postorganizer. The authors have no vested interest in promoting the procedure or maintaining its existence in the research literature.

In effect, we have done nothing more than define and study a process that we designed to assist our students' learning.

What is important is that the chapter lends additional insight and support to the unifying topic of the entire text: spatial learning strategies. Taken together, the chapters presented in the present volume provide clear evidence for the efficacy of this type of learning activity. Additional research may result in better understanding of how this learning occurs.

REFERENCES

Ausubel, D. P. (1963). *The psychology of meaningful verbal learning.* New York: Grune and Stratton.

Ausubel, D. P. (1968). *Educational psychology: A cognitive view* New York: Holt.

Barron, R. F. (1969). The use of vocabulary as an advance organizer. In H. L. Herber & P. L. Sanders (Eds.), *Research on reading in the content area: First year report.* Syracuse, NY: Syracuse University Press.

Barron, R. F. (1972). The effects of advance organizers and grade level upon the reception learning and retention of general science content. In F. P. Greene (Ed.), *Investigations relating to mature reading.* Milwaukee, WI: National Reading Conference.

Barron, R. F. (1981). *A systemic research procedure, organizers, and overviews: An historical perspective.* Education Resources Information Center. (ERIC Document Reproduction Service No. ED 198508)

Barron, R. F., & Cooper, R. (1973). Effects of advance organizers and grade level upon information acquisition from an instructional level general science passage. In P. L. Nacke (Ed.), *Diversity in mature reading: Theory and research.* Clemson, SC: National Reading Conference.

Barron, R. F., & Schwartz, R. M. (1980). *Teacher acquisition of semantic relationships about reading instruction.* Paper presented at the Annual Meeting of the National Reading Conference, San Antonio, Texas.

Barron, R. F., & Stone, V. F. (1974). The effect of student constructed graphic post organizers upon learning vocabulary relationships. In P. Nacke (Ed.), *Interaction: Research in college adult reading.* Clemson, SC: National Reading Conference.

Cronbach, L. J. (1943). Measuring knowledge of precise word meanings. *Journal of Educational Research, 36,* 528–34.

Earle, R. A. (1970). Reading and mathematics: Research in the classroom. In H. A. Robinson & E. L. Thomas (Eds.), *Fusing reading and content.* Newark, DE: International Reading Association.

Estes, T. H. (1972). Effects of advance organizers upon meaningful reception learning and retention of social studies content. In F. P. Greene (Ed.), *Investigations relating to mature reading.* Milwaukee, WI: National Reading Conference.

Estes, T. H., Mills, D. N., & Barron, R. F. (1969). Three methods of introducing students to a reading-learning task in two content subjects. In H. L. Herber & P. L. Sanders (eds.), *Research on reading in the content area: First year report.* Syracuse, NY: Syracuse University Press.

Hayes, W. L. (1963). *Statistics for psychologists.* New York: Holt.

Herber, H. L. (1978). *Teaching reading in content areas* (2nd ed.). Englewood Cliffs, NJ: Prentice-Hall.

Keppel, G. (1982). *Design and analysis: A researcher's handbook* (2nd ed.). Englewood Cliffs, NJ: Prentice-Hall.

Ryle, G. (1949). *The concept of mind.* London: Hutchinson.

Simon, H. A., & Chase, W. G. (1973). Skill in chess. *American Scientist, 61,* 394–403.

Stauffer, R. G. (1969). *Directing reading maturity as a cognitive process.* New York: Harper and Row.

Tobias, S. (1982). When do instructional methods make a difference? *Educational Researcher, 11* (4), 4–9.

PART IV

Spatial Strategies: A Critique

CHAPTER 14

Spatial Strategies:
Implications for Applied Research

CLAIRE E. WEINSTEIN

INTRODUCTION

When the editors of the present volume first invited me to prepare a chapter discussing possible implications for applied research of the work that has been done investigating or teaching spatial learning strategies, I was delighted. When the editors prodded and reminded me that I now had a complete set of chapters in my possession and that it was time to start reading them so that I could write my own chapter, I became apprehensive about my task. When I began to read the chapters I became excited. My thoughts began to wander around in a quagmire of my own knowledge about learning strategies. These tangential cognitions temporarily focused my attention on broader conceptions of learning strategies, the thoughts and behaviors that contribute to focusing perception, encoding, storage, and retrieval of new information. Explicit in each of these chapters is a set of suggestions concerning present or potential uses of spatial learning strategies for learning from text; however, implicit in each of these chapters are suggestions for how spatial learning strategies could be used to enhance learning by impacting other aspects of the study process. It is to this latter theme that I now turn my

SPATIAL LEARNING STRATEGIES
Techniques, Applications, and Related Issues

attention. First I describe briefly an eight-category scheme developed by Weinstein and Mayer (in press) to classify learning strategies, and then I discuss the potential role of spatial learning strategies in each of these eight categories. Finally, I identify a number of general issues or variables needing further research.

CATEGORIES OF LEARNING STRATEGIES

Successful students use a variety of strategies to selectively attend to new information, to encode it using processes and in a form that will then facilitate storage, and to recall this new information on either a short-term or a long-term basis (Dansereau, 1983; Ryan, 1981; Weinstein & Mayer, in press; Wittrock, 1978). Although these strategies are best used as part of an integrated study system where component as well as emergent properties can contribute to their effectiveness, for purposes of discussion, a categorical scheme developed by Weinstein and Mayer (in press) is here described. In this arrangement, eight categories of learning strategies are proposed. The categories are not meant to be exclusive (or exhaustive) but merely to serve as focal points for conceptualizing the field and for directing discussion. A listing of the category labels is presented in Table 1.

REHEARSAL STRATEGIES FOR BASIC LEARNING TASKS

When presented with a set of items to remember and later recall, such as the names of the states that joined the Confederacy or the metric equivalents of the American system of measurement, students often use some type of rehearsal strategy. The use of a rehearsal strategy implies that the student

TABLE 1

CATEGORIES DEVELOPED BY WEINSTEIN AND MAYER TO
CLASSIFY LEARNING STRATEGIES

Rehearsal strategies for basic learning tasks
Rehearsal strategies for complex learning tasks
Elaboration strategies for basic learning tasks
Elaboration strategies for complex learning tasks
Organizational strategies for basic learning tasks
Organizational strategies for complex learning tasks
Comprehension monitoring strategies
Affective strategies

actively recites the to-be-learned information. A primary goal for this type of activity is to help transfer items into a buffer, or working memory, so that more meaningful processing can then take place.

REHEARSAL STRATEGIES FOR COMPLEX LEARNING TASKS

With more complex learning tasks, such as studying a chapter in a history textbook, rehearsal strategies often take more involved forms. Underlining main ideas, copying important phrases or sentences, and rereading all come under this category. The use of these strategies helps the learner both to focus on important information in the text and to transfer this information into working memory for further study.

ELABORATION STRATEGIES FOR BASIC LEARNING TASKS

Many types of basic learning tasks, particularly list-learning tasks such as acquiring foreign language vocabulary or remembering the names of the organs in the digestive system, can be performed more effectively by students using elaboration strategies. The use of an elaboration strategy implies that the learner creates some type of symbolic construction to help add meaning to the to-be-learned information. For basic learning tasks this product is often a mental image or verbal string (a phrase or sentence) that helps to create associations between or among the items to be encoded and recalled. For example, to remember that tomatoes are in the fruit category of foods (and not in the vegetable category!), a student could picture a juicy tomato dripping all over a bowl full of luscious fruits. Using these strategies helps students to actively process to-be-learned information and to incorporate it into new or already established schemata by creating meaningful relationships within the new information and/or between the new information and existing knowledge.

ELABORATION STRATEGIES FOR COMPLEX LEARNING TASKS

More complex learning tasks, such as listening to a chemistry lecture or studying a play, require the use of elaboration strategies such as paraphrasing, creating analogies, generative notetaking, and integrative imagery. A primary goal for using these strategies is to relate knowledge currently in semantic memory to the incoming information by instantiating schemata already established and creating relationships between parts of these schemata and the new material. Much of the discussion in other chapters in the present volume focuses on strategies falling into this category.

ORGANIZATIONAL STRATEGIES FOR BASIC LEARNING TASKS

The task of remembering the major battles of World War II becomes easier if we divide the battlefronts up into different geographic areas such as Europe, the Pacific, North Africa, and so on. Using this type of strategy involves creating or adopting an organizational framework. The inherent relationships among items within and across categories in this framework helps to reduce the memory load involved in recall tasks and also helps to establish new schemata or relate to-be-learned information to already established schemata.

ORGANIZATIONAL STRATEGIES FOR COMPLEX LEARNING TASKS

When studying a chapter of text assigned for the next biology class, students spend a great deal of time identifying main ideas and important supporting details, and then trying to relate these to each other and to their already existing knowledge about biology and its associated areas (such as chemistry). Organizational strategies used to perform this type of task effectively include many of the techniques described in this book. Networking, concept structuring, schematizing, mapping, and graphic postorganizers are all different ways of representing to-be-learned information and the relationships among the subcomponents of this information as well as between this new information and already existing knowledge.

COMPREHENSION MONITORING STRATEGIES

The strategies in this category are used by students to monitor their own understanding and determine if a comprehension failure has occurred. To effectively use these monitoring methods a student must first establish learning goals for an instructional activity, then assess the degree to which these goals are being met, and, if an error is detected, modify the means being used to meet the goals. Performing this executive control function involves using strategies such as self-testing while reviewing for a French test and using headings in a math textbook to create questions that will be answered while the student studies the section.

AFFECTIVE STRATEGIES

The more recent descriptions of the teaching–learning process tend to emphasize the active roles of students in creating, monitoring, and controlling much of their own learning. In order to use effectively most of the learning strategies we have already discussed, students must also be able to focus attention, maintain concentration, manage performance anxiety, establish and maintain motivation, and manage their study environment and study schedule. Examples of strategies in this category include using positive self-talk to control test anxiety, using behavioral management techniques to maintain a study schedule, and using images of success to maintain motivation.

WHERE DO SPATIAL LEARNING STRATEGIES FIT IN THE CATEGORICAL SCHEME?

In the previous description of the eight-category classification of learning strategies, spatial learning methods were highlighted under the "Elaboration Strategies for Complex Learning Tasks" and the "Organizational Strategies for Complex Learning Tasks" sections. However, I would like to argue that spatial learning tasks can play an important role in *each* of the eight categories. It is the nature of these roles, the mechanisms by which they operate, the instructional procedures needed to teach students how to use spatial strategies for these different tasks and goals, and the interaction of the processing required by the use of these procedures with cognitive individual difference variables, that need to become the foci for applied research in this area.

Some of this work has already begun. For example, Dansereau and his colleagues (Dansereau *et al.,* 1979; see also Holley & Dansereau, Chapters 1 and 4, present volume) have adapted the networking techniques, which they developed to help students learn from expository text, to create a method for helping students to disrupt the mechanism by which high anxiety negatively affects test performance. The use of networking to represent problem components, potential solution plans, and probable outcomes, as well as the relationships within and among the concepts and actions in each of these categories, can be a powerful strategy for managing a number of affective variables. Long's work with hearing-impaired students (see Long & Aldersley, Chapter 5, present volume) focuses on organizational strategies as well as elaboration strategies. Some of Armbruster and Anderson's work (see Chapter 9, present volume) focuses on metacognitive strategies.

Much of the applied research focusing on learning strategies involves projects designed to develop either classroom applications or adjunct programs that can help students become more proficient in using learning strategies. For example, Jones and her colleagues (Jones, Amiran, & Katims, 1983) have concentrated on embedding learning strategies instruction into regular reading curriculum materials. Dansereau (1983), McCombs (1981), and Weinstein (Weinstein & Underwood, 1983) have all focused on creating adjunct, or stand-alone, programs to help post-secondary students in either job or college settings. These experimental, integrated learning strategies instructional programs have been used to investigate a number of variables. Some of this work has included examining the role of spatial learning techniques both as an instructional vehicle and as a component in the other types of strategies taught. For example, in an experimental learning strategies course developed by Weinstein and her associates (Weinstein, Butterfield, Schmidt, & Poythress, in press), the role of spatial strategies for representing affective and metacognitive learning strategies has been addressed. Spatial constructions have been used to identify and relate the components which contribute to creating and maintaining motivation and to develop plans for comprehension monitoring. Although the process of creating these aids helps students to identify and focus on the relevant variables, the product serves as a guide and checkpoint system for behavior change and self-control practices.

Although these research programs represent some promising steps toward investigating the potential roles of spatial techniques in each of the eight categories of learning strategies, this work has barely begun. As our understanding of the theoretical constructs underlying the uses of spatial techniques increases, so will our ability to understand the mechanisms by which these strategies operate (see Part I, present volume, for discussions of the current state of the art in relevant theory development). As we come to understand more about the underlying mechanisms, we will be able to expand our investigations of variables affecting the acquisition of these strategies, the use of these strategies, and the issues of transfer and generalizability. Conversely, as the applied research into instructional, individual difference, and assessment variables continues, this work will inform the more basic research probing the underlying principles and characteristics (see Parts II and III, present volume, for discussions of the current state of the art in applied research).

GENERAL METHODOLOGICAL ISSUES INVOLVED IN CONDUCTING SPATIAL-LEARNING-STRATEGIES RESEARCH

A common theme running through each of the chapters in the present volume is the need for improving the experimental methods used to study spatial learning startegies. Similar comments could generally be made about the entire field of learning strategies research. For example, Surber (Chapter 10, present volume) presents a good discussion of the uses of mapping methods to help diagnose students' conceptual errors in declarative knowledge, but we know little about how to assess a student's entry-level ability to use spatial strategies. Tailored training or remedial programs require the accurate assessment of entry-level skills (Schulte & Weinstein, 1981). In addition, the evaluation of the training programs themselves, as well as the students who participate, requires accurate assessment devices.

Dillon and Schmeck (1983) have identified a number of individual differences and individual difference variables that affect cognitive processes, particularly learning strategies. However, few studies have investigated these factors and how they interact with experimental, training, and performance tasks. Studying these factors and how they relate to other experimental variables can improve our understanding of the mechanisms underlying the use of spatial strategies and the instructional techniques needed to teach them to students. Related to this issue is the problem created by relying almost exclusively on group data. The application of the case study approach and ethnographic methodologies could also potentially enhance our understanding of the effects of individual difference variables.

A different type of methodological problem arises when one examines studies designed to teach students to use these strategies in their coursework. Many research investigations in this area are of relatively short duration and/or fail to examine performance levels over time (after the training has concluded) or in different contexts (to see if the training effects generalize). Without adequate training it is difficult, if not impossible, to evaluate the effectiveness of the technique, the instructional procedures, or the learner outcomes. Without examining transfer of training issues, particularly generalization to different educational contexts and course contents, the usefulness of the techniques is greatly restricted.

This discussion was in no way meant to be exhaustive. Rather, the purpose was to raise some methodological issues that need to be addressed if work in this area is to continue progressing and to stimulate the reader to consider other issues that require investigation.

REFERENCES

Dansereau, D. F. (1983). Learning strategy research. In J. Segal, S. Chipman, & R. Glaser (Eds.), *Relating instruction to basic research*. Hillsdale, NJ: Erlbaum.

Dansereau, D. F., Collins, K. W., McDonald, B. A., Holley, C. D., Garland, J. C., Diekhoff, G., & Evans, S. H. (1979). Development and evaluation of a learning strategy training program. *Journal of Educational Psychology, 71,* 64–73.

Dillon, R. F., & Schmeck, R. R. (Eds.). (1983). *Individual differences in cognition* (Vol. 1). New York: Academic Press.

Jones, B. F., Amiran, M. R., & Katims, M. (1983). Embedding structural information and strategy instructions in reading and writing instructional texts: Two models of development. In J. Segal, S. Chipman, & R. Glaser (Eds.), *Relating instruction to basic research*. Hillsdale, NJ: Erlbaum.

McCombs, B. L. (1981). *Transitioning learning strategies research into practice: Focus on the student in technical training*. Paper presented at the Annual Meeting of the American Educational Research Association, Los Angeles, April.

Ryan, E. B. (1981). Identifying and remediating failures in reading comprehension: Toward an instructional approach for poor comprehension. In T. G. Miller & G. E. MacKinnon (Eds.), *Advances in reading research*. New York: Academic Press.

Schulte, A. C., & Weinstein, C. E. (1981). *Inventories to assess cognitive learning strategies*. Paper presented at the Annual Meeting of the American Educational Research Association, Los Angeles, April.

Weinstein, C. E., Butterfield, P. J., Schmidt, C. A., & Poythress, M. (in press). *An experimental program for remediating learning strategies deficits in academically underprepared students* (Tech. Rep.). Alexandria, VA: U.S. Army Research Institute for the Behavioral and Social Sciences.

Weinstein, C. E., & Mayer, R. E. (in press). The teaching of learning strategies. In M. C. Wittrock (Ed.), *Handbook of research on training* (3rd ed.). New York: Macmillan.

Weinstein, C. E., & Underwood, V. L. (1983). Learning strategies: The how of learning. In J. Segal, S. Chipman, & R. Glaser (Eds.), *Relating instructions to basic research*. Hillsdale, NJ: Erlbaum.

Wittrock, M. C. (1978). The cognitive movement in instruction. *Educational Psychologist, 13,* 15–29.

CHAPTER 15

Spatial Strategies:
Critique and Educational Implications

W. J. MCKEACHIE

SPATIAL STRATEGIES: PERSONAL
OBSERVATIONS

How can I help students become more effective learners?

In the fall of 1982, I began teaching a new course for beginning university students called "Learning to Learn." In our syllabus we state, "The goals of this course are two-fold: One is to teach you basic concepts of cognitive psychology, and the other is to have you learn to apply them to your own learning here at the University."

Thus, a book on spatial strategies is very relevant. As a teacher I have to ask myself, "Should I teach spatial strategies as a part of my course?" "If so, how much course time should I devote to them?"

My answer to the first question is yes. The authors of the present volume have convinced me that spatial strategies should be a significant part of an armamentarium for skilled learners. But the second question is more difficult. Can spatial strategies compete effectively for course time against elaboration strategies, test-taking strategies, and methods of improving attention, moti-

SPATIAL LEARNING STRATEGIES
Techniques, Applications, and Related Issues

vation, self-management, and learning in groups? Each topic competing for time also has the backing of research and theory. Given a limited amount of class time and study time, how much should be allotted to each?

Here, I fall from grace so far as the disciples of spatial strategies are concerned. Not only do they present evidence for the effectiveness of spatial strategies; they also present evidence that it takes a good deal of practice before spatial strategies can be used effectively—more practice time than I feel able to allocate.

That learning spatial strategies requires practice should not be surprising; the development of any skill takes practice. I became acutely aware of this when I tried to introduce spatial strategies in a single class period and asked students to take notes using a spatial strategy. It was apparent that despite the students' belief that spatial strategies would be valuable, their attempt to use spatial strategies was disruptive to information processing. To listen to the lecture while trying to remember and record important concepts spatially was a disaster. The two tasks simply overloaded the information-processing system. Thus I learned from my own mistake what the authors have demonstrated in their research—that a good deal of training is needed. Fortunately, I was able to salvage from my failure in teaching spatial strategies an important point for the students to learn, the concept of limited capacity of the information-processing system. I pointed out that one can carry out two complex tasks at the same time only if at least one of them is relatively automatized. Their conventional systems of note-taking have been practiced for years and are probably well-learned. To replace them with something new cannot be done by simple substitution.

I suggested that those interested in developing skill in schematic note-taking might practice on easy reading material in a situation in which steps could be retraced and corrections made without time pressure.

I think most of my students were convinced by my lecture that it would be desirable to employ spatial strategies, but I doubt that many have adopted them. Why have my students not carried their belief into action?

The answer is not laziness or lack of motivation. In fact the problem may well be an excess of motivation. Students at the University of Michigan have been successful in elementary and secondary school. They ranked in the top quartile of their high-school graduating classes. Thus they had developed learning strategies that worked well for secondary school demands. At the University they find that the work is much more difficult. The majority plan to go from their undergraduate studies to medical school, law school, graduate school, or to some other form of advanced education. They are greatly concerned about getting good grades. A grade of "B" will not be enough to gain admission to the school to which they aspire. Taking a chance on a new method of study is thus risky. Not only is the time required a high cost, but there is the very real danger that before the new skill is mastered the student will have performed poorly on an important achievement test, thus jeopardizing a precious grade. Small wonder that adoption of schematic strategies is rare!

Lindquist, Greenberg, and Chickering (1983) present evidence that educational innovations are seldom adopted in toto but are rather adapted for use in new situations. The extent of diffusion depends upon the ease of adaptation—for example, the ability to use *part* of the innovation with an increase in effectiveness.

Adoption of spatial strategies seems to me to be analogous. Identification of key elements that can be effectively adopted without the major commitment involved in developing skill in an entire system seems likely to be a key to the spread of schematic strategies.

WHY DO SPATIAL STRATEGIES WORK?
WHAT ARE THE KEY FEATURES?

In Chapter 1 of the present volume, Holley and Dansereau present a clear exposition of the theoretical models upon which spatial strategies are based. They suggest that spatial strategies compel learners to process information at greater semantic depth and facilitate greater elaboration of the material to be learned. Such strategies also provide a mechanism for retrieval of the material learned. Holley and Dansereau also suggest that spatial strategies facilitate the building up of top-level schemata from bottom-up processing of difficult material.

The three types of spatial strategies described—networking, mapping, and schematizing—share the attribute of being relatively content-independent. Thus they share the practical advantage of being applicable to a variety of subject matters—an attribute which may not be important to the scholar working in one discipline, but an obvious asset to university students studying a variety of subjects. Moreover, because they require representation of relationships between concepts they facilitate abstraction and deep processing.

On the other hand, such schemes may be cumbersome and time-consuming when students must master large blocks of material. Does this imply the use of different strategies, breaking the material into smaller units, or some simplified adaptations of these strategies to be used in larger tasks? Breuker's discussion, "What is special about spatial?" (in Chapter 2, present volume) gives us some clues to the answers we are seeking. He points out that spatial learning strategies provide an almost unlimited external memory.

Breuker's point is well taken when spatial strategies are used for taking notes from a lecture, but if they are used in connection with printed text, the text itself provides unlimited external storage. Thus spatial strategies must provide something else if they are to facilitate effective information processing and retrieval. The answer to this criticism, according to Breuker, is that structure hidden in the original text can be made explicit in spatial strategies. The learner must engage in active analysis of the structure in order to construct a spatial representation.

TEACHING SPATIAL STRATEGIES

What does this suggest about the process of teaching the learner to use spatial strategies? I suggest that the first step must be to look for clues to structure, perhaps beginning by training students simply to identify the main points of a passage.

Once a spatial representation has been achieved, operations can be performed in steps, using a structure such as that in the examples cited by Breuker, which come from the fields of mathematics or physics.

But many areas of learning do not have the spatial "grammar" that mathematics and physics have developed. What then? Can the learner develop an adequate spatial representation? Can the learner use the representation effectively once it has been developed?

I am convinced that spatial strategies are effective if the learner develops enough skill in their use so that little information capacity must be devoted to the system, leaving ample capacity for reading or listening. But which of the three systems described in this volume is easiest to learn? Does any one of them provide rewards for the learner during the process of developing skills?

Breuker suggests that spatial strategies ease the problem of learning by reducing the number of topics and by assisting in producing greater coherence in the structure; that is, more relations between topics. But the ability to make the inferences necessary for adequate spatial representations depends upon previous knowledge. How can a beginner get started?

As Goetz points out in Chapter 3, present volume, our schools do not teach students how to get information from reading. We expect students to learn from assigned readings, but we do not instruct them in how to do it effectively. When systems for studying have been presented, they have been prescribed without much effort to find out how students carried out the prescription. Goetz's review of the meager research on the effectiveness of study strategies reports little research on the effectiveness of imagery in learning from meaningful nonnarrative text. It seems possible that spatial strategies are effective not because they provide an image, but rather because in constructing a graphic representation the learner carries out activities such as analysis, encoding, and organization that are themsleves effective regardless of whether or not they result in a spatial representation.

If so, the critical elements to be taught to students may not be the spatial scheme itself but rather the steps taken in constructing a spatial representation. What are these?

Goetz suggests the following:

1. Select material to be mapped. Goetz's primary criterion for selection is that the material requires intensive study.
2. Decide the level at which to represent the text. Here the criterion is primarily the size of the unit for which a representation is needed. In order to decide, the learner probably must survey or skim the material to determine its difficulty and the density of concepts.
3. Identify at least two concepts and the relationship between them. This points to the importance of looking for relationships.
4. Graphically represent the concepts and relationship.
5. Identify and graphically represent new concepts and the relationships among the enlarged set of concepts.
6. Continue until all concepts to be represented are represented—which obviously is a function of the level selected (Step 2).
7. Check the map to see if it matches the text.
8. Store the graphic representation.

Goetz concludes that the processing involved in these steps is consistent with research-based theories about what improves comprehension and memory. Whether the spatial aspects add anything beyond what would be achieved by a nonspatial method involving the same kinds of processing is unclear.

Nonetheless, our original question about how to teach spatial strategies has been clarified, and both Goetz (Chapter 3) and Vaughan (Chapter 6, present volume) have some specific suggestions about ways to teach their systems. One of these is to train students on actual assignments rather than simple sentence or paragraph examples. A second is to explain why spatial strategies are being taught. A third is for the teacher to model spatial representations by using graphic aids in presenting material. Vaughan suggests that the teacher ask for student suggestions while modeling the use of spatial strategies. A fourth suggestion is to encourage students using spatial strategies to include concepts and examples from their prior knowledge.

A fifth insight comes from Holley and Dansereau's finding (Chapter 4, present volume) that the number of types of relationships to be represented needs to be limited. As one would expect, they found that 6 relationships were more learnable than 13. But Holley and Dansereau agree with Goetz and Vaughan that (contrary to my intuition) it is ineffective to use a "building block" approach to training—that is, beginning training with simplified materials. Rather, they suggest beginning with practice in identifying key concepts, laying them out spatially, but filling in relationships only after further training. Holley and Dansereau also describe techniques of modeling, such as providing a network with annotations indicating how it was constructed or watching an expert produce a network. Finally, Holley and Dansereau and Vaughan found that when networking is part of a learning strategies course it works best if taught early rather than late in the course and is practiced frequently.

Armbruster and Anderson (Chapter 9, present volume) suggest that the learner's approach to mapping or spatial representation depends upon the learner's prior knowledge. With little prior knowledge, learners have little chance to use a top-down approach in which one starts with the general structure and main ideas of a chapter; rather they must start with individual propositions—a bottom-up approach. Similarly, texts in which there is little structure or coherence may prevent the learner from using top-down procedures. But even with relatively familiar, structured material the learner's goals may determine the most appropriate approach and level to be used— perhaps top-down for an essay test, bottomup for a test on detailed facts.

WHO BENEFITS
FROM USING SPATIAL STRATEGIES?

Very few educational methods are equally effective for all students. It would be surprising if spatial strategies were a panacea for all. One might argue either that successful students already have strategies that work and would thus not benefit from spatial strategies or that such students are those who will be able to learn and benefit most from spatial strategies ("to whom that hath shall be given"). Holley and Dansereau's results (Chapter 4, present volume) suggest that the former may be true. High-GPA students who used networking did more poorly on multiple-choice and short answer tests measuring details than did control students, while low-GPA students benefited from networking. Both high- and low-GPA students who used networking made higher scores on essay and cloze tests of main ideas.

Further experiments showed that high-ability students benefited from less structured spatial techniques in which they developed their own links between concepts, but low-ability students required the more structured networking with prescribed standard links such as "part," "leads to," and so forth.

Camstra and van Bruggen (Chapter 8, present volume) found an intriguing interaction effect in that students with low ability using schematizing did more poorly than controls on an easy passage but better on a difficult passage. Perhaps schematizing is a distraction for such students on material they understand, but helps maintain attention and improve comprehension on material that cannot be comprehended on a first reading.

Other individual differences among students have apparently not been investigated as aptitudes interacting with spatial strategies. With spatial ability, for example, would we find that high-spatial ability students benefit most from the use of spatial strategies or would we expect low-spatial ability students to need spatial strategies more? One might expect high-spatial ability students to be trained more easily, but would they be able to develop spatial representations of their own that would be more effective than the standard methods?

Surprisingly, the authors do not emphasize teaching students theory and concepts explaining why spatial strategies work. Because the spatial strategies have largely been identified with application of cognitive psychology to learning, I would have expected the authors to have more faith in the value of student understanding of the cognitive theory underlying the use of spatial strategies.

WHAT KINDS OF LEARNING BENEFIT FROM SPATIAL STRATEGIES?

Holley and Long and Aldersley (Chapter 5, present volume) have found that the most significant effect of spatial strategies is on recall of main ideas, but as the preceding studies indicate, other kinds of learning—memory of details, for example, may also be aided for less able students.

FOR WHAT KINDS OF MATERIAL IS SPATIAL STRUCTURING MOST USEFUL?

Long and Aldersley have suggested a text classification system differentiating three types, roughly corresponding to descriptive, narrative, and expository text, and crossing these types with four modes of writing—informative, personal interpretation, personal opinion, and persuasion. Intuitively, some of the resulting cells seem more likely than others to benefit from the use of spatial strategies, but the evidence for this is generally lacking.

Vaughan begins with the plausible assumption that readers need the most help with difficult material and that expository textbooks often provide too few links between facts, and between facts and main points. Thus the unskilled, inexpert reader is left with a welter of details, facts, and principles which must be comprehended and remembered as separate pieces of information. Spatial strategies are most valuable in learning difficult, unfamiliar, expository material, but this may be the kind of material most difficult to represent spatially.

WHAT ARE THE COSTS
OF A SPATIAL STRATEGY?

Vaughan demonstrated that, once learned, his ConStruct Procedure could be used without increases in study time beyond that normally used by conscientious students, but his adolescent students required 20 sessions of instruction to learn the ConStruct Procedure, although medical students learned it in four 2-hour sessions. Mirande (Chapter 7, present volume) and Camstra used six 2-hour sessions of instruction, plus 10 hours of homework. They found that students having difficulties with studies did not learn the system if given an individual study program rather than supervised group study instruction. Students become discouraged early in training on schematizing and need much encouragement to continue.

Once learned, the use of spatial strategies for studying also takes time, and Mirande reports that students view spatial strategies as too time-consuming. Schallert, Ulerick, and Tierney (Chapter 12, present volume) describe vividly the drudgery involved in discourse analysis—the sense of slowness, the struggle, the need to make decisions about what to include and what relationships are involved. No wonder that even students who have learned a spatial strategy often fail to use it to maximum advantage.

How do students decide that the potential gains justify the cost in effort? I suspect that only the most motivated and disciplined use spatial strategies regularly and that the average student assesses the likelihood of satisfactory understanding and achievement with, and without, spatial strategies and weighs the cost in time and effort against the importance of the goal.

USES OF SPATIAL STRATEGIES
BY TEACHERS

Using Spatial Strategies for Testing

For many years I have thought that we should have better ways of measuring student learning than conventional objective or essay tests. When Runkel adapted Coombs's unfolding technique to measure student–teacher colinearity (Runkel, 1956), we began a series of attempts to try to measure the degree to which courses increased the dimensionality of student cognitive space. Our results were not encouraging (Lin, McKeachie, Wernander, & Hedegard, 1970). Not only did we fail to replicate Runkel's results, but we also failed to develop practically usable ways of measuring multidimensionality.

More recently we have been exploring the possibility that the Reitman and Rueter (1980) "ordered tree" algorithm used for laboratory studies of organization of memory could be used in classroom studies. The method does seem to work but is cumbersome, and we are now attempting to develop modifications that could be fitted into a normal classroom examination. Shavelson (1974) and his colleagues (e.g., Shavelson & Stanton, 1975) have used word association techniques and multidimensional scaling as well as card sorting and linear graphs to study cognitive structure. These techniques, too, are difficult to use in ordinary classroom situations. Thus I approached Surber's chapter (Chapter 10, present volume) describing the use of mapping as a testing device with much anticipation.

I resonated to his statement that traditional tests are insensitive to the structure of subject matter. Like Surber we have tried using a cloze technique in which students fill in missing concepts. His use of the test to diagnose patterns of misunderstanding seems to me likely to be useful as an aid to teaching.

But as with using spatial strategies for note-taking, there is a relatively large cost in training students in the mapping skills needed for taking a map test. Can the average teacher afford five class periods of instruction on mapping unless teaching mapping is a basic objective of the course? It seems unlikely that teachers in ordinary content subjects will be willing to divert so much time to training for testing, despite the values of mapping both in learning and testing.

Map-tests correlations with conventional tests are similar to those we obtain with our tree measures. Like Surber, we rationalized these correlations as being high enough to demonstrate the kind of relationship to content knowledge achievement that one might expect and low enough to justify the conclusion that such a test is not simply duplicating conventional tests.

Stewart (Chapter 11, present volume) presents a less demanding contribution—the use of spatial representations to guide test *construction*. When the teacher has constructed a map of the material to be covered on a test, the test is less likely to emphasize trivial details.

Spatial Representations in Curriculum Planning

The use of spatial representation in surveying the discipline content to be included in a curriculum would represent a much more systematic approach to curriculum-building than is typical in colleges and universities. The resulting curriculum is likely to be more representative of the discipline than less systematic approaches. Equally valuable may be the educational value to faculty members who develop the maps. Stewart suggests that these values lie not only in helping teachers become aware of areas difficult to map but also in developing empathy for the learners and problem solvers who must learn and use the content and procedures.

Spatial Representations Presented by Teachers to Summarize or Review Material

Stewart presents a useful discussion of the use of maps to help remind students of the conceptual organization of the material they have been learning in lectures and laboratories. Barron and Schwartz (Chapter 13, present volume) present procedures as well as empirical data supporting the use of spatial strategies as postorganizers, in which students complete partially constructed maps or diagrams, much as with Surber's testing devices.

A key feature of the Barron and Schwartz method is that students work in two- or three-person groups. Such group study activities are known to be particularly effective techniques of learning. Their results indicate that the method is particularly effective as a technique for review at the end of a course or completion of a textbook, but is not effective as a preview, or overview before study. The Barron and Schwartz method does not specify relationships of the complexity involved in networking and mapping. Thus students apparently do not require extensive training to use the method. If the method does, as Barron and Schwartz suggest, stimulate processes such as active comprehension, organization, and relating material to prior experience, it may well be a more efficient method than those requiring extensive training in the proper representation of different kinds of relationships. But if maps or other spatial representation can be used for review or can capture the key concepts and relationships in discourse, why should not students learn directly from the map rather than the text? Reder and Anderson (1982) have shown that students achieve higher scores on conventional classroom tests if they read chapter summaries rather than the complete chapter. Would not a spatial representation provide an even more efficient learning tool?

SPATIAL STRATEGIES IN LECTURING

A number of our authors have mentioned the importance of faculty modeling in student use of spatial strategies. Probably the foremost proponent of spatial strategies in lecturing from notes is Day of Duke University. Day (1980) not only describes types of lecture notes using spatial strategies but also develops a cognitive theory of the effects of differing formats upon the thinking and teaching of faculty members.

She points out that written-out notes lack needed redundancy and give students too few opportunities to catch their breath and think about the material being presented. A written-out lecture often decreases comprehensibility because of inadequate vocal and rhetorical cues to the structure of the lecture. An outline or list of major points may give students too few cues to connectives or too few cues to the lecturer on filling in examples and details.

Spatial organizations, such as trees, pictorial representations, or other graphic representations give the lecturer more cues to relationships and more opportunities for options to be taken depending upon verbal or nonverbal responses from the class. A tree diagram, for example, enables a lecturer to see where a student question fits into the overall organization of the lecture. Essentially lecturers ease their own information processing load by a system of note-taking which efficiently represents the relationships between concepts to be taught.

SHOULD AN ORDINARY TEACHER USE SPATIAL STRATEGIES?

What should average college teachers do about spatial strategies? First, they should study the present volume. Then they should try using each of the methods themselves. Unfortunately, I find that I, like the students of our authors, become easily discouraged. Even after reading and rereading a chapter I cannot plan a spatial representation that does not wander off the page or become overcrowded and too messy to follow without detailed study. Nonetheless the exercise did encourage me to fit some spatial representations into my standard lecture notes.

The exercise, however, also convinced me that in order for spatial strategies to have widespread use, the progenitors not only need to develop methods of training students but also methods of training teachers in their use.

Will I use spatial strategies in my own teaching? My answer is a qualified yes. In the year since the chapters of the present volume first began to appear in my mail, I have been incorporating more spatial representations in my own lecture–blackboard presentations and in my own notes. I have illustrated them to students and suggested their potential utility. But I have not substituted extensive training in spatial strategies for other elements in my course. I feel some guilt about this, because I think such training would be valuable; yet I find that I am unwilling to give up other aspects of the course, which also seem to me to be valuable, even though their value is less well-documented.

I suspect that some students and some faculty members will easily fit spatial strategies into their repertoire. For now, my use will be in those areas in which less training time is required, such as in Barron and Schwartz's graphic postorganizers or in the use of spatial representations in testing.

REFERENCES

Day, R. S. (1980). Teaching from Notes: Some cognitive sequences. In W. McKeachie (Ed.) *Learning, Cognition and College Teaching.* San Francisco: Jossey-Bass.

Lin, Y. G., McKeachie, W. J., Wernander, M. & Hedegard, J. (1970). The relationship between student-teacher compatibility of cognitive structure and student performance. *Psychological Record, 20,* 513–522.

Lindquist, J., Greenberg, M., & Chickering, A. (1983). Unpublished paper presented at the International Conference on Improving University Teaching, Dublin.

Reder, L. M., & Anderson, J. R. (1982). Effects of sparing and embellishment on memory for the main points of a text. *Memory and Cognition, 10,* 97–102.

Reitman, J. S., & Rueter, H. H. (1980). Organization revealed by recall orders and confirmed by pauses. *Cognitive Psychology, 12,* 554–581.

Runkel, P. J. (1956). Cognitive similarity in facilitating communication. *Sociometry, 19,* 178–191.

Shavelson, R. J. (1974). Methods for examining representations of a subject-matter structure in a student's memory. *Journal of Research in Science Teaching, 11,* 231–249.

Shavelson, R. J., & Stanton, G. C. Construct validation: Methodology and application to three measures of cognitive structure. *Journal of Educational Measurement, 12,* 67–85.

Author Index

The numerals in italics indicate pages on which the complete references appear.

A

Aaron, I. E., 200, *208*
Abelson, R. P., 29, 30, 31, 37, *43, 46,* 55, *77*
Actkinson, T. R., 9, *16,* 48, 49, 53, *74*
Adams, A., 49, *71*
Adams, D. K., 201, *209*
Adams, J. J., 206, *208*
Adams, M. J., 36, *43,* 131, *146*
Albanese, M., 134, *146*
Aldesley, S., 114, *123*
Alessi, S., 63, 70, *72*
Alessi, S. M., 49, *71*
Amiran, M. R., 296, *298*
Anderson, J. R., 5, *14,* 55, *71, 73,* 235, *250*
Anderson, M., 111, *123*
Anderson, M. C., 213, *230*
Anderson, R., 11, *123*
Anderson, R. C., 12, *14,* 34, *43,* 52, 54, 55, 56, 57, 58, 68, *72, 76, 57, 77,* 213, 229, *230,* 270, *271*
Anderson, T., 122, *123*
Anderson, T. H., 11, 12, *14, 15,* 21, *43,* 48, 59, 63, 70, *71, 72,* 128, *146,* 202, 207, *208, 209,* 216, 230, *230*
Andre, T., 53, *72*
Armbruster, B., 122, *123*
Armbruster, B. B., 11, 12, *14, 15,* 48, 51, 55, 63, 70, *72, 74,* 128, *146,* 202, 207, *208, 209*
Asarnow, J., 59, *75*
Atkinson, R. C., 52, *72*
Ausubel, D. P., 4, 14, *15,* 56, *72,* 100, *106,* 276, 277, 283, *286*

B

Baddeley, A. D., 5, 6, *15,* 36, 40, *43,* 52, *72*
Baker, B. L., 52, *75*
Baker, L., 59, 63, 69, 70, *72*
Balser, E., 8, *15*
Barclay, J. R., 58, *72*
Barnes, B. R., 56, *72*
Barnes, H. V., 134, *146*
Baron, J., 33, 36, *43*
Barron, R. F., 135, *146,* 273, 277, 278, 280, 282, *286*
Bartlett, F. C., 4, *15,* 31, *43,* 55, 56, *73*
Barton, W. A., 48, 49, *73*
Battig, W. F., 93, *106*
Begg, I., 52, 53, *75*
Belezza, F. S., 54, 55, *73*
Belmont, J. M., 71, *73*
Birnbaum, L., *46*
Birnbaum, M., 212, *230*
Bishop, M. S., 201, *209*
Bjork, R. A., 6, *19*
Black, J. B., 31, *43,* 56, *73*
Bloom, B. S., 53, *73*
Bluth, G., *124*
Bluth, G. J., 55, *75*
Bobbitt, F., 233, *250*
Bobrow, D., 7, *15*
Bobrow, D. G., 36, *45*
Bobrow, S. A., 53, *73*
Bogden, C. A., 234, 248, *250*
Borges, J. L., 149, *160*
Bourne, L. E., Jr., 4, 5, *15*
Bousfield, W. A., 8, *15,* 55, *73*
Boutwell, R. C., 9, *18*

Subject Index

321

EDUCATIONAL PSYCHOLOGY

continued from page ii

Ronald W. Henderson (ed.). Parent–Child Interaction: Theory, Research, and Prospects

W. Ray Rhine (ed.). Making Schools More Effective: New Directions from Follow Through

Herbert J. Klausmeier and Thomas S. Sipple. Learning and Teaching Concepts: A Strategy for Testing Applications of Theory

James H. McMillan (ed.). The Social Psychology of School Learning

M. C. Wittrock (ed.). The Brain and Psychology

Marvin J. Fine (ed.). Handbook on Parent Education

Dale G. Range, James R. Layton, and Darrell L. Roubinek (eds.). Aspects of Early Childhood Education: Theory to Research to Practice

Jean Stockard, Patricia A. Schmuck, Ken Kempner, Peg Williams, Sakre K. Edson, and Mary Ann Smith. Sex Equity in Education

James R. Layton. The Psychology of Learning to Read

Thomas E. Jordan. Development in the Preschool Years: Birth to Age Five

Gary D. Phye and Daniel J. Reschly (eds.). School Psychology: Perspectives and Issues

Norman Steinaker and M. Robert Bell. The Experiential Taxonomy: A New Approach to Teaching and Learning

J. P. Das, John R. Kirby, and Ronald F. Jarman. Simultaneous and Successive Cognitive Processes

Herbert J. Klausmeier and Patricia S. Allen. Cognitive Development of Children and Youth: A Longitudinal Study

Victor M. Agruso, Jr. Learning in the Later Years: Principles of Educational Gerontology

Thomas R. Kratochwill (ed.). Single Subject Research: Strategies for Evaluating Change

Kay Pomerance Torshen. The Mastery Approach to Competency-Based Education

Harvey Lesser. Television and the Preschool Child: A Psychological Theory of Instruction and Curriculum Development

Donald J. Treffinger, J. Kent Davis, and Richard E. Ripple (eds.). Handbook on Teaching Educational Psychology

Harry L. Hom, Jr. and Paul A. Robinson (eds.). Psychological Processes in Early Education

EDUCATIONAL PSYCHOLOGY

Delaware